OF
Tears

A
Personal
MEMOIR

CRUSONDA
(YVETTE) LIDY

Vivian White

I have lost many "best friends" to passing away over the years but I think Vivian White was by far the most unique, nonconformist yet purest ~of~ heart of anyone I had ever known. Being pure in heart involves having a singleness of heart toward God, and that she did! A pure heart has no hypocrisy and she certainly didn't. I knew of her failures but I also knew of the precursor in her youth that shaped her views of life and people. I'd be the first to say that Vivian did have her moments when she could irritate you to no end. Nevertheless, if a person cared enough to look beyond those flaws, they would discover a rare jewel that was priceless! We are all to strive to become more like Jesus and that's the Vivian I knew and loved. She had such a generous heart taking groceries to people in need. I drove her to take food to the homeless, people living in tents and out in the cold. She got out before daybreak taking her young children to sell donuts to raise money for her church. Unknown to most people, Vivian and her sister, Emma Lee worked together as a team. Vivian would seek out those in need, tell Emma Lee, then the two sisters would go to work being the hands and feet of Jesus. I can't help but believe God was smiling down from heaven saying: THAT'S MY GIRLS!

Life had taught Vivian to be tough, to survive, but she still had such a tender heart that could be deeply hurt, and was, many times, from those who only focused on her rough edges.

When I get to heaven and I get to see people I knew here on earth, the first would be my mother and then I want to see Vivian.

Yvette and Vivian

Myra Vivian White, age 78, of Dalton, Georgia passed away on Tuesday December 29, 2020. She was born on September 6, 1942.

Acknowledgements

Aslam M. Sandvi, MD: I'm so grateful to have you as not only my doctor but also my friend. You've pulled me through so many of my darkest days and helped me to believe the sun would shine again. Your encouragement and support for me to get my book out, saying it would help others, only reaffirms my faith that you are truly a credit to your profession.

Christine Sager, MD in Obstetrics and Gynecology, FACOG: WOW, where do I begin, you've been so supportive and encouraging. Thank you for reading my manuscript and sharing your thoughts. You said my story would help so many other women, and that has truly been my driving force in getting my book out. To say to other survivors, "I've been there, made it through the storm, and you can too," that is my hope.

Joseph A, Veys, MD, Urology specialist: A very special thanks for reading my manuscript and cheering me on. I will never forget you for performing the life-saving surgery on me in 2009 when all hope was lost. You are my hero.

Chandra D. Fears LCSW: You have truly embraced your calling. You've been ready and willing to help at a minute's notice and it's been so comforting to know I didn't have to pretend with you. You began as my counselor that evolved into such a great friend, for that I will always be grateful.

Jodi McDaniel Lowery, Author: I feel so blessed to have you in my corner. Thank you so much for all the hours you spent, the direction and guidance you gave on my manuscript completely out of the goodness in your heart.

Laura M. Cross: Thank you so much for drawing the customized artwork for my book cover. Also, your poem "My Safe Place" personifies exactly how I felt. You are truly an undiscovered talent, and I am blessed to call you, my friend.

Dedications

This book is dedicated to my children: Danny Lidy, an avid hunter and a dedicated Georgia Bulldog fan. Who is, without a doubt, the best dad and Christian father I know. I'm so proud to call you my son. Sabrina Lidy Burnette, my beautiful daughter and dedicated Steelers fan. Who is so smart and mechanically inclined she can fix anything she sets her hand to. My darling grandson, Tyson Burnette, I love the way your face lights up when I walk into the room and when you put your arm over my shoulder; I'm truly the happiest grandmother in the world. My grandson, Little Danny, our "all-star athlete," so proficient in sports, skilled and accomplished in wrestling, cross-country, and all-star football and baseball. My sweet granddaughter Madison, who is so gifted & skilled with your creative drawings. Then there's your love for reading that will always take you to new and wonderful places. You are already wise beyond your years and I'm so very proud of you. My granddaughter Emmaline, who just arrived from heaven. I'm so excited to get to know you and watch you grow into your own unique personality. Thank you *all* so much. You are my forever loves.

Table of Contents

River of Tears

A little girl once sat on a riverbank alone,
yet reflections in the water showed a woman now grown.
Through teardrops of sadness the waters did rise,
and no one could save her from the tears in her eyes.
She cried out, "Please help me, oh why can't you see,
the pain that life brought me, now I cannot get free.
I keep hoping tomorrow, yet tomorrow won't come, and
the dark clouds won't let me feel the warmth of the sun.
River of Tears, the pain is so deep,
memories that haunt me and torment my sleep.
The river is rising as it covers new ground.
If no one will save me, I know that I'll drown.
River of Tears, oh, river of fears,
you've rolled close beside me through forty-two years.
The time soon will find me when no longer I'll weep,
And I'll rest eternal in these waters so deep."

Written, composed, and experienced by
Crusonda Yvette Lidy (April 28,1997)

Introduction

WELL, IT IS 5:44 Wednesday morning, and Amanda, my fifteen-year-old, is running water in the tub while my oatmeal simmers on the stove. I am wide awake, even though I couldn't fall asleep until after one o'clock. It is a nippy October morning as fall once again pushes its way back into our lives, and I finally begin this scary journey into the memories of my past. Until now I have only considered this journey in my daily troubled thoughts with the slight hope that, maybe, if I speak the words out loud and see the pain right in front of me, then I'll finally be able to make sense, as to why; my thoughts, my reactions and my decisions were always based from inside a mind that operated from a place of fear.

For some unknown reason, I have felt compelled to write my autobiography for many years, even with the uncertainly that I could follow through with such an idea. When I opened my eyes this morning, it was as though someone was there with me, telling me it was time to write my story.

A peaceful hand seemed to silently lead me to my typewriter and insert the first sheet of paper. The word angel comes to mind and feels very appropriate.

I have been a recluse for many years, and I seem to find it almost impossible to trust anyone. I taught myself at a young age to wear a strong, confident look to give others the impression that I was fine and didn't need anyone. However, this was far from the truth, but it was my only defense against their cruelty. As I grew older, this artificial facade grew stronger and stronger until one day I sadly realized I didn't know who I was anymore.

I have wished many times that I had a strong yet comedic personality like my brother Jacob who could make you laugh in an instant while commanding respect by his very presence. Unfortunately, my brother Josh and I always seemed to be the butt of his jokes. Then there's my sister, Karen; you couldn't help but love Karen. She had the patience of Job, and she seemed so gentle and sweet that I could not imagine anyone not liking her. And, last but not least, Josh was the youngest of the family and definitely the Red Delicious apple of Mother's eye since it was a well-known fact that he was her favorite. Josh was extremely honest and well-versed in most any subject one might want to discuss. So, in consideration of all this, it is easy to understand why Mother has been so obvious in her love for my two brothers and sister. I was my father's only daughter, and Mother told me many times I was just like his sister, Arleen, whom she simply despised. Mother's anger towards my aunt Arleen was very justifiable but I was nothing like my aunt. She always seemed to like me and I really needed that in my life. I just wish mother would have found a place in her heart for me, but it was always obvious she would never feel or display the affection for me that she did for my siblings.

In 1987, I developed a full-blown case of agoraphobia, and I accepted my life of isolation, yet I have a great need to tell my story for my emotional healing. However, there's another reason it's so important to me, and that's my two children, Hunter and Amanda. Because of this deep-seated fear I've lived with since childhood, it affected my relationship even with them. My prayer is that maybe not now but someday, they will sit down and read about my journey and what held me back from participating in the life I so desperately desired to share with them. I pray they have forgiven me for my flaws and my failures. I know I'm much harder on myself than they have ever vocalized. Still, I hope they will have a better understanding as to why they were deprived of so many thing's children get to enjoy when they're young. I also wanted them to have the security of a good home life like other kids but for many years our only income was what I made at the carpet mill. I kept believing tomorrow would be better, but sadly, tomorrow came too quickly and all the things I planned in my heart to share with them, they had suddenly outgrown. I was emotionally imprisoned in my home but in so many ways, so were they. I was trying to cope with my agoraphobia and my fear of life and of people and sadly, my children bore the weight of my illness while trying to understand what was wrong with their mother.

There were many nights when my son, Hunter, at twelve years old, and my daughter, Amanda, seven years old, sat by my bedside while their mommy clung to her Bible afraid to fall asleep. I wasn't able to leave our home and venture any farther than the mailbox without running back in fear to my bedroom, my safe place, where no one could hurt me. Singing Christian songs to the bluebird and redbird that perched each day outside my bedroom window as I tried to hold on to my sanity. I felt as if my mind would snap into a million pieces, yet, I prayed for deliverance and held tightly to the promises of God. Even now, thirty-one years later, my nights still find me weeping in regret and shame for what my children suffered because of me.

My son, Hunter, and I visited Eleventh Avenue Baptist Church, and he looked up at me and asked how to be saved. He asked me if I would go to the altar with him to pray. I was terrified to walk forward past all of the people to get to the altar. As soon as I made it there and the preacher began to pray with us, I rushed back to my seat in sheer panic while my eleven-year-old son stood before the church and accepted Jesus Christ into his heart. When little Hunter stood up from the altar, Pastor Guffey asked him if he would like to speak. He took the microphone and, in his sweet voice, shouted out to the congregation, "That Devil ain't gonna slip that Hippocrates shoe on me!" He was referring to an old gospel song I had taught Amanda and him when they were very young. It's called, "There's No Hiding Place Down Here." I was extremely proud of Little Hunter but felt so inadequate myself. My heart still grieves with regret because I was too afraid to stand there with him. I had such a struggle being in crowds and did everything to avoid them. No one but God knew how afraid I was of people and to be outside. Only God knew of the tears I cried from feeling like a worthless mother. As the years moved on with each slowly passing day, I waited alone, isolated in my existence, for the change to come. My fear of life and people along with the embarrassment I felt for having a mental illness held me emotionally captive and caused me to withdraw from relationships even more. Being so afraid of everything made me feel ashamed and weak as a human being. I didn't want anyone to know just how damaged I was. Years later, when my granddaughter, Madison was born the doctors gave us little hope that she would survive. I felt I had to see her before her open-heart surgery but because of my agoraphobia I couldn't get in the elevator without coming unglued. So, I took the stairs while someone held open the first floor door. I also had claustrophobia and could barely breathe in confined spaces along with severe panic attacks. When I made it to the filth floor I discovered the N.I.C.U. door was locked. Having agoraphobia and claustrophobia was living in hell on earth while trying to keep it secret from a world that would not understand. When I would go to church to find comfort I would be met at the door by my P.T.S.D. and all the abusive memories of my youth would come rushing back to remind me I was not welcome in this place they called: The House of God. When I was desperate enough to admit to a religious person what I was coping with, I was reminded that fear is of satan, which left me believing they thought I was too. This caused me to doubt myself and my value as child of God even more. My hope in writing my story is that it will help other women who have gone through trauma's they felt they couldn't talk about. To know someone else has been there too and understands their pain. Since this is about my life experience and in no way a desire to hurt anyone, I decided to change as many names as possible to deflect the reader from those who may have played a negative roll in my life. I've spent my whole life staying silent while stuffing my pain. Always being afraid of making someone angry with me if I spoke out. I was born afraid but by the Grace of God I don't intend to die afraid. Regardless of the many storms in my life and the tears that felt like an endless river in my heart, I always knew with profound awareness that I was not alone. I had never been alone because God had been right there with me in every devastating crisis that had ever occurred in my life.

1

Born Afraid

WHEN MOST PEOPLE write about their lives, I have noticed they tend to start with their childhood. However, I think I will take a step even farther back and begin shortly before I was born in DeKalb, Bowie County, Texas.

During my mother's pregnancy with me, her world was dictated by a fear-based religion called the Church Assembly, located in Dalton, Georgia, one of the largest yet least known religious cults in the United States.

Science has discovered that the unborn child can hear its parents' voices while it's still in the womb, and I can't help but believe I was born afraid. I believe the fear was instilled in me before I ever took my first breath. I have always been a very nervous person although I have tried hard to hide it from others. I believe this nervous condition stems from as far back as my pregnant mother's affiliation with this church. While Mother was pregnant with me, she lived in a world of fear enforced by the Stratton's, and since Mother grew up in this church, she believed and trusted in it completely.

Rev. Chaney Theodore Stratton was the founder of the Church Assembly with his son, Rev. John Winston Stratton Sr., who was second in command, and in later years, it would be Rev. John Winston Stratton Jr. The church was handed down to each forthcoming generation, completely controlled and dictated by the Stratton family and their descendants. I am convinced that sincerity and good intentions were the mindset of the Stratton's in the beginning. However, with many members comes money and with money comes power, and in that process everything went awry. It inevitably resulted in extreme mind control, abuse, extortion, corruption, cruelty, and permanent emotional problems for many of their victims.

Since the Stratton's had churches all over the United States, a ministers meeting would take place three times a year, and all the churches would convene in Dalton, Georgia. It was May 1954, the year I was to be born, and Mother wanted to buy a bedroom suite, but her pastor told her no; he said just put your clothes in boxes. He said Jesus would return and the end of time would come before the next assembly, which was only two months away. The Ministers Meeting would be held July 4, 1954, and I wasn't due to be born until July 9, 1954. Mother didn't even have clothes to put on me the night I arrived.

Mother's entire pregnancy with me was spent in a frightened and nervous state brought on by the church, which was waiting for the end of time and the arrival of Jesus to come. She believed all the while that she would never gaze upon the tiny face of the unborn child she carried in her womb.

My mother's parents (James and Laura Hoskins) donated their time and land in Harlan, Kentucky, and by their own hands poured and shaped the mortar into cement blocks to build a church as an offering of their faith. In later years, the Church Assembly, aka the Stratton's, offered to sell back to them this same property my grandparents originally donated. The church involved itself in every aspect of its members' lives, especially when it involved the almighty dollar.

The minister's meetings took place three times a year and during these meetings, ministers and deacons were repositioned to the state they would pastor in the future on behalf of the Church Assembly churches. Also, vicious rebuking was the order of the day.

The members who had fallen slack of what was expected of them were cruelly reprimanded. It was not uncommon to see members of the church grabbed by their heads and shaken viciously while the preacher warned them of the horrible ways God was going to punish them. When the women were shaken by their heads, many times their long, combed-up hair would come tumbling down.

Constant accusations against targeted members were coupled with vicious physical attacks on their person. You could especially be singled out for not paying your pledges since money was the driving force of the greedy recipients. I was present the Sunday morning Rev. John Winston Stratton Jr. cradled in his arms one of the oldest members and then threw him out of the sanctuary onto the sidewalk. Grown men crawled underneath pews to avoid the physical and violent rebuking.

When a man confessed to a sexual indiscretion, he had to stand before the church, give the name of the woman or women he had sex with, and give details. It was commonplace for the minister to randomly pick a member to accuse of sinning and build the entire sermon around that person. Members would walk to the altar in shame with tears streaming down their faces and confess; even if they weren't guilty, they had to say they were. If you were singled out, all eyes would be on you and what a fearful experience it was being screamed at, and all the shouting that ensued was terrifying.

Fear and brainwashing made it possible for the church to maintain control of your life and finances. Constant threats of hell, fire, and brimstone were never tempered by the amazing love of Christ. The "God of Fear" was the God we served. It still astounds me to know firsthand the emotional damage that can be done to a small child in the early years of life. Even my father, who was a minister in the church, tried to kill me while I was still in the womb. While my mother fought him with every ounce of strength she had, he held her down on the floor and tried his best to put turpentine on Mother's navel, hoping she would miscarry.

Abuse of the Elderly

As I was sitting on the church pew at a Sunday night church service, Harry and Matty (Matthew) Stratton, the two youngest sons of Rev. John W. Stratton Sr., began preaching to Sister Gaddis, telling her she had a bad spirit and to "get out!" I believe Sister Gaddis had emotional problems because she would always punch her side and mumble underneath her breath when the ministers were preaching. Nevertheless, she was harmless.

Sitting in a corner pew in the main aisle of the sanctuary, Sister Gaddis did not attempt to get up from her seat and leave. Suddenly, the teenage boys, Harry and Matty Stratton, ran off the platform with several other boys following close behind, heading toward Sister Gaddis. They grabbed her and began pulling her from her seat, all the while screaming and shouting as they pushed her toward the door, making her fall down. They continued to scream and shout that she had a bad spirit, and no one dared defy them. Everyone was shouting right along with them as though God was condoning what was happening to this little old lady, whom they decided was possessed by the devil because a Stratton had said she was.

Each time she attempted to get to her feet, she would be pushed again and again to the floor, and because she was old, she didn't have much of a chance to regain her footing.

This happened on a regular basis at the Church Assembly in Dalton, Georgia, and almost everyone was smothered by the fear that loomed over this church controlled by the Stratton's. The cruel and physically abusive tactics used to strip away at the victim's self-esteem were proclaimed in the name of God! Four services a week kept us in line and dreadfully afraid. We were living in hell, waiting to go to hell unless the Stratton's saw fit to approve our admittance into God's kingdom. I remember John Winston Stratton Sr. declaring one night at church, "If you people fool with me, I'll take my family and leave here!" We knew if he did, there would be no hope for us, and we would be doomed to hell. The Stratton's had their own toolbox full of fear tactics to keep us in line and in submission.

Unless the member was physically thrown out of the church and not allowed to reenter the building, the member would sadly make his or her way to the altar (which exhibited a picture of the general overseer, the Reverend John Winston Stratton Sr., and his wife, Moreen Stratton, and never a picture of the Holy Christ). As you knelt at the altar, those were the two faces that stared you down while holding the Bible in their hands, and those same eyes were there to judge you as you raised your head from praying. You were programmed to believe they were your only hope to make it to heaven. In later years, when Rev. John Winston Stratton Sr. died, Moreen continued controlling people's lives but at a much more extreme degree. She immediately made certain her eldest son, Rev. John Winston Stratton Jr., would be the new general overseer, she was always pulling the strings.

I'd see her sitting in the church dining hall where we all gathered to buy and eat her egg salad sandwiches. She would be verbally rebuking a terrified woman who was down on the floor whimpering at her feet, while the other women were shouting, which intensified the fear. This scene was not uncommon in our church dining hall or Sister Moreen's Sunday school room as everyone just stood and stared at the member being reprimanded. Sister Moreen was also personally responsible for many verbal and physical abusive messages that took place during the preacher's sermons. If you were simply observing an incident, you did not dare show any compassion for the member being chastised. The brokenhearted member would stand before the congregation while the preacher would proceed to shame, discredit, and degrade the church member. The hostile attack would grow to a fever pitch when suddenly the minister would grab the member viciously with his hands and shake the person violently by their head. It didn't matter if this humble Christian reached heaven with his or her cries; if it did not touch the preacher's heart or Sister Moreen's, the member was in for a great deal of shunning by fellow members.

We were not allowed to sing songs with the name "Jehovah" in them. Rev. Chaney Theodore Stratton wouldn't allow it because it made him think of the Jehovah Witness churches. For over fifty years, that unspoken rule has stayed in place. Also, we could not sing "I'll Fly Away" because our religion did not believe in the Rapture of the church. Nevertheless, the fast songs we sang were often expressed in such a threatening tone that they evoked fear in the hearts of all who heard them—songs such as "You Gotta Move!"

As the singing became louder and the fear escalated, church members would be standing, sobbing, and shaking in their shoes. They would begin moving from their seats to stand at the altar looking up at Sister Moreen like a terrified rabbit hoping for mercy. As everyone shouted, I'm sure they were wondering if they were going to be the one chosen to be emotionally ripped to shreds at that particular service. Most of the services needed a sacrifice, and I just kept praying it wouldn't be me.

Sister Moreen Stratton was a short, chunky woman whose look could send daggers and fear straight through your trembling heart because you knew what she was capable of. She destroyed many marriages within the church because she would decide if a person was married to the wrong spouse and should be married to someone else that she had chosen. Even the women called her "Mother Moreen" as they bowed in front of her with their newborn child and have her name the baby.

They taught us what to think, feel, and believe. We believed we were servants of God when, in reality, we were servants of the Stratton family. There were occasions where you signed over your homes and/or property and lost everything you had. Yet, Sister Moreen's "ladies" from the church would escort her to her waiting limousine or Mercedes Benz. We were expected to live a life of sacrifice and even poverty, such as turning in your father's life insurance or giving up your home, while Sister Moreen and the Stratton family lived a life of luxury. They owned their own airplanes, which they needed to pick up the monies from their feeder churches in other states.

I was a member of the church brass band, and I played the alto saxophone. Sister Moreen kept us busy on the streets and going door-to-door selling peanut brittle, donuts, candy, and many other projects to raise money for the church, and, of course, the Stratton's were the church. We each tried to sell as much as we could, many times buying a lot of it ourselves out of fear of Sister Moreen if we hadn't sold enough—also just to get a smile or small gesture of approval from her. Little children made their regular stroll through each pew every Sunday morning with their envelopes, asking for money in their sweet young voices that said, "Vote for me!" Sunday school consisted of Moreen Stratton's lady servants collecting and counting money diligently to raise a few million dollars, specifically to pay for John Stratton Jr. and his family's new million-dollar mansion on Dug Gap Road. When they decided to sell it, they sold it to a local carpet business owner, whose daughter was a famous anchor for _Inside Edition_ and CBS News. She also worked as cohost of _Today_ on NBC.

In every room down the hall and even in the sanctuary, people were busy collecting, counting, and raising money for the Stratton's. You paid your pledges, which far exceeded any reasonable tithes most churches expected. _This_ was their version of Sunday school.

Below are some of the rules that were implemented, and should members stray from obedience, these rules were enforced by cruelty.

- Members were prohibited from associating with ex-members even if they were your family, such as parents, children, or relatives.
- No smoking or tobacco products of any kind were allowed— no alcoholic beverages and no medical treatment (excluding eyeglasses, false teeth, and setting of a broken limb).
- No medicine or vaccinations of any kind were allowed for any reason.

- Members could not use hair curlers, dyes, or perms.
- They also could not use hair sprays or tease their hair.
- Women were prohibited from cutting their hair.
- Men were prohibited from wearing their hair down their necks or longer.
- Women had to wear their dresses one inch below their knees (no longer and no shorter).
- Fingernail polish, lipsticks, and makeup of any kind were not allowed.
- Members were prohibited from taking part in any worldly functions or activities, such as sports, movie theaters, the circus, etc.
- Women were required to wear stockings when going outdoors at all times.
- Members were prohibited from dating or marrying anyone who was not a member of the church.
- Members were prohibited from wearing swimming suits, short pants, or sleeveless dresses. Women were prohibited from wearing slacks (pants of any kind, excluding underwear).

There were many other rules I haven't named. Also, some rules were not listed in the church's rule book, such as women not being permitted to shave their legs or underarms since that was considered vanity.

2

When Daddies Die

WHEN I WAS three years old, my family lived in Harlan, Kentucky, and attended one of the Stratton's feeder churches. My father was a preacher in the church but had chosen to leave it and go back to Texas. He called my mother saying he had a good-paying job and would like her to join him. He said she should leave us kids with our grandparents until they could financially get back on their feet. She refused to leave us kids or the church. He told her if she refused to come to Texas, he would go to Mexico and start a new life, and she would never hear from him again. About two weeks after this conversation transpired, Mother was told by the authorities that my father was dead. They said he was deep-sea fishing off Corpus Christi, Texas, in the Gulf of Mexico with only the captain and him aboard the ship. A storm began to rage, and the waves were twenty-five feet high. Then, through the blinding rain, my father in his bare feet slipped and fell into the raging waters below.

He was an excellent swimmer, so he began to swim toward the life preserver that the captain of the ship threw to him. Just as he reached to retrieve it, something from below jerked his helpless body underneath the cruel waters never to be seen again. Some believed it to be the jaws of a shark or an octopus. His body was searched for, to no avail, for forty-eight hours. The only other theory was that if my father did indeed survive, he may have hit his head on a rock or something, causing him to have amnesia and making it impossible to return home to his family.

A great amount of mystery surrounded my father's death. For example, when my mother and father lived together, she offered to buy him a new wallet since the one my father carried was so ragged. He adamantly refused to carry any wallet other than his precious cowhide billfold that his father had bought for him when he was eleven years old. In that wallet he carried a picture of me, his only daughter. After his demise, his personal belongings were returned to my mother. A new wallet was among his clothes with no trace of the cowhide billfold my father refused to part with. The picture he always carried of me, his only daughter, was no where to be found. Also, why would two men venture out on the ocean with such a dangerous storm brewing? I would surely assume that a captain of such a boat would keep abreast of the weather forecast. It is also my understanding that my father had a large amount of money on his person that could have possibly paid the captain for his silence. For many years, my mother waited for my father's return.

My mother grieved for many years over the loss of the love of her life, but no one would ever know how many tears his only little girl shed for him. I always believed in my heart that my daddy was out there somewhere waiting for me to find him. I never talked about my feelings regarding my father to anyone, yet I was constantly  searching for him in every man I would see.

I was informed that my father had beautiful, curly, dark-brown hair and had served in the military. He was extremely handsome and sang with a beautiful voice. I vividly remember, when I was eight years old, standing inside the door of the JCPenney department store at Bryman's Plaza in Dalton, Georgia, and looking up at the tall, handsome security employee. As I gazed upon his face, I was wondering, "What if he is my father and he just doesn't know it?" Although I was only three years old when my daddy disappeared, I spent my entire childhood secretly looking for him and my adulthood trying to pick one out for myself.

My Daddy

He wasn't here to love me
or guide my tiny feet.
I have no memories of him
or something I could keep.

But one day up in heaven
his face I'll finally see,
the man who was my father,
who died when I was three,

Though I am growing old now,
my tears still fall the more,
still waiting for my daddy,
to come walking through the door.

Written and composed by Crusonda Yvette Lidy

One of the secret hurts I carried in my heart as a child, and as a young woman, was the fact that I didn't have a grave that I could visit. The church wouldn't allow Mother to spend her money on a headstone. Still, I needed to believe there was a special place for my father as a way to acknowledge he ever existed.

My dad's father, Daddy Joe, as we called him, lived at and operated Praters Mill in Dalton, Georgia for over thirty years. He drove my mother to Texas to pick up the $10,000 life insurance check from the death of my father. In 1957, $10,000 was a very large amount of money compared to today's market. My mother gave my grandfather $5,000 with the understanding, it would be used, so he would have the honor and privilege of turning it over to Brother Stratton since the Church Assembly was waiting for the money. Mother took the other $5,000 to the church office and handed it to Rev. John Winston Stratton Sr. He looked at my mother with an angry frown, and in a vicious tone, he said, "Is *that* all there is?"

Daddy Joe kept the $5,000 and bought himself a new truck and a washer and dryer. My mother never kept a dime of the money. In later years, when my grandparents died, there was no mention they ever had a son. The two daughters, Arleen and Maxine, kept the entire inheritance after bringing papers to my two brothers and me to sign, forfeiting any rights to our inheritance. My aunt Arleen reassured me that I would get my inheritance, which was a lie. My brothers said if our grandparents didn't want us to have any of the money, they didn't want it either. My grandfather could have at least put my father's $5,000 insurance money in a trust for my two brothers and me for when we came of age, but he chose not to. Mother left the Church Assembly for several years but would eventually return.

When Churches Abuse

The church obviously had bad feelings toward my father for quitting the church before he died. One night when we were at church in Harlan, Kentucky, Rev. Ted Stratton (Rev. John Winston Stratton Sr.'s brother) was preaching. He suddenly directed his attention toward my brother Jacob, who was five years old at the time. Rev. Ted Stratton grabbed my brother by his head and shook him violently while screaming at him, "You had better get that Johnny Cooper spirit out of you," implying my father was evil. I am sure this must have terrified my brother, but the church could and did get pretty violent on most occasions. Even with children, a common statement they abided by was "beat them with a rod and they will not die."

Our church took this Bible verse literally. It was not uncommon for a minister to beat his children and his wife, so the members would follow the examples they were given. Women were not allowed to read the Bible, nor were there Bibles on the pews in our church. When the word was being preached, a woman could be at the altar until her legs went numb. Many of the men had the attitude that women were simply created to serve them and their needs, bear children, and keep their mouths shut.

3

The Only Home I Ever Knew

MY FONDEST MEMORIES as a child were spent in a beautiful house located at 225 Mountain View Drive, in Dalton, Georgia. This was the only home my mother ever owned. The rest of our future would be spent in rental houses. This house was white and sat at the top of a beautiful green, grassy hill. I was seven years old at the time, but I remember vividly lying on the ground at the top of the hill and rolling down to the bottom, laughing all the way. When I reached the bottom of the hill, there were four majestic trees hovering over the yard and street. I know a couple of them were pine trees because of the many pine needles and pine cones that fell to the ground. I believe one of the trees was an oak tree. I used to touch the sticky stuff that ran out of the trees and thought I would never get it off my fingers, but it smelled good. Standing gracefully beside the brilliant green grass in my yard stood several lovely dogwood trees with pink petals. Even though their growth had been stunted, they stood proudly as if to say they knew what they represented and who created them.

When I remember my home, it is always of being outside in the yard with a cool breeze blowing through my hair.

Fall was always welcome in my heart because it turned the leaves to so many beautiful colors. After they floated to the ground, I would collect them, choosing the most colorful ones that had not been injured in their plunge to the earth. I would paste them on crepe paper and take them to school. My teacher, Mrs. Turner, would help me discover what kind of tree each leaf represented. There was something so wonderful about that house and yard to me, and even now, after all these years, if I could afford any home I wanted, I would buy this same house on Mountain View Drive.

Over the years, when someone at church sang "I've Got a Mansion Just Over the Hilltop," I would always think of the house on Mountain View Drive that, for a fleeting moment, had once been my home. On sentimental days, I still drive by this house slowly, just looking at it and wishing it were mine. I guess it's because it represents the only time in my life that I truly felt in my heart that I belonged somewhere.

Randy Henson lived next door to me, and even though our neighborhood was referred to as the opulent section of town, Randy was the only rich kid in our neighborhood. He had a trampoline to play on, and I thought that was the greatest thing I had even seen. Randy was an only child and spoiled rotten; he didn't want for anything. One day we walked to town to go to the movies at The Wink theater to see Elvis Presley in *Viva Las Vegas*. Before the movie started, Randy said he wanted us to have a party when we returned home, so he took me to McCrory's Department Store to buy some balloons.

When we entered the store and I walked over to where he was getting the balloons, he handed me a tiny bottle of perfume and told me to put it in my short pants because he wanted to give it to his mother as her birthday present. In other words, he was telling me to steal the perfume. Since my family wasn't going to the Church Assembly during this time, I wore black shorts with a bright-yellow sleeveless top with big black dots on it. I nervously put the fifty-cent bottle of perfume in my shorts as Randy had demanded. I was so scared as I stood at the counter since I had never before stolen anything. I was lucky that my arms were hanging down at my sides instead of on top of the counter because suddenly the tiny bottle fell out of the leg of my shorts onto the floor. I pretended to have dropped it out of my hand and nervously looked up at the clerk as I sheepishly pretended to change my mind about purchasing the perfume. I never forgot that incident because it scared the daylights out of me, and it taught me to never let anyone talk me into stealing again.

4

The Little Straw Shoes

WHEN I WAS five years old, I recall receiving a pair of white straw shoes, with a little pink bow on the front center of each shoe, for my birthday. My sister, Karen, also received a pair since we were both born on the same day. Mother looked down at me with her stern eyes as she said, "If you walk on the sides of these shoes, I will give them away." My heart was broken at the thought of giving up my beautiful new shoes to some other little girl. I tried very hard to walk straight and keep from running over the sides of those shoes, just as I had tried very hard to stay awake at night to keep from wetting the bed. Nevertheless, my feet were just like my Grandma Cooper's, and sure enough, my feet began to lean to the sides.

I remember watching as my mother took those little straw shoes and gave them away. Many years have passed since then, and I've tried to tell myself that since I was so young, maybe Mother really didn't give my shoes away; maybe the fear of Mother's threat caused me to remember it differently. But I remember pulling into a dirt driveway that swooped downhill, displaying a gray wooden house with a very long front porch that belonged to a member of the church. A woman wearing a long dress was standing on this porch with a little girl who accepted the straw shoes that Mother took from me.

It's Chicken-Plucking Time

Mother used to buy live chickens because they were cheaper than chickens that had been processed. She would have a huge pot of boiling water sitting in the backyard, and we would each take a live chicken by the neck and wring it in the air until its neck was broken. We then placed the chickens into the boiling water for a few minutes until their feathers softened. Next, we would pluck all the feathers out of the bird before using an ax to chop off the chicken's head. Mother would string it upside down by its tied feet and let it hang from the clothesline until the blood drained out of its body. In my mind's eye, I can still see myself as that seven-year-old little girl wringing that poor chicken's neck, which made me very sad. This process was not uncommon because I remember other people doing the same thing.

Frightened and Alone

Mother used to have an elderly lady by the name of Susie Coffee babysit me while she was away working. Even though I was only seven years old, Susie would make me walk to the Town & Country store over a mile away. I was terrified because about the time I rounded the curve at Rev. Chaney Theodore Stratton's home, several dogs would chase me up the street. Many times, Rev. C. T. Stratton would be standing outside by his fence, and he would talk to me real friendly, which helped me not to be so afraid. Each time I had to make these trips to the store for Susie Coffee, I would hope and pray I'd see that old preacher standing in his yard when I came around the corner.

My panic attacks must have started back then because I remember being so terrified that I could barely breathe. If it wasn't bad enough having those dogs on my heels, the meanest-looking one was a pit bull. One day in particular, there was a man about thirty-five years old on Pine Hill Drive following me in his car. I kept waiting for the man to pass by me, but instead, with each step I took, he would barely move his car forward right behind me. My only thought to save myself was to go into someone's yard and walk up to their door as though I lived there. Unfortunately, when I knocked on the door no one was home. I stood there between the door and screen door terrified. The man went on up the road, thinking he had missed his chance. Yet, if he had lingered for a moment longer, he would have realized I wasn't getting into the house. I stayed worried sick in fear of the next time Susie Coffee would force me to walk to the Town & Country store.

5

Afraid to Close My Eyes

AS A LITTLE girl I was a bed wetter and received some awful beatings because of it. Mother would wake me up in the middle of the night hitting me with a leather belt, which would terrify me because I wouldn't be completely awake. I was so nervous I would try desperately to stay awake because I knew once I fell asleep, it was too late. It is burned into my memory sleeping on that little bed with Mother hitting me while I slept, and I would awake terrified, trying to pull my thoughts together as to why she was beating me. Then I would feel the wet-soaked sheets beneath me, and I knew. Often, she made

me pull the wet sheets off the bed, and at times she would shove the wet sheets in my face and make me smell the urine to shame me for what I had done.

She once told me that was what Brother Dennis did to his daughter, and I guess she hoped it would stop me from wetting the bed. I'm sure Mother believed she was doing the right thing. Yet, even back then, it seemed so unfair, and it only made me even more nervous and afraid.

When I wasn't awakened for wetting the bed, Mother would be shaking me awake with that fearful look in her eyes, telling me someone outside our window was trying to break in to kill us. My memories are so vivid of Mother marching through the house in the middle of the night with her loaded pistol, shouting in a loud voice that she had a gun and didn't mind using it.

I also recall one incident in particular when Mother had cashed our Social Security checks earlier that day, and that night she shook me awake saying someone was outside. I knew she was right because as we lay there on the bed next to the open window, someone was blowing cigarette smoke through the screen.

All through my childhood years, and even after I married and had my son, Mother would shake me awake with the gun in her hand insisting someone was outside trying to get in to harm us. Many times she sat on the edge of my bed with the gun in her hand and refused to let me dose off as sleepy as I was; she didn't want to feel she was alone.

My life was never my own because Mother moved in with me, even after I married, and always took charge. I was so afraid of her, whether I was five or forty-five, and she took full advantage of that fear.

Karen

My sister, Karen, was the oldest, and Mother loved her so much, it was as though she only had one daughter. I adored Karen and secretly believed if I could be like her, Mother would love me too, but Mother would never express the love toward me that she did my sister.

One of my earliest memories of Karen was when I was seven years old, and Karen was walking to the store with her girlfriends. I was running up the street behind her, begging her to let me go with them as she angrily told me to go away. There are no memories of Karen lovingly fixing my hair or helping me dress or treating me special, anything at all that would bring sweet memories to mind of my big sister, yet, oh how I adored her. As the years progressed, I spent my life begging her to love me, but nothing I would ever do could make Karen love me in return.

Mother hired a man by the name of Wallace Regan to build some kitchen cabinets for us. Even though Mother had a good income, she was not prudent in managing her finances. Wallace Regan was an extremely poor man and a member of the Church Assembly. He was, however, smart enough to convince my mother she needed him, so she agreed to his marriage proposal. Wallace Regan bought my two brothers and me a new swing set, which I'm certain was to get our seal of approval on the upcoming marriage. Shortly after they married, everything went downhill, only this time I wasn't laughing. He was very mean to Mother, and we were scared to death of him.

I hated green English peas, and Mother accidentally put some on my plate one night at suppertime. Wallace always made us kids eat everything on our plates, and this day was no exception. He demanded I eat those terrible green peas, but as I started to chew them, I felt as though I would throw up since they tasted so gross to me. Mother secretly came to my rescue after Wallace had left the table. She slid the peas off the plate into her hand and threw them in the trash.

Once, my brothers, sister, and I planned a surprise birthday celebration for Mother, and we asked Wallace to keep her in their bedroom until we kids finished setting the table. When he finally brought her out of the bedroom, she was in tears because he had talked to her so mean and just laughed about it. Wallace was always threatening my mother and trying to scare her.

The most outstanding thing that happened in the year of 1963 was shocking for everyone who followed the life of President John F. Kennedy. However, our church did not want him as president, and our church leader always told us who to vote for. You would be in serious trouble at church if you were brave enough to make your own choice in voting and were ignorant enough to let anyone know who you had voted for in the election. Our people were Christian people, so the Stratton's knew when they made the members raise their hands to vote for a particular candidate, the members would keep their word.

I didn't go to school that day. As I sat in front of the television, the shocking news was reported: President John F. Kennedy had been shot in Dallas, Texas. I leaped off my seat and ran as fast as I could up the street and down past Brother C. T. Stratton's home and up the embankment to Goodwill Drive/Union City to tell my grandmother, who was about three blocks away, that our beloved president had been shot. President Kennedy was so loved that even children mourned his death.

Turn the Television On!

As members of the Church Assembly, we were not allowed to have televisions. Nevertheless, it was discovered in the early 1960s that Brother Ted Stratton owned a television set and was attempting to keep it hidden by covering it with a long tablecloth. Instead of bringing an immediate Stratton family member to task and realizing the huge profit margin to be made by selling tv's to the church members, they decided to allow all the church members to have televisions that year. To be purchased at the Church Assembly Auction and furniture stores. I remember it well because I failed the second grade (Mrs. Turner's class), and my brother Jacob failed the third grade (Mrs. Davidson's class) that same year. My mother was called to the East Morris Street school for a parent/teacher conference. The teachers explained to Mother: You can ask Jacob or Yvette about any movie on television, what the actors' names are, and what each actor's real name is, and they can tell you. However, ask them about their studies or homework, and they don't have a clue. I distinctly remember staying up until the television would play "The Star-Spangled Banner." We sat there looking at the screen that had suddenly become completely still, and only then did we go off to bed.

Mother

Because of the disparaging way mother treated me, I tried to figure a way to write my life story and leave my relationship with her out of it. However, I cannot, no more than I can delete her from the pages of my life. She was there, a dominant figure in shaping me into the person I am today. I am a product of my past, and she is my past. She began shaping my mind as a little child, just as surely as God took dust from the earth and shaped Adam.

My mother had a really good heart and was taken advantage of by all the slave labor she performed for the Stratton family. In addition to all the money she gave over the years and the thousands of dollars she handed them from the death of my father. She was born into and grew up in the Church Assembly with all the emotional abuse and violence it presented. Neither she nor my grandmother believed it was wrong to beat a child with a thin stick until the blood would run down their back and legs.

My mother's family was a group of people with brilliant minds but emotionally trapped in a religious cult that denied their need to cultivate their own God-given creativity that was born into them. It was in their genes to love classical music, it was in their genes to be artistic, and it was in their genes to crave knowledge with no hope of satisfying their appetite to learn.

I have always believed the saying "Ignorance is bliss," yet when God has blessed you with such a powerful insight to see things as they truly are in so many situations, it is so painful to be stuck in a station of life where you know you do not belong. My mother would give you the shirt off her back if she believed you needed it, and I believe her attitude in this was from growing up with so little. She was so used to giving and serving others that she never had any concept of money, and that's why she never succeeded when she did escape the church's rule.

I saw Mother as someone who was good to everyone, except me.

She has always maligned my character to anyone she believed might care about me, even my own siblings. Mother was a decent God-fearing woman, yet extremely apprehensive.

When she stole from me, she made it clear that it wasn't stealing since I was her daughter, yet she did it in secret. Mother didn't treat me like a daughter but instead she treated me like she "owned" me and I had no rights as a human being. Whether she was unfairly slapping me in the face or stealing my money, mother felt she had total rights to my life and I had none, regardless, of my age. It would be so much easier to judge her if I could convince myself that she was consciously aware of her guilt, but I am uncertain that she was.

When I would tell her, I didn't believe she loved me, in hopes of some kind of reassurance from her that I was wrong, she quickly reminded me of all the times she bought me new dresses to wear to church when I was dating Chaney Stratton. Sadly, in my own mind, I believed she did it to make herself look good in front of people that had made her feel inferior. There was so much constant judgement in our church and especially considering the abuse mother endured I can easily understand if that was her true motives.

Even so, my heart was crying out for affection and understanding with no one to dry my tears.

I know my emotions are fragile, but all I ever wanted was no different from anyone else, I wanted to be loved. I felt I was always standing at the window of Mother's heart just watching as she fed my brothers and sister with her love, yet when I looked at my own plate, it was always empty.

My Beautiful Pink Dress

My sister, Karen, graduated from Dalton High School in 1964, and Mother was so very proud of her. Karen was very smart, and everyone liked her. Mother bought me the most beautiful pastel-pink dress with three layers flowing down the front from the waist to wear to Karen's graduation. I loved that dress so much, and I felt so pretty when I wore it because it made me feel like a little princess.

However, after the graduation ceremonies were over, Mother took my beautiful dress to the cleaners located next to Stafford's grocery store to have it dry-cleaned. Once Mother dropped off the dress, she never went back to pick it up. For years to come, when I would ride by the Orchid Cleaners, I would sadly remember my little pink dress and how much I had loved it.

6

Mother's Generous Heart
(1965)

MY FAVORITE PLACE in the world was Dalton, Georgia, because I thought of it as home. However, I would quickly have to learn that every time I began to feel safe and comfortable, I would be yanked up and taken to another state. It seemed that every time I blinked my eyes, Mother was taking us kids to visit my sister, Karen, in Indiana. Karen and Mother always shared a special understanding and closeness that regretfully never existed between my mother and me, or even Karen and me. Karen moved to Kokomo, Indiana, after she married Lance Mullins, who was also a member of our church.

On one occasion, when we traveled to Indiana for the birth of my sister's baby, Mother decided to stay permanently. This broke my heart because Dalton, Georgia, was the only home I'd ever known.

After living in Kokomo, a short while, Mother landed a job at Hank's grocery store, which also had a bakery. Mother became a professional cake decorator, and she was also an exceptional seamstress. When Mother began to work at Hank's grocery store, she didn't own a car so she had to depend on other people for a ride to and from work. When the store would have day-old bread and bakery items, Mother was quick to bring them to the more unfortunate people in our church.

A memory that stands out in my mind so vividly is one freezing-cold day, as the deep snow lay on the ground, Mother found herself at work without a way home. She called the pastor, Brother Howard, of our church and asked him if he would mind coming to pick her up. He sternly replied that he would not come for her because he was meditating on the Bible.

With a grocery cart full of day-old bakery items, Mother started walking home in the snow for five miles without snow boots. She was freezing cold by the time she arrived, yet she was eager to give the food to Ellis and Anita Flood and their six children.

7

The Intruder

WE LIVED ON Vaile Avenue in Kokomo during my fifth-grade school year in a house that was over one hundred years old. The two-story house Mother rented was so old that it had withstood the Civil War. It was a spooky-looking old house that many of my friends from school swore was haunted. I'm not sure that was true; however, there were some really bad incidents that occurred during the time we lived there.

We had a very long porch that went halfway around our house, so we had two doors on the porch. One door opened into the living room, which had a lovely bay window I used to sit by and watch outside. If you stayed on the porch and walked a little farther, you could enter the other door, which took you into the kitchen. I remember the ceilings being so high, nothing like they are today. We had two telephones, one in the kitchen and the other—a pink princess telephone—in mine and Mother's bedroom upstairs. There was a little light on my princess telephone that would come on if someone picked up the receiver downstairs. One day, when Mother was in the kitchen with the outside door open, she looked up from snapping green beans and gasped. A man was standing there, reaching his hand for the screen door in an effort to come in. He wasn't aware I was standing a few feet behind him. In a stern voice, she quickly asked him what he wanted.

He stepped back and said, "Could I call me a cab?" Mother replied, "I will call it for you!"

Later that night while we lay in bed, someone tried to break into our house. Mother had my two brothers come into my bedroom with us and bolt the door by sticking a knife between the door and the door facing. She then attempted to call the police, but every time she picked up the receiver to dial the number, someone was picking up the telephone downstairs from inside our house making it impossible to dial out.

Since the house was so old, there were no locks on the bedroom doors, so Mother had us remove the drawers from the dresser and put them in a line leading from the door to the wall. The stairs leading up to my bedroom door were so old that each time you stepped on one of them it would creak loudly.

Suddenly, we heard someone coming up those steps, obviously trying to tiptoe, but it never worked because we could easily hear him. This time she knew that whoever was in our house was on the stairs, so Mother quickly dialed the number for the police station. While she was talking to the chief of police, the little light lit up on my telephone, so Mother knew someone was listening in from downstairs.

When the police came, they searched every room but the attic, so the police assured us that whoever was in our house was now gone. After the police left, we settled back down to sleep, but we still kept the door bolted with the dresser drawers.

Suddenly, we heard pieces of plaster falling from the ceiling inside my bedroom closet. Someone was coming down from the attic through the hole in the ceiling. Mother and we kids quickly grabbed drawers from the chest of drawers in my room and lined them up from the closet leading to the bed.

Then we heard sirens and people's voices right outside our window, so I opened the window and hollered down at my neighbors on the sidewalk and asked what was going on. They said there had been a horrible accident, and someone was killed. The EMT turned over the body and discovered it was his own sister.

We shouted at my neighbors to get the police because someone was trying to break in on us. We immediately heard our intruder pull himself up the inside of my closet, as lots of plaster was falling, and we heard his feet running through the attic overhead. The police came once again, checked out our house, and determined the intruder had escaped from the attic by jumping down though the adjoining bedroom. He then climbed out of the window onto the roof, then jumped onto the lower roof, and then onto the ground.

Chased by Evil

A few days later, Debbie, my best friend and neighbor, came over to my house to show me her new bicycle with a banana seat and butterfly handlebars. She was so proud of it and wanted me to go to town with her to buy her mother some earrings for her birthday at the five-and-dime store. Debbie said we could take turns riding her bicycle, so I agreed. It was about three miles to Kresge's department store. We first passed the high school parking lot, then crossed a bridge, and passed Kokomo High School, which was to the left of us.

Once we arrived in town, I was riding through a parking lot when suddenly a man with curly dark-brown hair in an old blue car almost hit me. Automatically, I wondered if this man was my father. After all, he did possess the curly dark-brown hair. I swerved to keep from being hit by his car. On we went to Kresge's and I thought no more about the incident other than wonder if he was my dad. Debbie bought the earrings, and then we headed for home.

After we got out of town, we once again passed Kokomo High School, and I was riding the bicycle across the bridge. Then it would be Debbie's turn to ride. At the end of the bridge, I got off the bike and Debbie got on. As we looked up and to our left, that old blue car that had almost hit me in town was sitting in the vacant high school parking lot. As we looked at him, he slammed on his gas pedal, spinning his wheels in the dirt in an effort to hurriedly get to us. We panicked and took off down a side street that was downhill to our right. Debbie was on her bike and I was on foot, but I was running faster than she was pedaling. We ran into someone's yard, and since they didn't have a telephone so we could call home, we stayed until we thought it would be safe to leave.

8

On a Greyhound Heading West

REV. HENRY STRATTON came to Kokomo to hold a revival at church. During this time my brother Jacob, who was in the seventh grade, had been caught smoking cigarettes and skipping class. He would also spend his free time with our brother-in-law, Lance Mullins, who allowed Jacob to drink beer. The pastor of our church advised my mother to send Jacob to the church farm in Arizona to get him away from Lance's influence so Jacob's soul wouldn't be lost and go to hell. At first, Jacob was the only one who was supposed to go to the church farm. However, Mother realized she couldn't bear to let him go, so she decided we would all go.

Jacob was the only one who looked forward to the trip to Arizona because he really looked up to Brother Henry Stratton since he remembered him from when he was a little boy. We couldn't take all of our clothes on the bus, so Mother left behind a huge box in our living room with an agreement from Ellis Flood that he would ship it to us, but that would never happen. Instead, he kept our belongings— this church member whom my mother had fed, along with his wife and six children, so many times with day-old bakery items she pushed home in the snow to keep them from going hungry.

Mother had bought a station wagon, so the first thing she did was sell the car and liquidate all our assets which were few, into cash for our trip out West. She was told that the church would build us a home in Arizona, but we would later learn that promise would never be carried out. Mother packed a couple of suitcases and walked away from everything we had acquired. Then she bought tickets on a Greyhound bus heading west for all of us, including Jacob, age 13; Josh, age 9; and me, age12.

9

A Little Girl Lost

IT WAS 1966 and I was twelve years old. This was the third day I had been riding on the Greyhound bus, and although I was extremely anxious to get off, in the back of my mind I felt very afraid. I didn't want to go to the church farm and leave everything that was safe and familiar to me behind. I knew how scary the meetings at church were when the preacher grabbed and shook people by their heads amid warnings of what horrible ways God was going to punish us for our sins and even for what we might be thinking. I felt such a great dread of what life on the farm was going to be like. The church would be in total control of our lives and every move we made.

As I looked outside the window of the bus, it seemed as though we were slowly leaving civilization as I knew it. The trees began to gradually disappear. We rode for miles and miles without seeing any sign of life. This was my first trip to the white sandy desert. After riding for three days and two nights, we finally arrived in Phoenix, Arizona. With an extremely tired and aching body from trying to find comfort in every position possible on the bus, my eagerness to get off overpowered my fears of what lay ahead. It was two-thousand miles to our destination, so sitting on a bus for three days had become quite uncomfortable.

Sister Jeanette Stratton, Rev. Henry Stratton's wife, picked us up at the bus station in Phoenix and took us to the farm, which was 125 miles away in the middle of nowhere.

The little town of Bouse, Arizona, was ten miles from the Utting farm. Bouse had a post office, a small motel, a telephone, and a one-room school. The closest grocery store was thirty miles away in Salome, Arizona. As we approached the church farm, the tension within me began to mount, but nothing in my wildest dreams or worst nightmares could have prepared me for what I would soon discover was in store for us. There were no telephones on the church farm, and the mail was picked up in Bouse by Florence Carter. When we arrived at the farm, I saw no trees, no grass, or much of anything except for a few houses lined up horizontally. It was so terribly quiet, you didn't hear any of those little sounds of everyday living, such as motors, horns, or even God's little creatures like birds. Heck, they must all be dead! I felt like a trapped rat, knowing I was caught and wondering if I would ever be able to get away.

As I looked all around me, it was hard to believe that people really lived here. The highway we came in on was the only highway for at least 110 miles. I would later refer to this highway as the highway to freedom. Everything around me looked so barren and desolate, just sand as far as the eye could see.

Suddenly, I saw real trees, real green grass, and a beautiful yellow brick house right in the middle of nowhere. The grass and trees were constantly irrigated by cool waters spraying all around me. The house belonged to Rev. Henry and Jeanette Stratton. Mother, my two brothers, and I were permitted to stay at the preacher's home for the first two nights. I ended up with only three dresses because the rest of our clothes would never be sent to us as promised by the church members in Kokomo, Indiana.

The Arizona sun was so hot that I learned very quickly to keep my shoes on, but there was another reason. There were these weird-looking stickers hidden in the sand called goat heads. The painful sharp stickers were similar to those you find on rose bushes only harder. If you picked up one, you would understand. It looked like a real goat's head.

On about the third day, Sister Jeanette took us to see where we would be living. We were taken across some railroad tracks on a hill that ran along the one and only highway that passed by the church farm. Just as we went over the hill we could see the other side, and there were eight buildings, including the shop (where the churchmen worked on farm equipment), a little white church with a small junkyard behind it, a building called the shower house (where we would bathe), and an outhouse about two-hundred feet from the church. There also were four shabby houses and the worst looking one was to be ours. It was a shack they had set up on blocks, simply a square wooden box nailed together. We were told that when the church farm was first started, they put up these tar-paper shacks for the people to live in. There was also a clothesline, a little Cessna airplane that belonged to our pastor, and an airstrip. The wood on our house looked like the ancient gray wood you see on outhouses; it was cracked and shabby, and it was long but not very wide.

Our house was used as a toolshed before we moved in, so it desperately needed a roof to keep out the rain. There were no steps to assist you in getting into the house; instead, you had to kind of step up and leap forward as though you were trying to get in a pickup truck that sits high off the ground. Upon entering the house, I observed a creaking wooden floor that was literally covered with inches of sand. There were so many wide cracks in the walls and floor that everywhere I looked, I could see the light of day beaming through the holes. I felt as though I was in a glass prism looking at little reflecting lights.

As I entered the kitchen and looked to my left, I observed a huge sink. Above this sink was what appeared to resemble a window, but it had no glass. However, there was a singular spigot that protruded through this opening in the wall. Over to my right was another one of these square holes in the wall that went directly outside. In front of me was a little white gas stove, and there was a very small refrigerator. Our house consisted of three rooms, and we were told that we should feel fortunate because at one time several families had to share those three rooms.

There was a total of six windows without any glass in them, which would really be a problem when the sandstorms came. At one point, I looked down at the floor, and as I did, out of the corner of my eye, I saw something move on the top of my shoe. As I looked directly down at my feet, there, in the midst of my horror, sat a huge scorpion with a large stinger.

Sister Jeanette took me and Mother behind the church to a small junkyard. There she chose a tabletop with no legs for us to eat on, a crate to put under it for support, and lard cans to be used as chairs. The tabletop was warped by the sun, Mother couldn't set food on one side of it because it was so bubbled up, and the other side wasn't level either. She put only a small amount of pinto beans in a bowl at a time so they wouldn't spill out. It was now time for Sister Jeanette to make her exit and go to her beautiful home. How easy it seemed that she could just simply walk away and leave us in that horrible place. It was very close to living outside because there wasn't anything outside that couldn't get into our house.

I remember so vividly sitting there in front of that hole in the wall in the kitchen with my mother and two brothers eating our first meal, which consisted of pinto beans. At this point we experienced our first sandstorm. It was so strong that it moved Brother Henry's little Cessna airplane about outside our window. The storm blew sand in our food, faces, hair, and everything around us. In my mind's eye, I can still see my mother's powdery-looking beige face and the dirty tears that rolled down her cheeks as she said, "I can't believe this is really happening to us." Then suddenly, she began to laugh hysterically as though she were losing her mind.

I wore a thin headscarf over my eyes, ears, nose, and mouth to keep the gnats from tormenting me while I hung out the laundry. By the time I moved from one end of the clothesline to the other end, the clothes were almost dry. The shower house was shared by four families, and someone had tied a rope around one of the wooden beams in the ceiling. So, for fun, when it was time to bathe, I would swing through the ice-cold water holding on to the rope. The water was just too cold to stand there and freeze your butt off while trying to wash yourself. The outhouse was separated from the shower facility farther out in the desert. The walk from our house to the outhouse was a frightening experience because of all the poisonous critters that lurked in the desert.

10

Please Find My Mother

MANY DAYS I would spend my free time going into the church and playing what few, tunes I knew on the piano. The church was empty and spooky, but there just wasn't any other way to entertain myself; after all, we didn't have a television. You can never imagine the loneliness I felt; it was so quiet and life seemed so empty. I remember one day when I was permitted to go to Parker, Arizona, with one of the church members for supplies. As I stood there on the sidewalk and looked around at all of the Indians mostly old, I wondered if I would ever get to go home to Georgia. I remember thinking, "Someone please come and get me and take me back home," but no one ever came.

I felt as though I was behind an iron curtain. I spent many nights looking up at the stars and wondering if the people in Dalton could see the same stars. I needed desperately to believe that they could. Mother took a job in Parker, Arizona, as a butcher at Pinky's market. She worked like a man, carrying sides of beef weighing fifty pounds across her shoulder. Mother was a very ambitious and talented woman, putting her whole heart in whatever job she had to do. I always saw her as a perfectionist. She could use a meat saw as well as any man.

One evening as she waited for Willie Carter to pick her up and return her to the church farm, the minutes turned into hours. Neither

Willie nor anyone else showed up to take my mother home. It began to get dark, and Mother was very afraid. Pinky's market had closed at five o'clock, and now it was going toward eleven o'clock as Mother stood on the street hovered in a corner, terrified and very much alone. Suddenly someone was shining a spotlight in her face and said in a deep voice, "Lady, what in the world are you doing here? Don't you know how dangerous it is for you to be here alone at this time of night?" It was a police officer, and after she told him she was waiting for someone to pick her up from work, he assured her that he would patrol this particular area and keep her safe until someone showed up to take her home.

I was back on the farm trying to find out why no one had brought my mother home, but no one seemed to be listening or show any concern. That night at church, I told Marlana Douglas that no one brought my mother home, and she was the one person who seemed concerned. She was very angry that no one had done anything to help. Right away she jumped in a car and hurried to rescue my mother. I have always felt very grateful toward Marlana for her kindness.

11

Human Targets

I RECEIVED SOME very harsh whippings from my mother during the time we were on the Arizona church farm. Once, when I was riding a horse across the railroad tracks to the other side where the decent homes were located, Ronnie Gaddis told my mother that when I crossed the tracks riding the horse, he could see my knees. This was the only time I was ever fortunate enough to even get to ride a horse on the church farm. I was given one of the worst beatings of my life by my mother, who believed she was doing the right thing.

The next time was when I walked out to the shower house to bathe. I knocked on the door before attempting to enter, and a man's voice made me aware that the shower house was not empty. I returned to the house with my towel to wait for the shower house to become available for me to use. The man in the shower house was Donnie Gordon. His wife, Gracie, told my mother that I was trying to peek at her naked husband. I was twelve years old with no interest in seeing her short, chubby husband. It's easy to resent being punished for things you're not guilty of and not easily forgotten.

Brother Henry enjoyed the luxury of having everyone do his bidding and fearing his every word. My brother Jacob looked up to Brother Henry and would tease him by calling him "Hubcap" just to get Brother Henry's attention. One day, after washing Brother Henry's airplane,

Jacob started calling him Hubcap, and Brother Henry grabbed a BB gun and began shooting at Jacob. Brother Henry hopped on the back of a pickup truck, and while brother Tucker Davis drove for him, Brother Henry shot Jacob in the back three or four times as he and another boy ran across the desert as though they were animals. Brother Henry was laughing as he aimed his gun and used my brother for target practice. Jacob said it really hurt when Brother Henry shot him, but he had Henry's attention, and Jacob wanted so much to please Brother Henry since he didn't have a father of his own. At the time, Jacob said he just felt special because it was him whom Brother Henry was shooting at. Jacob used to massage Brother Henry's feet for hours. Brother Tillis used to do it before we came to Arizona, but now Jacob massaged Henry's feet while Brother Tillis massaged his head.

One night, when Jacob was at Brother Henry's massaging his feet, the men were talking about how strong Jacob was. Even though he was only fourteen years old, he worked as hard as a man on the hay trucks. Brother Henry said, "We're going to see just how strong Jacob is." So, he made Jacob hold his arms straight out to his sides while they placed a catalog in each of his hands. The cattle catalogs were about four inches thick. Jacob held the catalogs so long that his arms ached and he wanted to put them down. Each time his arms began to get heavy, he would slowly begin to lower the catalogs. Brother Henry Stratton held a broken-off antenna from his portable television in his hand, and he would whip my brother across his legs and back with it. Jacob held back his tears regardless of how much pain Brother Henry inflicted on him. Brother Henry just kept laughing because he thought it was funny.

Jackrabbits and Jacob

Jackrabbits were real pests on the church farm because they would eat the alfalfa the church would be growing, and the church also grew soybeans. There were so many jackrabbits that the churchmen would load up their pickup trucks at night and go hunting. Brother John Winston Stratton Sr. would come to Arizona with the intention of inspecting the church farm. He would also bring important ministers— his entourage—with him to go hunting for jackrabbits. Even the church women would get together and go jackrabbit hunting.

Since the jackrabbits were wild, it was only for sport and to keep them out of the fields, not for human consumption. When the men shot a jackrabbit, they would shine a big spotlight that was hooked up to the truck's battery on the injured jackrabbit. Then they had one of the young boys they had brought along get off the truck and kick the jackrabbit in the head until it was dead. This game plan would save on their bullets. The churchmen would kill as many as fifty to one hundred jackrabbits a night. On one occasion, Jesse Blackford told my brother Jacob to get off the truck and kick the jackrabbit in the head. As they shined the spotlight on him, suddenly someone spotted another jackrabbit in the distance. Without waiting for Jacob to get back to the truck, they hurriedly drove off without him.

It was about ten o'clock at night and always very snaky. Being terrified and alone, my fourteen-year-old brother began to walk toward the main dirt road. There were always snakes out at night because, unlike during the day, it would be cool at night, and so it was not uncommon to see deadly poisonous snakes stretched across the width of the dirt road.

My brother was a tough cookie and was always reluctant to let anyone see him cry. I am sure, since he was all alone and no one would see him, he did cry as he asked God to watch over and protect him. Jacob finally made it to the main dirt road and began to walk in the direction of the church farm with no light except for the one God had provided (the moon),

With about a mile left to go, the truck that had left him in the desert suddenly pulled up beside him, and Jesse Blackford told him to get on the truck. When the men had left Jacob in the desert, he was very afraid, but now he felt only anger at what they had done, so he refused to get in the truck with them. The next night at church Jacob got his hide busted. When they rebuked him at church, they told him he had a spirit against Jesse Blackford because he had refused to get back on the truck.

One day, when the churchmen were branding and castrating the cattle that had just arrived, Jacob was sitting on top of the fence watching. As the churchmen clipped the horns of the cattle, the blood would spray up into the air at which point the hot iron would be applied, causing the blood to stop. Tucker Davis would hold a pan underneath each bull and cut off its testicles. He would then take these testicles home and eat them for supper.

Brother Henry held a long buggy whip in his hand as he popped the cattle on their rears to control them. Once, as he yanked the whip back with his hand, the whip caught on the fence behind him. As he jerked it forward, it caused him to hit himself in the eye with his own hand and knock off his glasses. Jacob and the churchmen begin to laugh at Brother Henry. He was furious as he shouted, "Shut up!"

The men immediately became silent except Jacob, who was still laughing. Brother Henry took the buggy whip and lashed my brother across the back, causing Jacob to drop off the back of the fence to the ground as though he were dead. Once Jacob was himself again, he heard Brother Henry call out to the churchmen, "Get him!" Jacob began to scramble underneath the fence to escape to safety but not before Brother Henry lashed him with the buggy whip once again, only this time across the back of Jacob's legs.

Jacob was bleeding and in a lot of pain, but Brother Henry still wanted to inflict more pain on my brother. One of the churchmen, D. W. was in reach of Jacob when suddenly Lance Mullins stepped in front of him, making it impossible to reach Jacob and allowing Jacob to escape to safety. Now, thirty years later, Jacob still wears those scars across the back of his legs and his back as a reminder of how life was for him on the Arizona church farm.

12

Arizona School Days

I **TRAVELED TEN** miles a day across the desert to our one-room school on a little school bus along with my brothers and the other church kids from the farm. The school also had a small stage at the head of our desks. Each row of desks represented the grade you were in. If there were only three first graders, the first three desks would be the first grade; the next seat would begin the second grade. There were two other buildings; one was the lunchroom with Lucille as our wonderful cook, and the other was a small house for the one teacher we had, who taught from the first grade to the eighth grade. On many occasions the teacher would permit me and sometimes one of the other girls to get out of class by going next door and cleaning her house.

There was no recreational equipment at our school, except for one monkey bar, so the kids would make up their own games to play. One fun thing to do was climb the two big old trees on the playground and swing out onto the ground. The most popular game was when the first and second grade kids would search for snakes underneath the many rocks on the playground. The two eighth grade boys (my brother Jacob and his friend Chuck) would hit the snakes in the head with a railroad spike, which looks like a very large nail, and then rip out the snakes' guts and hang the skins up to dry. When the snake skins were dry, the boys would place them around their cowboy hats. These snakes were deadly poisonous, and if any child had been bitten, they would die because our faith didn't believe in seeking help from doctors. Besides, we were so far out into the desert we couldn't have made it to a doctor or hospital anyway.

It was against our religion to wear slacks, short pants, or sleeveless dresses, so the clothes we had to play in were really uncomfortable. One day at school, my friend Darlene took a safety pin and pinned her long skirt between her legs. She wore her long hair in a bun with some of her ponytail hanging out of the center. She climbed up on the only monkey bar on the playground, wrapped her skinny legs around the bar, and hung upside down with her body swinging in the air, unaware that a huge Red Racer snake was underneath her dangling head. The snake began to crawl away into some rocks.

13

Living in Fear

I **REMEMBER COMING** home from school many times and seeing my mother lying on the old wooden floor in front of the cooler with a wet cloth over her mouth trying to breathe. The cooler was an ugly contraption with a big wheel rolling around while water dripped down on it from a water hose in an effort to cool the dry hot air. The house stayed dusty with sand because every time we had a sandstorm, the sand would simply blow through the cracks in the walls and cover everything in the house. It would get so hot at our house that Mother would send me up to the shop with a large stainless-steel pan to fill up with crushed ice from the ice machine.

One day as I was headed to the shop, I suddenly heard a gunshot as though someone was shooting at me. This scared the daylights out of me. It was Brother Collins shooting a pistol right in front of my feet. As I moved the pan to my side, I saw why he was shooting his gun. There was an extremely large, black, hairy tarantula spider, and when it was turned over, its belly was a bright orange color. I was told their bite is extremely painful. I always dreaded going to the outhouse each day because it was a pretty good distance from our tarpaper shack. Furthermore, with so many dangerous creatures living in the dessert you never knew what to expect. I felt nervous being inside the outhouse with all the big spiders spinning up and down on their webs but mostly I was always afraid of meeting up with a snake. I had heard my aunt say when she lived on the church farm in Texas, she always looked inside the hole before she sat down. She said one day when she looked in the hole, there was a huge rattlesnake curled up on top of the poop. Knowing this, I always looked in the hole before sitting down. I was inside the outhouse and when I opened the door to step out and leave. I came very close to stepping on an enormous Western diamondback rattlesnake. It was six foot long and looked like it could have put half my foot in its mouth. I screamed only to hear my brother Jacob laughing close by. He thought he killed the snake before dragging it in front of the outhouse in his attempt to scare me. Unfortunately, what he did not know is a rattlesnake's bite reflex can be triggered hours after the snake is dead. Jacob always treated me badly growing up but he would have never gotten over it if he was responsible for getting me killed.

God was truly protecting me while living on the church farm in the middle of the desert.

Since we didn't believe in medical treatment, the state sent out pamphlets to the farm each month explaining the dangers and what to expect should you be exposed to the venomous bites of the creatures that lived in the desert. I vividly recall a picture of a man's hand after he had been bitten on the index finger by a tarantula. The wound turned black, and bubbles began to form all the way up his hand as though it was rotting off like some form of cancer.

We never had very much to eat around our house. I do remember eating a lot of pinto beans but no meat. When I would go over to Darlene's house, I felt very lucky to eat with her family because they not only had pinto beans, but they also had fried potatoes and corn bread every day, and fried chicken on Sundays.

I remember being at Shelly Stratton's home one day as she opened her refrigerator, and there sat a huge glass jug of orange juice. My heart ached just to have a sip of it, and I remember thinking they were so very rich because they had orange juice. For years to come,

I believed that people who could afford orange juice were wealthy.

Mother was a professional when it came to decorating cakes and sewing. She had made about everything in life that could be made with a needle and thread, including parachutes and Catholic robes. Mother made a dress for a lady named Janice Brock on the church farm who insisted that my mother line the entire dress. Mother had never lined a dress before, so this was something new and difficult to do by hand. After sitting up all night and working so hard to make and line the dress to perfection, the dress was finally completed. When Janice came to pick up the dress, she handed my mother one dollar for her labor. Even in 1967 that was insulting, but Mother never said a word.

14

Slave Labor Religion

WHILE WE LIVED in Arizona, Mother made seat covers for all the seats on both the church buses; there were fifty-six seats on each bus. They utilized Mother's talents in the kitchen as well, making Brother Henry's favorite sweets, such as Martha Washington candy. She was also a fabulous cake decorator and made a huge wedding cake for Brother Henry's sister-in-law Meg Blackford, as well as the wedding dress and all of the bridesmaids' and flower girl dresses. Mother believed in her heart she was being a servant for God when, in reality, she was being a servant for the Stratton's.

Mother was always sewing for the Stratton's, many times paying for the material with the Social Security checks she received from the death of my father. Except for the dollar, I never knew of even one time when they paid her for the work she did. When it was getting close to the ministers meeting, Mother made Jeanette Stratton and each of her four sisters a different dress for every service of the assembly. There would be seven services (two a day) of the ministers meeting, so Jeanette and her sisters wanted a different new dress for each church service, which totaled thirty-five dresses. I never before or since have seen anyone sew as much as Mother did. It seemed that every time I saw her, she was sitting at a sewing machine.

She never had time to sew for me. One day I went to Mother

and asked her if Sister Anderson could make me a dress. It hurt my mother so much because she later told me she felt ashamed that she had neglected my needs for other people. After that she made me the prettiest floral skirt I had ever owned. She gave me a soft blue blouse with ruffles down the front and a small ruffle on the collar and sleeves. At thirteen years old I wore this outfit to church with my first pair of high heels, which were also soft blue with tiny white straps across the top. I loved that skirt so much, and I realized it was because I appreciated it so much.

Working on the Farm

The church farm had hayfields, cattle, soybeans, etc., so the church needed their members to work these farms. Before daybreak Brother Tucker Davis would come by in a sand buggy to pick up my younger brother, Josh, and me to work in the fields for fifty cents an hour. The fifty cents an hour that Josh and I made was expected to be returned to the church in the offering plate. I really don't know why they even bothered giving us the money in the first place.

A sand buggy is an automobile that has had the top and trunk cut off. It has the appearance and capabilities of a truck. All Josh and I had to do was step on the back and hold on tight. Because Jacob, my fourteen-year-old brother, was so strong they used him to stack bales of alfalfa on the hay trucks. They paid Jacob sixty dollars a week, which averaged out to two dollars and fifty cents a semitruck load, and each bale of alfalfa weighed about 160 pounds. My brother didn't have a daddy, and he was willing to work his tail off for the love and approval of the churchmen. The money he made went straight to Mother to buy us food and pay our pledges.

One day Bobby and Darlene Davis came over to play with my brother Josh and me. Suddenly, a Gila monster came running out of a cactus bush and headed right for me. The Gila monster is the most dangerous animal in the Arizona desert. It's a very scary-looking and an extremely huge lizard. Furthermore, the venom of a Gila monster is poisonous. I began to run as fast as I could because they're so big and scary looking. I accidentally knocked Darlene into a cactus bush. I felt so sorry for her because I had fallen into one on the first day, I had arrived at the church farm. I knew just how painful the needles were. When it happened to me, I was told if I didn't pick all the needles out of my leg, they would work their way through my leg and come out the other side. As I was running, my brother Josh took out his railroad spike from his pocket and hit the creature on the head and killed it. Those kids were really good shots with those railroad spikes.

15

A Little Boy's Nightmare

OUR CHURCH HAD branches all over the United States, so there were people who lived on the farm from different parts of the country. There was a real sweet yet poor family with six children that was recruited in Kentucky to move out to the church farm. I learned that before they moved out to the farm, one little boy by the name of Timmy Sanders had some bad nightmares of being bitten by a snake. His mother said he would wake her up in the middle of the night screaming and crying. He would tell her he had once again dreamed a snake was biting him. He pleaded with her, "Mommy, please don't take me to the church farm in Arizona because I know I will be bitten by a snake and die." Everyone loved Timmy because he was such a sweet-natured child and never gave anyone a problem.

When Timmy's family arrived in Arizona, Timmy and Josh immediately became great friends. The entire farm was snaky, but the area of the farm where Timmy lived was extremely snaky. The back of his house sat high off the ground.

One day, when the children were playing in their backyard, Timmy's little sister's kitten ran underneath the house, and she started in after it. Timmy stopped her and said he would retrieve the kitten for her. It was during dog days, when the snakes shed their skin. During this time, the old skin covers the snake's eyes making it unable to see. Because of this, they will strike many times out of their own fear. Timmy was crawling under the house behind the little kitten, and the kitten was sniffing along behind an extremely large rattlesnake. Suddenly the rattlesnake whirled around and began biting Timmy. He was bitten several times in the mouth and several times in his private area. How utterly horrible it must have been for him not being able to get away and having that monster biting you in the face. Even now it makes me shiver to think of what that child went through and what must have gone through his terrified little mind. He truly lived his nightmare.

Timmy lived in a house where someone could walk completely around in a circle and not hit a wall. His mother was cleaning when Timmy walked in the door. When she looked at him, all that was noticeable was a little trickle of blood on his mouth. He was obviously in shock and never said a word. Instead, his mother said, "Timmy, you've been on that white propane tank again and fallen off, haven't you?" Not waiting for his reply, she went on to say, "I have told you to stay off of it, so you go over there and sit down on the couch and don't you get up!" Timmy silently complied. His mother resumed her cleaning, and on one of those trips around that inside circle of her home, she suddenly stopped and looked directly at her little boy as an overwhelming fear gripped her soul. She cried out, "Timmy, you've been snake bitten, haven't you?"

As she spoke these words, he was rising to his feet, and before he could speak, he began to vomit up this terrible-looking green stuff. As her heart fell to her feet, she grabbed her little boy up in her arms and ran toward one of the few vehicles on her side of the church farm. She hurriedly took her son to Brother Henry's home and laid him on the sofa. The word spread quickly about what had happened, and all of the other church members headed for Brother Henry's home. As she and her husband and their other five children gathered around Timmy, everyone began to pray frantically.

Brother Henry was away on one of his many trips, so George Hollis was in charge. He started preaching to everyone there in the living room. "Bless God, if there's anyone in here that doesn't believe he will live, then get out of here!" The truth is, if you didn't have the faith to believe that Timmy would be miraculously healed, there is no way you could admit it, and you did not dare leave that room. Timmy had four snake bites on his lips and mouth, and red streaks quickly began to run up his face toward his temples. His grieving father held up little Timmy's head and tried to feed him a sip of Mountain Dew soda pop. You could see he felt helpless, not knowing what to do, and Timmy wasn't saying anything. His lifeless little body just lay limp while he slowly died without the slightest ounce of medical help.

His mom and dad and five brothers and sisters had such a loving bond for each other that it was difficult and sad for me to kneel there beside the kids and watch as they had to see their little brother suffer and die. There was so much fear in that room with George preaching on top of what was happening to little Timmy. I saw George as a mean and hateful person, but I guess he was as afraid as the rest of us. Yet he spoke so mean that I never did like him, and I was scared to death of him. Our religion was definitely one that was held together by great fear.

I remember Timmy's fourteen-year-old brother, Ronnie Sanders, going a little berserk and taking off to his home, screaming, "I'll get that snake or it'll get me!" He left before anyone had a chance to stop him. Ronnie took a pistol, crawled underneath their house, and shot the rattlesnake that bit his brother. He brought the rattlesnake over to Reverend Henry Stratton's home where we were all still watching Timmy dying. Ronnie held the rattlesnake up in the air for all to see. The rattlesnake was so big and long that, with Ronnie's hand held high in the air, the snake still hung down to the ground.

Timmy was eight and a half years old, and the rattlesnake had eight rattles and one button, which meant it was the same age as Timmy. Knowing about the dream Timmy had before coming to Arizona, I believe the rattlesnake was just waiting there for him.

Even after Timmy had died, no one wanted to admit it. Eventually, George placed a mirror over little Timmy's face for signs of his breath steaming the looking glass, but there was no sign of life, and they had to admit the little boy was dead. I have never heard such sad cries in my life. Most of the children were in their teens.

To see such helplessness in a mother's face, to know she was doing everything in her power to live the kind of life she thought God wanted her to live, and then to see her hold the lifeless body of her precious little boy in her arms, you knew she would never be the same. She wouldn't cut her hair, and she wore her dresses below her knees. She wore no makeup, and as poor as she was, she gave her money to the church. She had given up all her worldly goods and lived her life for God. She had packed up her life in a few suitcases and brought it to a desolate desert believing this was what God expected of her and so much more.

And I was sure, as she gazed upon the face of her precious little son, she probably heard his still small voice ringing in her ears, "Mommy, please don't take me to the church farm in Arizona because I will be bitten by a snake and die." His sixteen-year-old sister, Sharon Sanders, ran into Brother Henry's bedroom alone, but everyone in the house heard her cries. She screamed such a sad, pitiful, and helpless scream that surely those sad screams rose above the clouds and touched the ears of Jesus.

Mother stayed up all night sewing clothes for little Timmy's brothers and sisters to wear to their brother's funeral. My brother Josh, who was ten years old at the time, was a pallbearer for his little friend Timmy Sanders.

16

The Tumbleweed Christmas Tree

AFTER TIMMY DIED, I was always afraid that what had happened to him might happen to me or one of my family members. Late one evening, Brother Henry sent word to my mother to come over to his house and make him some Martha Washington candy. Transportation was not sent for us, but it never was, so we had to walk. It was dark outside, and I was so afraid to go. Nevertheless, I didn't want to stay home alone either in that spooky little house across from that spooky little church. Brother Henry wanted something for his sweet tooth, so off we started, Mother, Jacob, Josh and me, for his home. We didn't own a flashlight; the only light we had to light our path was the moon. There was a slight breeze blowing sand in my mouth, and as I clasped my teeth together, I could feel the grit between them.

With each step I took, I silently watched the ground for snakes and S's. Sidewinder snakes make lots of S's as they quickly move across the sand. No one talked; we were all afraid. We just held hands and walked while we silently prayed and strained our ears listening for snakes. Since the front of our house faced the dark and spooky little white church, we had to walk behind our house to head toward Brother Henry's house.

As I stepped down to the ground, I looked to my right where I would take nightly outdoor trips with my mother because she would throw up about every night after she had eaten. I would stand a few feet away from her while she made herself vomit. I never understood why she did this since I had never heard of bulimia nervosa. I used to wonder if she was dying. I would keep watch for her for snakes and anything that moved. While I would stand there in the dark, I would eagerly wish that she would hurry up.

As I looked at all the ugly around me, my eyes always made their way up toward heaven. In my heart, I never thought of God as someone who loved me unconditionally. Everything around me was so dreary, so I spent every chance I had looking toward heaven at all the stars in the sky because that was my only connection to the life I once knew.

The farm was so isolated from the rest of the world that you can't imagine how deserted and lonely I felt without experiencing it for yourself. It was my idea of what it felt like to be behind the Iron Curtain, having no contact with anything you once loved. I now sometimes wonder if that's why I developed agoraphobia because I panic at even the idea of being very far from home. It is as though something inside of me is terrified that I will never be able to get back to my safe place.

As we rounded the house and headed toward the main highway, I continually reassured myself that if I would just keep walking, it wouldn't be long before we made it to Brother Henry's home. We passed the clothesline, and over to our right was the shower house. We then headed across the sandy desert toward the man-made hill that supported the railroad tracks. The farm equipment shop was close to the hill.

As we reached the top of the little hill and our feet stepped over the rails, I quickly surveyed the rails for railroad spikes to use as a weapon, but it was just too hard to see much of anything with only the light of the moon.

As we walked down the opposite side of the hill, we came upon a fence lined with barbed wire on the top and bottom. My fears intensified to the point that I felt as though I wasn't getting enough air to breathe. I already knew this fence was here, but seeing it at night and knowing we had to crawl under it with our faces only an inch or two above the ground, terrified me. Mother held up the barbed wire as my two brothers and I took turns and crawled through, praying all the while we wouldn't be bitten in the face by a snake. There was just something about the idea of being bitten in the face by a snake that far surpassed any horrible fate I could imagine.

After Jacob, Josh, and I had made it through safely, Mother got down on her knees and started crawling through. She was kind of heavy, so we had to hold up the barbed wire as high as we could to try to keep her from cutting her back. Once we made it past the barbed wire, the paved highway was just a few steps away. I remember looking down that highway longingly and hopelessly wishing I could leave this desolate place.

After we crossed the highway, we continued on through the desert and sand for a short distance until suddenly we saw lights and what looked like an oasis in the middle of the desert. It was Brother Henry's beautiful yellow brick home surrounded by big trees and real green grass, with cool waters breathing precious life into his little portion of the earth. Mother, Jacob, Josh, and I just stood there in silence, holding each other's hand, at the edge of the graceful emerald-green yard stretched out before us. We were mesmerized by its splendor. The brilliance of the colorful lights in the big picture window was my only way of knowing it was Christmastime. I was truly a little girl with her nose pressed against the window in my desires, with no hope of a better day.

As we reached the front door, knocked, and were permitted to enter, the first sight that grabbed my attention was their glorious Christmas tree with all the magical presents underneath it. Mother headed toward the kitchen to our right, and we were told to go into Brother Henry's bedroom and sit on the floor. Brother Henry was sitting on his king-size bed, propped up with a cushion that reminded me of the back of a chair. The bedspread was gold, and this was the first king-size bed I had ever seen. He truly looked like the big chief that he was.

We sat quietly on the floor, and the fear was so great in that room that you could cut it with a knife. It was always that way in a Stratton's presence. We watched the movie that Brother Henry was watching, *Splendor in the Grass*. How ironic that the title of this movie expressed just what I had been experiencing earlier while I stood outside in the dark in his yard.

That night, when we returned home, we were determined to have a Christmas tree too. Putting their own fears aside, Jacob, age 15 and Josh age 11, ran across the desert chasing tumbleweeds. Mother and I stood in the doorway of our shell of a house waiting and watching as they eagerly struggled to procure one of the many pitiful, round and brown tumbleweeds blowing across the desert in hopes of transforming it into a festive Christmas tree. I remember the light of the moon beaming down on the tops of my brothers' heads and their long skinny shadows running beside of them with each step they took. Suddenly, they reached out to grab one of the tumbleweeds, but the night breeze blew it farther away as if it were a bouncing ball. The tumbleweeds had sharp edges, so they were hard to grasp. Jacob and Josh spread out a little and closed in on one with no thought for their own safety. Finally, they had won our prize. We were so excited as I helped the boys confidently and proudly drag the tumbleweed into the house.

Mother had lots and lots of scraps of material from sewing for the Stratton's. We began to make little bows and homemade ornaments and whatever our wonderful imaginations could come up with. We raced around the house collecting beans, buttons, and anything else we could find. Even though there wasn't one present around that tumble tree, we were happy. Even though you could see outside through the cracks in the walls, and many times we heard snakes rattle inside those walls, we were happy. And even though, when we laid our heads down to sleep at night with the uncertainty that we would ever wake up again, still we were determined to enjoy this moment of our little Christmas celebration and the birthday of our Savior.

17

Submerged in Sadness

MOTHER WENT TO Parker, Arizona, and bought some plywood on credit (since she had given her money to the church). She needed to build a closet to protect our clothes from the sandstorms since the churchmen never got it done as promised. Mother was severely rebuked for buying the few pieces of plywood on the church credit account. Yet, I had seen on occasion, Mother sign the check she received from the death of my father and place it in Brother Henry's hand.

Mother made a homemade closet by using a sheet of plywood. Then she used a bedsheet and sewed a string through the top of it. She then nailed it to the wall in the corner area of the room to shield our clothing. She bought two extra sheets of plywood, which were vital to us when the sandstorms came. Each time the sandstorms started we would run with our sheets of plywood to the side of the house in which the wind was blowing. Since we didn't have glass on our windows, Mother and Josh would hold each end of the plywood up at one hole in one room, and Jacob and I would hold up the other sheet of plywood in the other room. The wind would howl as it blew so hard and strong that my arms would ache to put the plywood down. It seemed to take forever for the dirty winds to cease.

Everything in the house would be covered with sand, including Mother, my two brothers, and me, when suddenly the rain would begin. There I sat already covered with dirt and sand, and now rain was pouring down on top of my head. Each time I washed my hair, I would feel granules of sand covering my scalp.

I don't know if I can express the total sadness, I experienced from living on the church farm. There were no small pleasures that most people experience living in a regular town in a regular community. We lived in constant fear of God. Hell, fire, and brimstone were the only things our God seemed to represent. At such a young age, I saw life as living in hell and waiting to go to hell for something as small as thinking the wrong thing. Yes, *fear* was what God represented to us. I remember nothing about a loving God! Fear of God and fear of the Stratton's seemed one and the same.

When I was barely thirteen years old, I decided I would rather die than go on living on the church farm. I convinced myself I could "accidentally" drown myself since it was a sin to take my own life. I remember going swimming in an irrigation ditch (they were extremely large) with Tiny Stratton. She was an older lady whom I dearly loved. It was in this irrigation ditch that I tried desperately to drown myself, but every time I swallowed too much water, I came up coughing and struggling to catch my breath. I wanted to die, but I was too afraid to just let it happen. It was on this church farm that I truly lost my reason for living; a lot of who I was simply closed up inside, and I became very withdrawn.

18

Belts and Bullies

ONE DAY WHEN I got on the church school bus and stepped into the aisle, my arm bumped a little redheaded girl's arm on my left. I quietly said, "Excuse me," and silently headed for the back of the bus to sit down. The little girl's name was Tonya; she was George Hollis's daughter. That evening, while my mother was at Sister Anderson's house sewing, I was out in the yard when George pulled up in his big pickup truck. He reached across the passenger's side of the truck, opened the door, and said in a stern voice, "Get in!" I quietly complied. Not saying a word, he drove me to his home, got out of the truck, and went inside as I followed behind. He then got out a man's large, thick, leather, western-style belt so he could whip me. His daughter, Tonya, had told him that I hit her on the school bus when, in reality, my hands didn't even touch her skin.

Someone went to find my mother and told her that Brother George had me at his house and was going to whip me. My mother was a tall, large-framed woman, and I believe she could take care of herself if the situation called for it, or she would at least go down fighting. When she walked in the door, it was obvious she was upset. At once she began to try to make Brother George realize it wasn't his place to whip me. Nothing she said seemed to faze him. He had his big, thick leather belt in his hand eagerly waiting to stripe my back.

Mother continued to argue with him, and at some point, his facial expression and shouting appeared to indicate he would enjoy using his belt on my mother.

Suddenly, she spoke the magic words: Brother John W. Stratton Sr. doesn't allow anyone to whip his kids unless he leaves them in their care! This was like saying, "God doesn't allow you to whip His children unless He leaves them in your care." Brother George wilted, turned to his own daughter, and began to question her further. Tonya admitted she lied about me, so I left for home, unharmed, with my mother. However, Brother George was furious with my mother for "bucking" him. That was the expression the churchmen used to describe someone talking back and not accepting their decisions. That night was a church night, so Mother was in for the George Hollis wrath.

Our little white church had wooden floors, and for some unknown reason, the floor was covered with thousands of dead flying termites. I remembered it well as I walked across the church floor with the sound of crunching dead insects beneath my shoes as though I was walking on cornflakes. The setting was perfect for a hell-raising, preacher-shaking, fire-and-brimstone meeting. It was dark and dramatic outside the shaking church windows as the strong winds whistled an eerie tune and the lights kept flashing off and on to the shouting of Brother George Hollis's voice and his hostile eyes as he pointed his accusing finger at my mother. "Bless God, everybody Look at this woman! She will be bitten by a snake tonight, then rigor mortis will set up in her, and she will be *dead by morning*!" Everyone began to scream and shout, which made it so scary.

When a member was rebuked in this manner, it would make you feel like you were nothing. You would feel like you wanted to crawl into a hole somewhere and hide from all this humiliation. Mother, my two brothers, and I left the church that night feeling dejected and shunned by the rest of the congregation. When you walked down the aisle toward the door, people would stare at you without cracking a smile. As we silently walked home together and went inside, Mother broke the silence by saying with a chuckle, "Rigor mortis is something you get after you're dead!" She laughed as though she thought Brother George wasn't too smart.

We all smiled with relief because we knew she wasn't afraid, so that chased away our own fears. Jacob dragged a mattress off his bed and brought it into the middle room at the foot of Mother's bed so we could all be together to talk and try to keep cool by the cooler. We stayed awake most of the night talking about many things. Mother and I slept with our heads at the foot of the bed so we would be closer to the boys' heads and better hear what each of us said. That night we heard a snake in the wall, but this wasn't unusual. Even though I believed God was an angry God, I still believed He would keep us safe.

19

What the Hell Am I Doing Here?

MOTHER WAS SHUNNED by many of the church members, which broke her heart because she had tried so hard to please and gain approval of the church congregation. She eventually got to the point where she didn't seem to care what they thought anymore. She was like a strong-willed horse whose spirit had been broken.

One day as my mother sat on the floor with our door open and her feet and legs dangling outside, looking very dejected, our next-door neighbor Fay Smithy walked by our house. With her haughty voice, she said to my mother, "Carolyn, what's wrong?" Mother replied, "I'm just wondering what in the hell I'm doing out here!" Fay not only had a husband to care about her, but she also had an indoor toilet, and that was awesome. Her husband was always building on new things to make her life wonderful and easy. Mother had obviously, and finally, given up because we just didn't say ugly words like that. I guess if you beat a horse down long enough, it will simply lose its will to go on, and I believe that is where my mother was at this point. I am sure Mother knew she was in serious trouble for making such a statement, but she just didn't seem to care anymore. Still, she continued to pray and serve the Lord.

The sandstorms continued to wreak havoc on our little shack while we continued to grab the plywood and hold it up to the windows. Then the rains would come as soon as the sandstorm ceased. The rain would pour into the house, turning everything to muddy water. My brother Jacob and Kenneth Anderson put a tar-paper roof on the house to try to keep the rain out, since it would literally pour in on our heads. The next time the sandstorms and rains came, they were so strong that they ripped the tar paper off the top of the house. Once again everything was covered with mud, only more so than usual. In order to clean up the house, Mother took the wet closet curtain sheet outside and spread it on the ground. We then carried the muddy clothing outside and piled it on top of the sheet.

This same day, Rev. John Winston Stratton Sr. was visiting the Arizona church farm. He drove by the front of our house in his big, fine truck on his way to go hunting. He never said anything then, but when we went to the next ministers meeting, he used what he saw that day to humiliate my mother to such a devastating degree that it would cause her to leave the church and never return. In front of hundreds of people with standing room only, he shouted that Mother would never be in heaven to clutter the streets of gold.

My fifteen-year-old brother Jacob was so desperate to get off the church farm that he came up with the perfect plan for us to escape, without arousing any suspicion. He turned on the tears as he stood up during a church service and proclaimed that he believed God had called him to preach. Brother Henry said we would have to go to the next ministers meeting on the church bus to Dalton, Georgia, so my brother Jacob could go on trial to be a preacher. Also, Mother was told she needed to come to the assembly so the general overseer, Rev. John W. Stratton Sr., could straighten her out.

My sister, Karen, and her husband, Lance Mullins, had recently moved out to the church farm and lived on the side of the farm where Timmy was snake bitten. After Timmy's death, the churchmen took gas cans to the building that was out behind Timmy's home. In this building, there were several toilets. The churchmen poured the gas down these toilets, and snakes came running out of them by the hundreds.

Lois Douglas lived next door to Timmy's home, and she was outside hanging clothes one day when a huge snake crawled beneath her clothesline. Lois was sweet but had to be a little crazy to do what she did.

She ran into her house and came back outside with a large kitchen knife. She chopped the snake in half, and as she did this, about a dozen tiny snakes came running out of the larger snake and began to strike at her feet. A few of the churchwomen carried little switches with them when they went outside. They said if they came upon a sidewinder snake and whipped it on its back, it would run away. These snakes were deadly poisonous.

Living in the desert along with so much fear of the Stratton-controlled church farm, Mother and Karen never confided their feelings of how miserable they were. Our religion was so extreme, with mind-controlling fear, that even a mother and daughter were afraid to admit their true feelings about the church to each other.

Finally Leaving the Arizona Church Farm

The morning we were to leave for the ministers meeting, Mother boiled eggs to make egg salad sandwiches so we would have something to eat on the two-thousand-mile road trip to Dalton, Georgia, since we had no money to buy food. We always used a pot during the night because it was too dangerous to go outside in the dark to the outhouse. On the morning we were to leave it was still dark, so Jacob and I begged Mother not to make us take out the pot or the eggshells. Mother said Karen had told her she would be coming over to the house that morning, so Mother left a note for Karen to take out the pot and the eggshells after we were gone. However, as soon as the church bus pulled out that morning, since they had a car, Lance and Karen immediately escaped to Kokomo, Indiana.

20

The Shepherd

AFTER WE RODE for two-thousand miles eating nothing but egg salad sandwiches, we finally reached Dalton, Georgia. I looked out of the bus window as we rode into town on Highway 41, where a huge billboard on the side of the road that read "The Church Assembly." You couldn't possibly imagine the excitement I felt seeing the buildings and homes, and hearing the truck motors, car horns, and noises of every kind signaling to my splintered heart that I had finally returned home, home to civilization. Although it was exciting to see, it was also very scary for me.

Being withdrawn, I was a very nervous young girl turning fourteen-years of age that same week, and I had been greatly affected by my life on the church farm. Yes, we had left the farm, but I would later realize the farm and the effects it had on me emotionally would never leave me.

When we first arrived in Dalton, we stayed at my grandmother's home. My aunt Arleen had discovered we were in Dalton, so she wanted to come and visit us. Arleen was one of my daddy's two sisters. As my grandmother started to pull out of the yard that evening to go to church, my aunt Arleen and my cousin Wayne ran over to the car and opened the door in an effort to hug my neck. When Wayne excitedly reached out his arms to grab me, I remember quickly pulling away from him in fright. I wasn't used to that kind of excitement, and all the new things that were going on around me made me very anxious.

As soon as the church bus arrived in Dalton, my fifteen-year-old brother Jacob ran away. He said he was so nervous in his attempt to escape, he kept hiding because he believed the church people were after him. Yet the church people never even realized he was gone. He called our uncle Ben and Maxine Waters in Chatsworth, Georgia, which was about ten miles away. He hid at their home during the ministers meeting and never went to the first service. He called Mother and told her that if she said he had to come in and return to Arizona, he would. However, he said he would just run away again. Mother secretly told Jacob to stay where he was.

Mother went to Brother Henry Stratton and told him that she could not find my brother Jacob. Brother Henry told her to come back to Arizona and he would get the law to find my brother and return him to the church farm, but she refused. The church rebuked her and preached at her, saying, "Bless God, the Bible says to forsake your father and mother, wife and children, and yea your own lives." They told her she should return to the farm without her fifteen-year-old son. She adamantly refused.

That same week some of the church members talked to a member of the church who had called from Arizona, and Mother was criticized for refusing to return to the farm. The member who called from Arizona said that Mother hadn't taken out the pot and the eggshells. That was just what they needed to present a hell, fire, and brimstone meeting to try to regain control of her.

My mother's spirit and self-esteem were already so beaten down from what she suffered on the church farm. Now she was in Dalton and getting preached at and belittled for the second night in a row in front of the huge congregation. Nevertheless, the abuse she would endure that night from the general overseer, John W. Stratton Sr., in front of the whole assembly would break her to the point that she would disassociate herself from the Church Assembly for the rest of her life.

That night the huge church was packed with people, even standing along the walls and outside the church windows during Rev. John Stratton Sr.'s fearful presentation of the Word. He recalled the muddy sheets and clothes that he had seen outside of our little tar-paper shack the day he was in Arizona on his hunting trip. Also, the recent information that our house smelled because we hadn't taken out the pot and eggshells before leaving for Georgia. He suddenly grabbed my mother by her head and viciously shook her many times, and in a cruel and heartless tone, he shouted, "Carolyn Cooper! You will never be in heaven to clutter the streets of gold!"

Oh, how he crushed my poor mother's spirit—to be so humiliated in front of so many people and to have the general overseer, Rev. John Stratton, say such devastating things about you. The people looked down on Mother as though God Himself had said those cruel words to her. That would be the last service Mother would ever attend at the Church Assembly. She relinquished her membership and would never return.

The sheep blindly follow the shepherd, trusting that the shepherd is following the voice of God. Rev. John Winston Stratton Sr. was our shepherd, and we too followed him with blind trust. When I wrote the following poem, I thought of him and found comfort in knowing God knows all.

This poem is in honor of my mother, Carolyn Cooper, and the many thousands of other dedicated Christians who dedicated their lives to the Church Assembly and in return were treated so cruelly and unkind.

The Shepherd

Woe unto the shepherd whose heart is fast asleep,
who had no thought of searching out
to find my poor lost sheep.
You're busy thinking of yourself,
You never knew he'd gone,
And now he wonders in the night
And cannot find his way back home.

I heard a soft voice weeping
Though my eyes just could not see.
I cried, "Dear Lord, please guide me
To where that lamb might be."
I ran through fields of clover
When suddenly I found
Where once had laid that injured soul,
Only blood now stained the ground.

I bowed my knees in sorrow.
I pray, "What can I do?"
I want to find that little lamb
And bring him home to you.
As darkness overtook me
And tears rolled down my face,
It was only then I realized
I never knew this place.
I heard a man, he called my name,
And then my eyes beheld
An angel standing in the place
To where the blood once fell.

He said, "Dear child, be not afraid,
lift up your heart in song.
For if you look beneath my feet.
You'll find the blood is gone.
It was me who you heard weeping
For the souls who've gone away,
And my shepherd who was to give you hope
He too has gone astray.
Yet you, my child, with a heart so pure,
You took the time to find
Not knowing then that lamb was me,
And the blood you saw was mine."

Written and composed by Crusonda Yvette Lidy, 1993

The diseased have ye not strengthened, neither have ye healed that which was sick, neither have ye bound up that which was broken, neither have ye brought again that which was driven away, neither have ye sought that which was lost; but with force and cruelty have ye ruled them.

Ezekiel 34:4 (KJV)

21

Leaving the Church
(1968)

MOTHER WAS DISILLUSIONED by the church, so right away she took me to town and we had our hair cut. Believe me, that was a big deal. I don't ever remember seeing my mother with her hair cut. I guess it was her way of rebelling, but whatever the reason, I was tickled pink. However, it would only be a short time before I would be the little lost sheep returning to the fold. The church had so much mind control over each and every one of its members that even though I was just fourteen years old, my belief in the church was unwavering. Furthermore, even as a kid, I knew without the Church Assembly I would be doomed for hell, and I was consumed by that fear. My grandmother, Laura Hoskins, allowed Mother and us kids to live in one of the two little houses she owned on Goodwill Drive. Goodwill Drive was the main street of Union City, the community and businesses that was owned by the Stratton's for so many years.

I guess my grandmother thought now that I was not going to church, I was going to be a bad girl because she kept warning me about boys. She told me that my knees were "the gates of hell" and having sex with a boy was like "sticking a hot poker in you." The kind of poker she was referring to was the long steel stick she always used to knock down the ashes inside her old coal stove in Harlan, Kentucky.

Finally, she got out the rubbing alcohol and told me to take it in the bathroom and wash my private area with it. I obeyed because she was my grandmother, and I had always been taught to respect her wishes. When I applied the rubbing alcohol to my genital area, it set me on fire. It burned so badly that I could hardly stand it. By her making me do this, it made me feel that she thought I was contaminated in some way, even though I was a virgin. Still, I loved my grandmother very much, and I believed that she loved me too.

My grandmother had to endure so much grief and humiliation during the church services, still she was steadfast. When she died, she left her home and property to Sister Moreen Stratton, even though my mother didn't have a home of her own after leaving the church farm in Arizona. Over the years, many people signed over their properties and homes to the Stratton's, so this wasn't uncommon.

For a long time, I would go to my grandmother's house and she would hand me a skirt through the front door since we couldn't wear pants in her house. Then, when the new rule was passed that dismissed members couldn't associate with church members, I would stand outside in the front yard of her house and talk to my grandmother through the screen door. I wanted to go in, put my arms around her, hug her neck, and just touch her skin, but I couldn't because she was too afraid of the Stratton's and going to hell.

Just up the street from where we lived was the A&W Root Beer stand, and oh, how I loved their food. As I sat in a booth eating a hotdog with a large, foaming root beer in a chilled glass mug, I was listening to three of my favorite tunes on the jukebox: "Crimson and Clover," "Traces of Love," and "Ruby, Don't Take Your Love to Town." Suddenly, an extremely handsome man walked in the restaurant and smiled at me. He sat down in the booth in front of me and continued to look at me and smile.

I was only fourteen, but I was very slender and well developed for my age, so anyone might assume I was sixteen or seventeen. The guy said hello and introduced himself as a minister. Although he didn't know me, I certainly knew who he was even though I never said a word. He said his name was John W. Stratton Jr. as he struck up a friendly conversation. Then he invited me to go to church that same night as his guest since he was holding a revival, and of course I knew it was the Church Assembly.

That night at church, as John W. Jr. was preaching, I could feel his eyes on me, and it was obvious he wasn't just trying to save my soul. Then suddenly he called out my name. As he turned his attention toward me, he asked me to come to the altar and pray. I did go forward and requested to be baptized since I had never been baptized. John W. Jr. announced he was to have his first baptizing, and he told me when we were alone that he wanted me to be the first person he ever baptized. I was very happy that I would be the first, but when we gathered at the river at Redwine Cove, a girl named Wanda Jackson deliberately stepped in front of me. I later learned she had her sights set on John W. Jr. for a husband.

A couple of nights after I had rejoined the church, I was walking to my house from the A&W Root Beer stand since it was so close. I had no sooner walked out of the A&W than John W. Stratton Jr. came riding up in his Ford LTD with Al Gantry. He stopped and offered to drive me the rest of the way home, so I got in the car. When he pulled up at my house, he offered to pick me up the next evening and take me to church, and I accepted.

The next evening, he never showed up, but Steven Todd happened to be at my house looking for my brother-in-law, Lance Mullins. Steven was leaving to go to church so, since John W. Jr. was already late, I rode with Steven. It was nothing personal, just simply a means of transportation. By the time we had gone as far as Cox's store, John W. Jr. caught up with us, burning rubber and squealing tires. He sweetly invited me to get in the car with him, so I complied. He looked a little angry and a lot jealous. After all, if you were a Stratton, you didn't take the back seat to anyone. I have to say, John W. Jr. was one of the best-looking boys I had ever laid eyes on; he made me think of Elvis Presley. In his youth, he was drop-dead gorgeous.

That night when I arrived at church, with my short hair and wearing a beautiful, lacy, soft-yellow dress, I walked into the church and everyone looked at me. They all knew that I was John W. Jr.'s love interest, so that made me special in their eyes. I had come from a dirt shack in Arizona, but tonight I was treated like royalty. After church, he kissed me for the first time and, *wow*, what a kiss. It was my first real kiss outside of playing spin the bottle when I was ten years old and Bobby King kissing me in fourth grade.

I was officially his girlfriend, and from then on, my favorite song was "Son of a Preacher Man." John W. Jr. and I would meet at the A&W Root Beer stand as often as we could to sit and talk, listen to the jukebox, and sip on an ice-cold, foaming root beer. He would drive me to church in his Ford LTD with the Temptations' music blasting and my heart soaring into the clouds. Oh yes, I was doing fine on "Cloud Nine," as the song says. The Temptations' music was so thrilling, and I loved it! Songs like "Kiss and Say Goodbye," "Runaway Child, Running Wild," "Papa Was a Rollin' Stone," and "My Girl."

One night after church when we were sitting in his car at the A&W, he kissed me and then dropped his hand down on my knee. I immediately knocked his hand off. Suddenly he was in love, and that's just about how quickly it felt like it happened for him. I think the Stratton's were so used to being obeyed and idolized by their members that they were stunned to have anyone deny them whatever they wanted.

He told me he loved me and wanted to marry me, but of course that would never happen as long as Mother Moreen had a breath of life in her controlling body. Furthermore, I was only fourteen years old and he was twenty-two.

Sunday morning church service rolled around, and after church I waited for John W. Jr. as he expected me to. After a while I was tired of waiting for him, so I asked Archie and Frances Wheeler to take me home. That night after church, John W. Jr. stood waiting for me outside by his car. He was angry because I had left church without waiting for him. He acted very disappointed when he informed me that he and I were supposed to have Sunday dinner that day with Jeb and Susie Wilson. I told him he should have let me know instead of leaving me waiting so long without telling me he was in a meeting.

John W. Jr. was so handsome, but he was a big kid too. He was used to having his way with girls, but he certainly never got his way with me. He came to see me the following Tuesday to tell me that his mother said he could not see me anymore. Even though I looked older, I was only fourteen anyway, so I was way too young for him. Within a few short weeks, he walked down the aisle and married Wanda Jackson. I didn't think I was in love with him, but oh, he sure was handsome, my very own Elvis Presley. After we broke up, I would listen to The Temptations singing, "Kiss and Say Goodbye," it was my favorite song.

22

Women Don't Read the Bible

THE CHURCH HAD more control over you than your own parents. Now, the church was announcing we could no longer associate with any of our relatives or dismissed members who had left the church. Without question, you simply complied with the new rules. However, with someone like me who was still underage, the church accepted the situation until you could legally leave home. When you looked at someone who didn't belong to the church, you felt pity for them because you knew they were going to burn in hell. It didn't matter if it was your parent or the Baptist preacher down the street because they were going to burn!

I always went to church with my grandmother, who was still a member and was until the day she died. When I entered the church, the music would be playing loud and strong. The members would clap their hands or tap their feet in unison. The men were required to sit on the rostrum facing the women. The women couldn't sit with their husbands and weren't allowed to read the Bible. The church taught that the women would learn from their husbands; they were to be seen and not heard. There weren't any Bibles in the pews like most churches provided. The altar exhibited a picture of the general overseer, Rev. John W. Stratton Sr., and Sister Moreen Stratton and never a picture of Jesus. So, when you knelt at the altar, it was Rev.

John W. Sr. and Sister Moreen Stratton's faces you saw when kneeled to pray. The same portrait also hung above everyone on the center wall for all to see and salute.

Many of the members would come to church as early as two hours and thirty minutes before the service was scheduled to start when it was time for the Assembly. There was a constant blanket of fear that hovered over the people; you could see it in everyone's faces. The church members, especially the front-row screamers, would constantly watch the door for the arrival of the Stratton family. Suddenly, John W. Stratton Sr. and his family would enter the building as the music played. The members would spot them after watching the door for hours and begin to clap louder and louder. Then they would rise to their feet and scream and shout. When there are so many men and women screaming and shouting at the same time, believe me, it is scary. The people would stand during all the excitement and fearfully move closer and closer to the front. I would be standing there wondering who was going to get grabbed by their head, rebuked, or have death pronounced on them. One night at church when I told one of the women in the front row that I didn't feel the spirit, she told me to throw up my arms and shout when everyone else did and eventually I would.

When the people rose to their feet, many times they would salute whichever Stratton had entered the building. It didn't matter if it was John W. Stratton Sr. or his family. they were saluted. If the Stratton's were out of town and none of them were present for the service, many times the minister who was preaching would stop in midstream and say, "I salute you, Brother Stratton," and then he would salute the air or Brother John Stratton's picture. The members would also salute his picture. If you didn't salute and they saw you, you could be grabbed viciously, shaken by your head, and accused of having a spirit against the Stratton's. There was definitely mind control in our religion.

When a visitor came to our church, the minister who would be preaching talked to them with such love and care, and with tears streaming down his face. It would make the visitor want to go to the altar, and before they knew what hit them, they would join the church. That love and concern would continue until that new member had totally accepted our way of life. I have never before or since witnessed such amazing mind control and brainwashing.

The Stratton's were truly the world's greatest manipulators. Even the younger Stratton children could turn on the tears with the blink of an eye. They could make you feel that no one loved you as much as they did. As the old saying goes, they could easily sell a bald man a comb. Ex-members who would visit our church either came to see their families or the church had accomplished such control over their emotions that even though they desperately tried to break away from the church, they couldn't seem to do it. When ex-members did come to visit, it would generally be a hell, fire, and brimstone meeting unless the Stratton's wanted them to rejoin the church for reasons such as the ex-member had a good income. Also, they had to be willing to submit and beg for forgiveness.

Our church didn't want just your income; they wanted your property or anything you had of real value. You gave it or signed it over if you planned to continue being a member or, should I say, "pay for your ticket to heaven." They wanted complete submission and control of your life. It was well planted in your mind that if you didn't stay with the church, you would burn in hell! They preached that the Church Assembly was the only church in existence that preached "the truth." They believed that if others on earth were to be saved, they would eventually find their way to the Church Assembly.

The members who either left or were thrown out of the church didn't seem to know how to function in regular society. They were convinced in their own minds that they were going to hell, so nothing mattered anymore. Without the church they had truly lost their identity. Many people went so wild that when they left the church, they would try anything. It was truly sad to witness the emotional damage caused by being a member of the Church Assembly.

When I was fourteen years old, I was grabbed various times by my head and shaken while being warned of the horrible fate that awaited me. I was being attacked because Sister Moreen wasn't happy that I was taking her son Jesse Stratton Jr.'s attention away from Wanda Jackson, the girl she had approved to marry her son. I spent many church nights at the altar praying to a God I didn't understand or even know if He was listening. I know that my mother's influence and my life with the church most assuredly determined my self-worth and greatly lowered my self-esteem.

Members who left the church experienced for the first time the feeling of being able to do all the things that they never could have considered doing before. The church members for many years were discouraged in obtaining a formal education, and I am certain this was an effort to maintain control and make sure the money went to the Stratton's. Many of the members were poor and neglected their own families in order to put their money in the church and pay their pledges. The Stratton family had the best and finest in regard to homes, cars, airplanes, and businesses, and when it came to clothes, no one dressed better than the Stratton's.

When I was seventeen years old, I saw Brother Willie Patton mowing lawns, and it was so hot I was afraid he would suffer from heatstroke. He was an old man and sweating profusely in the heat of the day to pay his pledges. I had been to his home with his daughter, Rita Patton, whom I went to school with, so I knew what pitiful living conditions he and his family had to endure.

Our church always spoke proudly and quickly that we didn't believe in paying tithes, but the truth is they wouldn't even consider accepting just 10 percent; they wanted it all. When I was a little girl, there was a time when the Stratton's had used guitar cases and even washtubs to collect their members' hard-earned income. If they didn't collect what they wanted in the offering, they would preach fearfully and warningly to their members, and then they would collect again until they got more, more, and all. I have heard them shout out, "Clean out your pockets!"

23

The Ugly in Uncles

IN 1969 I was fifteen years old and a student at Dalton High School. We lived on Chattanooga Avenue in Dalton, Georgia. Mother worked two jobs to try to make ends meet. She had her hair cut short and started wearing pants, which seemed very strange compared to her once long dresses and hair. Even though she looked like "worldly people," as we once called them, she was very much the same inside. I had spent a great deal of time with my father's sister Arleen whom Mother disliked. I loved my aunt Arleen very much, and I guess it was because she seemed to love me.

My trips to visit Arleen had become fewer and fewer because every time I came home from visiting my aunt, Mother would accuse me of talking about her. My mother possessed very little self-worth and was extremely insecure, but I guess anyone would be if they had walked in her shoes.

My mother's brother Sylas came to visit, and I was happy to see him since he had been away in the Marine Corps for several years. He was a handsome man with a jovial personality. Sylas was always laughing or teasing about something, making it a very pleasant experience to be around him.

Mother hadn't come home from work yet, so Sylas was talking to me about his wonderful life when suddenly he handed me a picture.

He laughed and said, "This is my girlfriend from overseas." As I gazed down at the picture, I felt shocked and stunned with disbelief to see my uncle Sylas lying naked while an Oriental girl was on her knees beside him obviously trying to swallow his erect penis. I just walked away; I had never seen anything like that before. I was baffled and confused about why my uncle felt the need to show me something so disgusting. Nevertheless, life would eventually teach me there would be no man I could ever completely trust but God.

24

Hiding in the Dark Rain

MY MOTHER'S UNCLE, James Taylor, had recently come to Dalton to live with his wife, Mary. Ordinarily, Mother was reluctant to let me go off with anyone, but since James was her uncle, she agreed to let me go home with him and Aunt Mary. I was tickled pink because it was very seldom, I got to go anywhere. James and Mary lived in a small trailer off South 41 Highway.

That night we had Kentucky Fried Chicken and biscuits for supper, and then James got a beer out of the refrigerator. I was definitely not used to being around alcohol. He suggested I taste the beer, so out of curiosity I took a sip. I hated the nasty taste, so I got up from my chair and went to take my shower to get ready for bed. Mary gave me a blue knee-length polyester robe to sleep in.

As I lay on the little half bed in the back of that crummy little trailer, I was staring up at the heavens and the starry sky through a tiny, square screened window above my head. Suddenly, my great-uncle James came into the bedroom and sat down on the edge of the bed. He offered me twenty dollars to let him have his way with me, and I was terrified. I nervously told him I was going to tell his wife on him, and in a lusty voice he laughed and said, "Mary isn't my wife, and not only that, I have had her and another woman in bed with me at the same time." I had never heard talk like that fall from anyone's lips before and I was terrified.

At this point, my feet hit the floor running. Out the door I went barefoot into the cold rain and darkness with nothing on but the little blue polyester robe and my panties. James was chasing me, and I hid from him. As I squatted down behind an old station wagon, with the rain pouring down on the top of my head, I peeked around the corner of the car. The words kept flashing through my mind: "I don't have a dime for a telephone call, and there's no phone booth around here anyway." Needless to say, I was scared to death.

James began calling out to me, "Yvette, come on in! If you'll just come on in, I promise I won't hurt you." I peeked around the bumper of the car and through the darkness and rain, I saw him leaning against the frame of the trailer door with the light at his back. I had no other recourse but to trust him to leave me alone until daylight would come and I could go home. He did keep his promise, so I made it home the next day unharmed.

Safe at Home

After mother left for work (her second job), Jacob, Josh, and I went searching for pop bottles to cash in for their deposit so we could buy some chocolate ice cream. This was a regular occurrence for us to search the ground for pop bottles to cash in. It didn't matter how nasty they were or how much muddy water had collected in the bottles because they were worth their weight in gold to us. We would get so excited when we spotted one. This particular evening, I told the boys of my terrible experience, and I left nothing out. In other words, I told them I had tasted beer.

The very next day at school, the counselor from the principal's office came to my homeroom class and told me I had a telephone call. I went to the office and discovered it was my mother on the phone. She never gave her reason; she simply demanded I wait at school when the bell rang and my two brothers would walk me home.

Although they had never come to walk me home before, it never dawned on me what was going on until I walked in the door to our house on Chattanooga Avenue. Mother was beside herself with anger as she held the leather belt in her hand and proclaimed that she was whipping me because I had drunk beer. I'd had less than a tablespoon of beer, but obviously that was irrelevant. She disregarded the fact that her uncle could have raped me. She never asked me any questions, not even one about what had happened that night.

Mother was a large-framed woman, and with the brutal force of her strength, she lashed my back, arms, legs, and any part of my body she could hit with the leather belt, and with no mercy. I felt so hurt and angry because I knew in my heart that I did not deserve the beating. My brother Jacob had told Mother what had happened at her uncle James's, so that's how she found out.

The very next day I expressed my hostility in front of Jacob for what Mother had done to me. I made the statement that I was going to run away from home, and Jacob said, "Mom will just call the police, and they'll bring you back." I said, "Then I'll get married!" Jacob replied, "You can't get married unless you're pregnant!" I said, "Then I'll get pregnant!" Well, at this point I had said a mouthful, but I hadn't really meant one word of it. I was just so hurt at what she had done to me.

When she came home, Jacob told her every word I had said. Once again, Mother beat me and beat me in the dining room until I thought she would never let up. She then made me go in the kitchen where we would be alone and warned me if I ever let a boy touch me, she would send me away to a girls' farm. She then told me horrifying stories that made me feel sick with fear, warning me of all the terrible tortures I would go through in such a place. After all she put me through, she then said the most emotionally devastating words to me that had ever fallen from her lips. Mother threatened to get me down on the floor and examine me to make sure I was still a virgin.

The thought of my own mother putting her finger inside of me was more than my mind could possibly absorb. I can't express how horrified those words made me feel. I was such a private person that since I had matured even Mother had not seen so much as my breast.

Covered with bruises, I went into the bathroom and sat down on the commode. Mother must have felt guilty or just concerned about someone finding out. As I sat there on the commode lid, she asked me to forgive her and made me promise to never tell anyone what she had done to me.

25

My Amazing Aunt Mazy

MOTHER HAD A sister named Mazy. Mazy and her husband, Rex, lived in Austell, Georgia. There, they owned and operated a little grocery store they called The Little Market. I loved my aunt Mazy dearly because she was always so good to me. She allowed me to visit her as often as I could, and I was always glad to get away from my mother.

During the summer I stayed with Aunt Mazy, Uncle Rex, and their two children, Michael and Jennie, and I worked in their grocery store. Aunt Mazy was always buying me things besides paying me to work at their store. There was no one I held with higher esteem than my aunt Mazy. She was my refuge from the rain. I say that because my heart correlates rain to tears.

However, Uncle Rex was a different story. Even though he was nice, generous, and affectionate, he was too affectionate. I quickly learned to never catch myself alone with him. Since my aunt Mazy usually went to bed early due to severe headaches, Uncle Rex was eager and insistent on showing me his collection of dirty movies.

I remember feeling nervous seeing them in his presence, yet I couldn't seem to stand up for myself. I was fifteen years old and very much a virgin.

I was, however, a little inquisitive about what was on the film since I had never seen a dirty movie before. When he turned it on, I felt very embarrassed and just wanted to get out of that room, but I didn't want to make Uncle Rex mad at me, so I just sat there waiting for it to be over.

The room we were in was my aunt's sewing room, which was next to the den on the ground level floor. As I recall, the film was on a reel-to-reel tape and didn't play very well, so the viewing was short lived. Later that night, while Aunt Mazy slept on the third floor and I was in the den on the sofa watching television, Uncle Rex returned and sat down on the sofa. He began talking affectionately, telling me how special I was as I perceived a father would be to his child. As he spoke, he lovingly suggested I come to his end of the sofa, so I did. He put his arm around me and hugged me close to his side. I was so starved for the need to feel loved, and now here I was safe and secure until his hands began to move toward places they did not belong.

I began to cry because I felt betrayed and scared. I told him I had always thought of him as the father I never had. It was apparent my words of disappointment made him feel guilty for what he tried to do. He said he was sorry, and what I had said about looking up to him like the father I never had made him feel ashamed of himself. As I cried, he began to comfort me and hold me in his arms again, tenderly. Things got out of hand as he once again began to rub my body because this time I didn't stop him as quickly as before. I wanted and needed the love I believed Uncle Rex and Aunt Mazy felt for me, so I didn't want to make him mad at me and take the chance of losing my place in their home and their hearts.

Although I didn't want him to, he was touching me sexually with his hand. I abruptly demanded he stop when I realized he was going to try to insert his finger inside of me, and he complied. When I returned home to Dalton, I was carrying this huge burden on my shoulders of what had happened in Austell with Uncle Rex. Yet I knew I wanted to go back to Aunt Mazy's the next opportunity I had to get away from my mother, but I was afraid to be alone with him. I wanted their love, but I was afraid of this new kind of love my uncle wanted to give me.

I desperately needed someone I could trust to confide in.

One night I stayed with my aunt Addie in her office at the San Quinton Motel where she worked. I told her I had a problem and I really needed someone to talk to. She assured me that she was the one I could trust. When I told her, what had happened with Uncle Rex, she sympathized with me and said she understood. After she left me, she immediately went straight to my mother and Aunt Mazy and told them that I was trying to seduce Uncle Rex. My mother treated me as though I was some kind of a slut. My aunt Arleen told me that my mother had sat at her kitchen table and called me a whore. I was barely fifteen years old and a virgin, and my loving mother called me a name like that! I grew to hate her for the way she treated me in my youth.

Addie said I was lying about Uncle Rex because he wouldn't do something so terrible to a kid. The next time she was standing on a ladder in the Austell grocery store, Uncle Rex made a sexual pass at Aunt Addie. After that, she believed I had been telling the truth, but the harm had already been done. Not once did my aunt Mazy throw it up to me, and she never changed toward me. I'm sure she knew Uncle Rex better than anyone did. I loved her with all my heart, and she loved me.

26

Silenced by Fear

ONE DAY WHEN Mother and I were at my grandmother's house, Aunt Addie was preparing to go out of town for a few days. As Aunt Addie picked up her luggage to leave, the suitcase fell open, and several articles of my clothing fell out on the floor. My beautiful pink dress and my peach silk pajamas Aunt Mazy had given me, along with several other articles of my clothing, were now lying on the floor as Aunt Addie scurried to shove them back into her suitcase and out of our sight. I started to shout, "Those are my clothes!" But Mother shut me up in a hurry and dared me to say another word as she gave me one of her forbidding looks.

Mother allowed my aunt Addie to get on a Greyhound bus and leave town with my favorite clothes Aunt Mazy had given me after working all summer in her grocery store.

27

No Safe Place

I **WAS SEVENTEEN** years old and a student at North Whitfield High School. I had a great friend by the name of Serena Mays, who not only went to North Whitfield High School too, but she also was a member of the Church Assembly. Mother had married a man by the name of Gerald Norris, and we lived in his trailer on McFalls Avenue.

One day I came home from school early because I was not feeling well. As I entered, I realized someone else had been there, but I never assumed they had broken in and were still inside. I softly walked down the hall toward the bathroom, and as I did, I observed my aunt Addie sitting on the bathroom floor with Mother's towels, sheets, pillowcases, and washcloths stacked between and to the sides of her legs.

She was stealing from Mother, so when Mother came home from work, I told her I had caught Aunt Addie stealing our towels and bed linens. Mother confronted Aunt Addie, and she responded, "Carolyn, surely you don't believe Yvette, do you?" Mother meekly said no. Once again Mother showed me that I had no value and wasn't worth defending. Many years later Mother admitted to me that she knew I was telling the truth, but even Mother didn't want to make Aunt Addie mad.

The trailer we lived in on McFalls Avenue while Mother was

married to Gerald Norris was a nice trailer but extremely hot during the summer. One night as I lay sleeping on the bottom level of the bunk bed at the far end of the trailer, it became unbearably hot, so I got up and went to sleep on the sofa in the living room thinking it might be cooler in there. The sofa was a western-style leather sofa with what looked like wooden wheels on each end. My body began to sweat and stick to the leather sofa, so I called out to Mother and asked her if I could come into her room and lie beside her since they had the only fan in the trailer.

I soon fell asleep with the breeze from the fan blowing on my face. After I had been sleeping awhile, I began to slowly wake up, and I felt what I believed to be my mother's hand lying on my stomach. I gently laid my hand over what I believed to be mother's hand. Then suddenly I was conscious enough to realize that the hand was not only rubbing my tummy but it was also covered with long hairs. I felt as though all the blood drained from my body. I was shocked and frightened to realize it was my stepfather's hand on my stomach. I quickly jumped up, and as I did, Mother woke up and asked, "What's wrong?"

I fearfully said, "Nothing," but I vividly remember all the angry thoughts flowing through my head: "If Uncle Bob and Uncle Jim were here and knew what you had tried to do to me, they would beat you up!" These were the two uncles who had *never* tried to sexually molest me, so I thought of them as my secret heroes. This was my uncle Jim (Mother's brother) and not my mother's uncle James, the one who tried to molest me when I was fifteen. Although I hadn't been around my mother's brothers in years, I found comfort in believing there was someone out there in the world who would protect and defend me if they knew.

Unbeknownst to me, before that night occurred, my stepfather had tried to persuade my mother to allow him to have sex with me. He even told her that he'd had intercourse with his last stepdaughter, who had been fourteen years old at the time. We later learned that my stepfather had sex with her after she was married. Gerald got her pregnant, and when her young husband found out his four-year old little boy was in fact his father-in-law's child, the young man committed suicide.

When I walked through the house, he would tell my mother that I looked like "a brick s%&* house with all the windows knocked out." My stepfather was a very unattractive, spooky-looking man who wore extremely thick glasses. He had recently been very nice to me and was promising to buy me my first car. Like most men, he too was evil and not to be trusted. Mother sent me to stay with my grandmother until she could leave.

28

Chaney's in Love

I **STARTED GOING** to the Church Assembly again with some of my friends, even though my immediate family didn't go anymore. The church kids were practicing for a Christmas play, and I was invited to take part in it. This particular night, all the members who had a part in the Christmas play were sitting on the stage at church waiting to be called up front to recite their parts for Brother Harry Preston. I had been chosen to be one of three angels who say in unison, "Glory to God in the highest, and on earth peace, good will toward men." Brother Harry began to read out of the Bible leading up to where we were to say our part. I thought it was time for the angels to speak because the words Brother Harry was saying were very similar to the real ones, so in a loud voice I cried out, "Glory to God in the highest," etc. Suddenly everyone began to laugh at me. Even though I was a little embarrassed, I really didn't mind because everyone was getting such a big laugh out of my mistake. There was, I would say, at least, 150 kids present, and my mistake seemed to have caught the interested eye of one certain young man by the name of Chaney Theodore Stratton III, who was named after his grandfather Chaney Theodore Stratton, founder of the Church Assembly.

Every time I looked up, he was standing close by looking at me and grinning. He was the son of Brother John Winston Stratton Sr.

and Sister Moreen Stratton, and even she had suddenly taken a special interest in me. She invited Shirley and Wilma Benton over to her house, but I later realized it was because I was riding with them. Apparently, the girl who lived in Sister Moreen's home had been brought from up North to marry Chaney. Unfortunately, the girl had treated Chaney shabbily, so Sister Moreen wanted to use me to make the girl jealous.

That night after band practice we went over to Sister Moreen's, and as we sat at her kitchen table with several other churchwomen, Sister Moreen asked each girl who they were interested in as a sweetheart. Everyone gave the name of the boy they liked, but when she asked me what boy I liked, I said laughingly, "All of them!"

I walked away from the table and Judy Bedford immediately asked, "Yvette, who do you like for a boyfriend?" Apparently, everyone was suddenly very concerned about who I liked. I didn't even have a boyfriend and wasn't looking for one, but that would soon change.

Sister Moreen began buying me presents such as sweaters and Youth Dew Eau de Parfum by Estee Lauder. I later learned it wasn't because she really cared about me at all; I was just a means to an end. When she realized her son, Chaney was interested in me, she wanted to use his affection toward me to make Judy jealous, but it backfired. Chaney fell head over heels in love with me just as I did him. Moreen Stratton spent every waking moment trying to come between us, and eventually she would succeed.

From that first time our eyes met, it was obvious to both of us that there were some powerful feelings between us. We were both shy and hesitant to look directly at one another. When I did catch his eye, I could feel my face turn red and burn. I appeared to be confident in front of everyone, but it was all a facade. Each time he looked at me my knees would suddenly feel weak, and I would feel an unexplained thrill in my stomach that I had never felt before, yet it was difficult for both of us to get up the nerve to talk to each other.

One night after church, when most of the members were in

the dining hall talking and eating, several of the church kids were outside in back of the church playing around in the snow—Serena Mays, Valerie King, Darnell Adkins, Bobby King, Donny Patton, Chaney Stratton and me, among a few others. We were having a snowball fight, laughing, and having a good time when suddenly all the church kids disappeared except for Chaney and me. Finally, we were standing face-to-face, and I timidly asked him, "Where did all the other kids go?" Chaney gazed into my eyes with a look that felt as though it reached down into my very soul. As he did, he reached out and, for the first time, held my hand in his. How wonderful to know God can create such a powerful feeling of love between two people. I felt as though I had met my kindred spirit, my soul mate.

Everything was great in the beginning of our love. I was seventeen and Chaney was eighteen years old. One night when we were standing in the dark, leaning against his mint-green Grand Prix, Chaney held me in his arms. With the intoxicating fragrance of his Brut cologne in the air, he kissed me so tenderly and told me he loved me. He said he wanted to marry me, but we would have to keep our plans a secret until his mother would approve of our love. Chaney hoped just as I did that eventually his mother, Sister Moreen, would accept me, but that would never happen.

I would go to bed at night thinking of him and knowing in my heart that wherever he was, he was thinking of me too. I would wake up in the mornings with a smile on my face, counting the hours until we could see each other again. We would write each other letters expressing how deeply we loved each other. In one letter, he said, "Yvette, I love you so much that I would die for you." When he saw me again, he put his black onyx diamond ring on my finger, and I felt like the happiest girl alive. Chaney and I had such a strong, unspoken emotional connection that it would be difficult to try to explain it. However, a dark cloud always hovered over our rainbow that we were both very aware of, even though we tried to ignore it. Chaney would always say, "Yvette, no matter what happens, just don't quit the church."

In our church, money was such a big issue, and each member was aware of what class they were in. You were always judged by what your material possessions were and what you had acquired in life. But it was difficult to hang on to what you had if you were a member of the church.

29

The Altar You Owned

THE MOST RESPECTED members outside of Brother John Stratton Sr.'s family were people who were related to the Stratton's either by blood or marriage. Even though I knew in my heart that Chaney truly loved me, I was still self-conscious of the fact that I was poor and lived in a trailer. I knew financially I could never measure up to what Moreen Stratton would demand of a daughter-in-law even though I was a virgin. When my father died, Mother never kept a penny of the insurance money but gave it to Rev. J. W. Stratton Sr. which was Chaney's father.

I have no doubt our lives would have been so much better had we never heard of the Church Assembly.

Very early in the relationship, Sister Moreen would do whatever necessary to keep Chaney and me apart. We stood in the hallway at the side entrance of the church building in order to talk to each other. The church had a brass band, and I played the alto saxophone, with practice on Tuesday nights. Sister Moreen would reprimand Chaney in front of everyone at band practice. It didn't matter where we stood and talked at church, Sister Moreen would find fault. Eventually we started hiding at the back of the church so we could spend a little time together. We would be at the back, keeping watch for Sister Moreen and her women as they headed toward her limousine parked underneath the awning. When we spotted them coming out, we held hands and ran through the night across the back of the church until we reached the other end that led into the kitchen area.

Chaney was given the responsibility of serving as pastor of the church in Maryville, Tennessee. Sister Moreen was relentless in doing whatever necessary to keep us apart. I was still a virgin, so it wasn't because I wasn't decent that she disapproved. However, if my mother had lots of money, she would have welcomed me with open arms. It began to seem that every time I walked in the church doors, I was the subject of a hell, fire, and brimstone meeting. I know they kept Chaney away from the Dalton church so he couldn't see what they were doing to me.

One night at church, Pratt Huggins was preaching when suddenly he directed his violent presentation of the word at me. While the huge congregation stood to their feet and screamed and shouted all around me, he pointed his cruel finger at me, saying, "Yvette Cooper, you've got a spirit against Sister Moreen!" To be accused of having a spirit against any Stratton, especially Sister Moreen, was like saying I had renounced our beloved Savior in the eyes of the people. I fell to my knees at the altar as I was expected to do. With tears streaming down my cheeks, I hid my face on the red velvet covered altar. In front of the picture of Rev. John W. Stratton Sr. and Sister Moreen. I begged God to help me to bear this shame because, even though I knew I wasn't guilty, in the eyes of the people I was. All Rev. Pratt Huggins had to do was say I was guilty and that made it so.

I waited there on the floor with my tear-stained, swollen face until the shouting and angry preaching had quieted down a little. I hoped that I might have permission to raise my head and stand on my feet. Suddenly, Pratt Huggins grabbed my head in his hands and shook me violently while threatening God's wrath to be on me. When I was allowed to speak, I begged for forgiveness as I was expected to do.

I was being accused at church and having to confess to lies, even though I wasn't guilty, just as Mother was always accusing me of things at home when I wasn't guilty. It's a spirit-breaking guilt complex that manifests itself when you endure this kind of abuse for so many years.

It devalues you as a human being. I know because that's what they did to me. I had become like a robot with a horrible guilt complex and a heart that grieved for someone to care. I knew Sister Moreen felt threatened by the love her son felt for me, but I never hated her or at least not at that time. I always longed for her approval but inevitably would never attain it.

This is the poem I wrote about her:

The Altar you Owned
Once there was hope once I believed,
Once I could love with a heart that was free,
But you took the faith that I had in you
and used it against me to look like the fool.

Tears flowed like a River at that altar you owned;
I wanted to please you but you wanted me gone.
My Savior, your weapon, your motive, your son,
Oh, the cross I have carried, oh, the damage you've done.

My spirit was broken though I fought a good fight
I smiled through my sorrow and cried through the night
I try hard to let go of the pain I still feel
I want to see Jesus and be in His will
But I'll never see heaven feeling this way
Let's deal with this now not on Judgement Day
I bowed in your altar, I confessed to your son
I begged for forgiveness, things I never done

Now, you'll never see me, kneeling to pray
I know that sounds awful but you made me this way
There once was a time it seems so long ago
I wanted acceptance but your heart said No

Written and composed by Yvette Lidy

The preachers and some of the prophesying women were aware of Sister Moreen's disapproval, so they did their part to not only make me feel unwelcome at church but also attack me at every possible opportunity. Chaney would call me at school and talk to me. He tried his best to comfort me and continued to plead with me not to leave the church, no matter what they might do. One day, when I was talking to him on the telephone, Brother John Stratton Sr. picked up the telephone in his bathroom where he was shaving. Brother J. W. Stratton was very cordial to me on the phone. It was obvious he was unaware of what his wife was doing to me at church, especially since he was out of town a great deal of the time. About the only time Chaney and I would be able to see each other was during the weeknights at church and even then, we had to hide.

30

Guilty by Accusation

ONCE AGAIN, CHANEY was sent out of town to preach. It was Sunday morning, and I walked into the church wearing a pretty new dress my mother had bought for me at Sears and Roebuck in Chattanooga. The electric guitars were playing loudly when suddenly John Stratton Jr. walked in the church doors. People rose to their feet as they clapped and shouted at the sight of him. The people responded as though he was bringing the Holy Ghost with him. The controlling power he held over the people from his presence alone was always astounding. While John Stratton Jr. was preaching, his wife, Wanda, suddenly started dancing around and shouting.

Once she danced her way to the altar, she proclaimed, "Yvette Cooper, you had better clean out your heart!" I quickly searched my mind and heart for something I may have done wrong since the last time I came to church, which was only three nights ago. There was no condemnation in my heart. I tried desperately to think of something I could repent for before the indignity increased. All eyes were on me as I walked toward the front of the church to stand at the altar and look up at the almighty Rev. John Stratton Jr. Suddenly, I saw Julie Stratton coming into the church from the corner door by the ladies' restroom.

Thoughts flashed through my mind. "I am offended by Julie

Stratton because she is always very unfriendly to me." That's it; that's what I can use to beg forgiveness, so I then say aloud, "I would like for the church to forgive me because I have a spirit against Julie Stratton." Well, this was all they needed. Everyone began to scream and shout so loudly that I was terrified of what might happen next.

My head raised toward Brother John Stratton Jr., and he sneered as he looked down at me from above, perched at his Bible stand. He said, disgustingly, "What has she ever done to you?" I felt like a cockroach about to be stepped on. I stood silently weeping with my head bowed while Brother John Stratton Jr. shamed and verbally rebuked me.

After church was dismissed that Sunday morning, I was hurt and angry because of the humiliation I had to endure in front of everyone. I needed to be defiant, so I had to decide just what horrible sin I was going to commit to make myself feel better. I decided to be really bad, so I bought a pack of cigarettes. When I got home from church and told Mother what they had done to me, she called Sister Moreen and had a talk with her. Sister Moreen told my mother to have me come to church again that night and everything would be fine.

When I walked into church that night, I felt proud and confident because I had a pack of cigarettes in my pocketbook. I remember thinking as I walked down the aisle of the church to sit down, "Ha-ha. Goody, goody, I am a smoker! So now what do you say about that?" This was only my seventeen-year-old mind thinking, so no one really knew I had the devil's tobacco in my purse. No one said anything to me during the service. However, after church was over, Wanda Stratton followed me outside. She asked me to forgive her for what she had said to me. She said she had been listening to talk, and apparently someone had lied about me. She never told me what had been said. I resented her for years for humiliating me that Sunday morning in front of the entire church and then privately that night asking me to forgive her. No one ever knew of the conversation that had transpired outside in the dark.

31

Church Abuse

IN YEARS TO come, Wanda Stratton would endure much emotional cruelty from Sister Moreen Stratton, who was her mother-in-law. I would get to know her twenty-three years later in an entirely different light. Through her own private hell being married into the Stratton family, she would grow to be the most precious, understanding, and gentle-natured person I have ever had the privilege of getting to know. She would die at the youthful age of forty-two years old from a brain tumor on September 17, 1994. She told me before she died that she had forgiven Sister Moreen for all the abuse she endured during her marriage to John Stratton Jr. Wanda loved me and I loved her dearly; she was my best friend. Two days after she died, I wrote this poem about her.

Wanda's Heart

Yesterday is just a memory, into our lives you came.
You always brought the sunshine and never saw the rain.
You radiated such energy of life like no one did,
a sweet and precious innocence, just like a little kid.

I've never known of anyone with a zest for life like you.
With each new task completed, you still saw more to do.
You searched out lost and injured souls,
you gladly took the blame,
but of all the heartaches you were given,
you chose to not complain.

If there's one important thing, I've learned from you
that in this life to live
is even though they never ask,
your heart it must forgive.

You were always in a hurry;
you never seemed tired or slow.
Maybe you knew something I didn't
that soon you would have to go.

I close my eyes and see you smile,
my tears they start to fall.
I call your name out, Wanda
but I hear no sound at all.
This dreadful sound of silence,
my heart can find no peace.
Your voice, your smile, your memory
stay with me in my sleep.

From the depths of my heart
like the song that you loved so,
I'd like to keep you here with me
and never let you go.

I opened my eyes with a sad heart
this morning to find you gone.

Then suddenly I heard him singing
and found peace within his song.
I ran over to the window and looked into the trees;
I saw the precious bluebird who came to sing to me.
His song he sang so glorious like none I'd ever heard,
though my lips can't sing its melody,
my heart knows every word.

And a voice I keep on hearing
but a face I just can't see, says,
"Yesterday she walked beside you,
but today she walks with me."

Written and composed by Yvette Lidy 09-1994

It seemed that every time I walked into the church I was being viciously attacked by the preachers. On another Sunday morning, as Brother George Huggins was preaching, he turned toward me and shouted, "In my vision, it is dark outside your trailer while you lie in your bed, and a black man (only he said "nigger") stabs you to death." Everyone started screaming and shouting. They all knew that Sister Moreen didn't want Chaney and me to marry, so they did whatever they could to please her by hurting me. There was a woman that walked up to me after services and would ask me if I was a virgin and I said yes. Then in a stern tone she said Well, one thing about it, if you're not, Brother Chaney will know it! One man and his wife walked up to me in the church parking lot after services and told me to stay away from Chaney so Chaney and Judy could get back together. They wanted to break me to the point that I would leave the church and never return. Yet, my true love's words kept ringing in my ears: "Yvette, whatever they do, don't quit the church."

Another time, when I was being preached to by John Stratton Jr., the tears streamed down my face as I walked to the altar and stood waiting for him to let me speak. When everyone was sitting, except for the preacher and me standing at the altar, it was extremely uncomfortable knowing everyone was staring at me. Brother John Stratton Jr. continued to preach, ignoring me, yet totally aware that I was standing there. It was necessary to cry a lot, so I had to keep the tears flowing.

After standing there for a great length of time, my tears dried up. Suddenly he turned to me and allowed me to speak and beg forgiveness, even though I hadn't done anything wrong. I don't recall what I said, but because I wasn't crying anymore, I caught holy hell. For me there was just no relief from their wrath. I remember him saying in a nasty tone that I had "dry eyes," and everyone started shouting.

The following Sunday morning it continued on, only this time it was Michael Branson shouting at me from the pulpit saying: Yvette Cooper you have a spirit against Sister Marla Stratton! Then everyone started shouting which was so fearful. Once everyone knew Sister Moreen Stratton had placed a target on my head the nightmare attacks were relentless and unending. Sister Marla was her daughter, my age, who I had no bad feelings toward at all. She was always nice to me, she even admitted to me one day at the Chatsworth church farm that she knew her brother, Chaney loved me.

It's devastating to be publicly Humiliated in front of people you love and respect and only want their approval. Even placing their judgement of me above my own. I was very attractive at seventeen years of age and tried very hard not to let these people destroy me. Yet, they just wouldn't give me peace or kindness of any kind.

After church dismissed, I was walking out the side door when someone called out my name. Yvette! It was Lucinda Cramer, Sister Moreen Stratton's niece. In front of several people, she viciously and verbally attacked me. She shamed and reprimanded me for wearing a dress that she claimed was not far enough below my knees. It was so embarrassing the way she talked to me in front of everyone since she was my own age. I felt rebellious once I got away from the church that day, going over in my mind what she had said and thinking of all the perfectly mean words I wish I had said to her.

I had spent so many years with these people beating down my self-esteem that I seemed to have lost something inside me that was important in dealing with people. I couldn't find the emotional tools within me to fight back or even talk back. Mother had taught me to never take up for myself, so I would always stuff my feelings somewhere deep inside my heart. I walked away from Lucinda without saying a word. I simply looked at her with no obvious expression.

When I got home, I once again rebelled in my own way. Mother sent me to the beauty parlor, and I wasn't at all reluctant to have my hair fixed for church that night, even though I knew it was against the church rules to go to the beauty parlor for any reason.

When I had lived on the church farm in Arizona, I would take a brown paper bag and tear it into several strips to make homemade hair rollers. I would fold the strips over many times, roll strands of my hair up on each strip, and then twist the brown paper once I reached my scalp. I would then pin it with a bobby pin. Other women would take strips of material and wrap their little girls' long hair around and around the material until it was tight. Several hours later they would take the material out, and the little girls would have the most beautiful long and perfectly curled ringlets around their heads.

However, tonight was my night to wear an obviously professionally curled beehive with lots and lots of that shameful stuff called hair spray. I walked into the church with my head held high, pretending I wasn't afraid of anything or anyone. My only thought had been "I will show them I am fine!" Yet, I apparently wasn't smart enough to realize it would be a no-win situation for me.

Brother Ted Stratton was preaching, and what a lusty devil he was. I think all he must have thought about was sex. I recall one Sunday morning church service when he stood before the huge crowd and told the men they should take a bath with their wives. He said, "I take a bath with Anita," who was one of his wives.

After the meeting was moving pretty fiercely and the screaming and shouting began, he ran down the aisle to where I was sitting and grabbed me by my pretty hairdo. He shook my head with his angry hands and shouted, "Bless God, you'd better move!" They said those words often when they were rebuking someone. That meant "get to the altar and change your evil ways." The public crucifying of Crusonda, or Yvette, as they called me then, continued.

Each time I walked into the church I suddenly felt like I wasn't getting enough air to breathe, like an imaginary cage had dropped down over my entire body. Their accusing eyes pierced through my very being as if to say, "We don't want you here; you don't belong. You are keeping Judy and Chaney apart, and that is making Mother Moreen angry, so that is making us angry too." There was such an obvious unwelcome feeling for me at church, yet Chaney's words kept ringing in my ears: "No matter what happens or what they do to you, don't quit." Still, it was almost more than I could bear.

I worked so hard at my artificial smile and my confident look that I appeared to say, "I am all right; I am okay." It was so difficult for Chaney and me to find ways to see each other since Sister Moreen was determined to keep us apart. Chaney would tell her that he and Jimmy Stratton were going to sell Bibles, which was true; however, his true plans were to meet me at Shirley Benton's house.

32

Never Good Enough

ONE MORNING AS I stood outside by the street in front of my trailer home waiting for the school bus to pick me up and take me to North Whitfield High School, I spotted Chaney in his mint-green Grand Prix driving down another street to my right and straining his neck looking for me. My first thought was to scream, "Here I am; come and get me." But I also thought, "Oh my God, there he is; I'm so ashamed." I wanted to run and hide. I didn't want him to see where I lived, yet my heart leaped at the thought of seeing him. I was desperate; I didn't know what to do or which way to turn. The most overpowering feeling was I can't let him see where I live because he will realize I'm not in his class, a nobody, and I don't deserve someone so special. The trailer I lived in was only a couple of years old, but it was a "trailer." Only poor people lived in trailers.

Rodney Clemmons, who was a member of our church and a first cousin to Wanda Stratton, had walked up to me after the service one Sunday and demanded I stay away from Chaney, telling me I wasn't in Chaney's class. Even though I knew deep in my heart he was wrong, my low self-worth accepted his cruel words to be true. I would constantly try to build myself up by reminding myself of the Bible scripture that said, "A virtuous woman's worth is far above rubies," and another Bible verse that said I should encourage myself.

I quickly surveyed my surroundings to try to decide just how it would look to Chaney. There was a field of tall weeds next to our trailer, and my stepfather's old green Studebaker (which was his pride and joy but about the ugliest thing I had ever seen) was parked close by. So, although my heart ached to hold him, I hid from him instead. I felt as if I would die inside. I kept telling myself that if I could get on the school bus, I could then let him see me get off as the bus stopped to pick up other students, and maybe he wouldn't have to see where I live. Sure enough, I made it on the school bus while he was going up and down the street behind me.

The school bus pulled off McFalls Avenue onto Cleveland Highway. The bus kept making little stops while I desperately tried to get up the nerve to get off again. After all, I would get in trouble with the school and the bus driver.

I went to the back of the bus, and Chaney was right behind us as we once again made a stop in front of the golf course on Cleveland Hwy. I began to beat my fist on the filthy back window of the bus to try to get his attention so I could motion for him to follow us until I could get off at school, but he never saw me and finally gave up and drove away.

For years to come I would carry that painful memory in my heart and the anguish I felt in the depths of my soul. In my mind's eye, I can still see myself trying so hard to get his attention while beating relentlessly on the school bus's window with my clutched fist. I couldn't seem to forgive myself for not disregarding everything and everyone, and running off that bus into the arms of the only man I would ever love. For many years I would wake up at night covered in tears and torturing myself for not approaching that day differently.

33

The Royal Rulers Returned

CHANEY'S FAMILY WAS planning a trip to the church farm in Arizona. In the beginning, Sister Moreen had encouraged the relationship between Chaney and me because she wanted to make Judy jealous, so she had invited me several months earlier to come with them to the Arizona church farm. Before the time for them to leave came, she realized her son was in love with me. Her plans took a sudden turn, and she told me I was no longer invited to go along.

The night Chaney and his family returned to Dalton, Georgia, from their trip out West was a big occasion for the church. That Sunday night, a red carpet was literally rolled out for them to walk on when they entered the church building, all the way down the center aisle. The church brass band was playing as they entered the building. I played my saxophone and eagerly, yet fearfully, waited to see my soul mate again. I could see him from a distance, but he was never able to get any closer to me than that. His little brother, Matty, called out to me in front of the entire choir/band, "Ha-ha-ha, Chaney is going to marry Judy." I felt as though my heart had just fallen to my feet—not because I thought Chaney no longer loved me because there was never a doubt in my mind about his true feelings for me, but because I knew Sister Moreen had finally accomplished her scheme to tear us apart.

When church was over, as I stood taking my saxophone apart, I looked to my right and saw Chaney coming in the side entrance leading from the men's restroom area and the hall that led outside. He was looking at me, and I could see he was coming to talk to me when, suddenly, Pratt Huggins took one of his arms and James Stratton took his other arm and forcefully escorted him out of the sanctuary. After that, the Stratton's made it impossible for him to even get close to me. I was informed by one of the church members, who lived on the Chatsworth church farm, that while Chaney was at the Arizona farm, he was driving a sand buggy with some of the young church boys on the back. A young boy by the name of Johnny Huggins fell off the back of the vehicle and cracked his head open.

That night, at the Arizona church farm service, Chaney was rebuked while being accused of lusting after me. They told him that was the reason the young boy fell off of the sand buggy Chaney was driving, and that it was a warning from God. They said his Bible wife was Judy Bedford. Even though nothing sexual had ever happened between Chaney and me, his mother treated me as though I wasn't good enough to be her daughter-in-law. I was still a virgin, but I was very poor, with nothing to offer but my heart. Besides, like she had done with so many other couples, Sister Moreen had already chosen whom she wanted to marry her son.

34

Love Denied

ONE NIGHT AFTER church, Chaney and I once again hid from his mother so we could be together, and this would be the last time we would ever get to talk to each other. As we stood there talking and holding each other close, he told me he would love me until the day he died. He said, "I'm not in love with Judy. It's just that she has lived in our house so long that I love her as though she were my sister. But, Yvette, even though I will truly love you until the day I die, I will do anything to please my mother, even if that means marrying Judy." Chaney had hoped that eventually his mother would accept us, just as I did, but it was obvious that was never going to happen.

When Chaney and his family returned to Dalton from Arizona, he made many attempts to try to talk to me, but Sister Moreen always had someone watching to keep us apart. A revival started in Maryville, Tennessee, so I went with Frances Clemmons to the tent service. After the service was over, I walked out to the car so I could be alone should Chaney attempt to talk to me. Suddenly, I saw him coming toward me, but by the time he was only one car length away from me, his sister Marla screamed, "Chaney! Mother said for you to come here right now!" On one occasion, Marla admitted to me that she knew Chaney was in love with me.

I was still wearing his ring and secretly engaged to Chaney as I stood in the dining hall at the back of the church when Judy walked down the center aisle loudly proclaiming she was marrying Chaney. She held out her hand with her new diamond engagement ring on her finger for all to see. I would say Sister Moreen most likely furnished the ring.

A few nights later, Chaney was allowed to come to the Dalton church, although, as usual, Sister Moreen would see to it that we wouldn't have an opportunity to talk to each other. After the church service ended, I was determined to talk to him. After most of the members went to the church dining hall, I discovered Chaney was still in the church playing a guitar with several churchmen crowded around him. Although I felt very distraught inside, I was at the point that no one was going to stop me this time. I walked right up in front of the altar and loudly exclaimed, "Chaney, I want to talk to you!"

The music suddenly stopped, and Chaney got up and walked down to where I was standing. As I removed his ring from my finger, I simply said, "Here, I guess you will be needing this," and then I quickly walked away. I was too young to realize what a coward Chaney was, so as I walked out of the church with my heart breaking inside, I only felt sad for us because in my heart I knew he loved me too.

Timothy and Glenda Stratton took me home from church that night as I sobbed in the back seat of their car. Timothy kept telling me I should have never given Chaney his ring back because he and everyone knew that Chaney really loved me. Timothy and Glenda were of lesser importance in the Stratton status, but they were my good friends.

Although Chaney and I were members of the same church, we could only gaze at each other longingly from a distance. I sat in the women's section, and he sat above the altar with the other ministers. Even though we were only about forty feet from each other, we could have been oceans apart with Sister Moreen keeping watch from the front row. Regardless of the circumstances that surrounded us, I knew he loved only me, and he knew I knew it.

Even though Judy was openly engaged to Chaney, it was obvious she was unsure of herself. One night after church, she approached me outside and asked, "Did Chaney ever ask you to marry him?" I replied, "No." Then she asked, "Well, did he ever tell you he loved you?" I replied, "No." She seemed very pleased not knowing I had just lied to her in order to keep my promise to Chaney. When Chaney proposed to me, he had asked me not to tell anyone until his mother approved of us, and I would have done most anything to protect him.

I was crushed inside my soul to the point that I couldn't stand to hear my name fall from anyone's lips. I had heard it called out so many times in church in such an awful tone, and the abuse that would ensue from the preachers attacking me was more than I could bear. My full name was Crusonda Yvette Cooper, but I had always been called by my middle name, Yvette.

After Mother took me away from Dalton, Georgia, I began to ask the new people I met in Indiana to call me Crusonda. I wanted to be anyone but Yvette Cooper, and this gave me the opportunity to pretend I was someone else. I had to find a way to forget—forget the church abuse, forget I wasn't good enough, and forget the only man I would ever truly love.

35

Intimidation and Fear

It was 1972 and I had finally arrived at my eighteenth birthday. For just a moment, I felt hope and joy rise up inside of me. I knew this would be my chance to finally get away from Mother, so I walked in the kitchen and calmly told her I wanted to live with my aunt Arleen. Mother turned toward me, raised back her arm, slapped me in the face very hard, and told me I wasn't going anywhere.

In my heart, I wanted so badly to stand up for myself, but Mother had conditioned me at a very young age to fear her. Also, the church certainly instilled fear in me of anyone with an authoritarian personality and definitely of God. Mother continually stripped away at my self-confidence and belief that I could make any rational decisions. She had destroyed something inside of me that is so necessary to survive in life. She never allowed me to defend myself, and she certainly didn't defend me either. Each time she allowed people like my aunt Addie to steal from me or my male relatives to try to molest me, Mother *never* protected me, and in doing so she taught me I had no value. With her reassurance, I always felt like everything was my fault, and she did nothing to make me feel good about myself. I don't ever remember my mother telling me she was proud of me. I was so afraid of her, and she knew just how to control me.

Later in life I realized that when I was confronted with a situation that demanded I stand up for myself, I would begin with the strong and powerful words that I needed to command respect for my feelings. Yet I would wilt inside before the confrontations were completed, so I would lose my battles and once again be controlled. I now realize this weakness was a result of the emotional and physical abuse I endured during my years with Mother and the church.

Mother purchased a bedroom suite in my name, without my knowledge, at Bates Furniture Company (since her credit was bad). She said she was giving it to me as a gift, but she would later use it to threaten and exploit me. The day she slapped me in the face, she also said something about that bedroom suite that frightened me, but I can't remember what it was. However, I do remember that once we got to Indiana again, and I wanted to return to Dalton, she told me that if I returned to Georgia, I would be arrested for taking the bedroom suite out of the state since it was legally in my name. I believed anything she told me, so I was an easy target for her to control and manipulate.

I worked at Mercury Mills, where Mother also worked. I worked more that year at the carpet mill than I realized was possible. I would work as many as sixteen hours a shift in some instances, go home, sleep three or four hours and return to the plant because the company had no governing stipulations on how many hours anyone worked. I had never filed an income tax return; however, I knew I would be filing one this year and hopefully get a nice return since I had worked so much the previous year. I waited and waited for my W2 form to come in the mail, but it never came. I was barely eighteen years old and very naive in regard to the way things operated in life. I now realize I could have gone to the company I worked for and requested another one.

I kept asking my mother, "I wonder why I didn't get an income tax form to fill out." Instead of advising me on how we could find out, she said, "I bet Mommy (which is what she called her mother) filed your income tax return and forged your name so she could get your money!" Believing what she said, I dropped the issue and accepted that she was telling the truth. Years later I began to believe that my own mother did just what she accused her mother of doing, and now there is no doubt in my mind that she was the guilty party.

The red brick house Mother had rented for us on Eaton Drive was very nice but very expensive. It rented for $190 a month, which was high rent in 1972. The average rental house rented for fifty dollars a month, which would have been in our price range. However, Mother said she wanted us to have the best, so even though she couldn't afford it, she rented it anyway. Decisions like that kept us in hock all the time. So, when things got bad and Mother didn't pay the bills, she would simply run away from the problem.

I will say that Mother was honest in her own mind and had good intentions of paying the bills at the time, but her intentions were like a bucket that had many holes in the bottom of it—it just didn't hold water! She didn't have a husband to help her, so I understand she had it hard, but when she did have windfalls, on many occasions she would not use the money responsibly. Instead, she would spend it like a child who had no cares in the world for tomorrow. I believe that was from growing up with so little.

When we first returned from Arizona, Mother received several thousand dollars of back-pay money owed to us by the government. She bought a beautiful Story and Clark piano for $700, and she said it was for me. My piano looked so elegant sitting in front of the picture window of our beautiful red brick house, which was on a hill overlooking the lake. I loved that piano so much, and I dreamed of learning to play it better than the few tunes I had taught myself in the little white church at the Arizona farm.

One day my uncle Rex knocked on the front door and informed me that he was there to pick up his new piano, which he had just bought from my mother. I was heartbroken as I watched him load what I had thought was my piano onto his truck and drive away, but this wouldn't be the last gift my mother would give to me and then hastily take away.

We inevitably had to move out of the house on Eaton Drive, so Mother persuaded my grandmother to let us move back into the little house she owned on Goodwill Drive.

36

Alabama, Here We Come!

AFTER LIVING IN the little house on Goodwill Drive for a short while, Mother announced to Josh and me that we would be moving to Alabama, along with Betty Blevins and her two children. During the time we lived on McFalls Avenue, while I attended North Whitfield High School, my brother Josh became acquainted with a boy by the name of Michael Blevins. Michael's parents lived directly next to the Cherokee Drive-In Theater in Dalton. Many nights the boys would sit on the roof of Michael's house and watch the movies playing next door on the drive-in screen.

One night, Michael's father was walking home drunk and passed out on the railroad tracks behind their house, and a train hit him and killed him instantly.

After her husband's death, Betty persuaded my mother to move to her hometown in Snead, Alabama. Betty painted a pretty picture for Mother of how wonderful it would be for us to live there too. Not true! In some ways, being taken to Snead, Alabama, was like being dropped back on the Arizona desert, and I now realize that even back then I had a mild case of agoraphobia. I felt so frightened being taken away from Dalton, which I thought of as my home, and brought to a place in which I had no idea where I was or how to get back home even if I tried.

As we drove down a secluded dirt road deep into the woods, I began to feel such panic inside that I thought I would smother to death. Then suddenly the car came to a stop. The house was sitting on cement blocks and had been abandoned. It would have surprised me to discover that my mother had to pay rent to live there. We were surrounded by the forest, and I heard no sounds except for the chirping of birds and crickets.

We lived on poke sallet (pokeweed) that we found in the forest. We would fill large black trash bags full of poke sallet, and Mother would find many different ways of preparing it for us. She would wash it several times, boil it, and fry it in grease. She pickled the stalks, and on a good day, poke sallet, fried potatoes, corn bread, pinto beans, buttermilk, and an onion were what we ate. Most often, however, we just ate poke sallet and a pan of corn bread because that was usually all we had.

Eventually, Mother began to pawn things, and the first to go was my typewriter. She pawned it for ten dollars. Next, she pawned my record player for ten dollars. It seemed that no matter what you presented to the pawn brokers in Alabama, they wouldn't give you but ten dollars for your merchandise. The pawn brokers also ended up with my treasured alto saxophone.

I went to the American Legion with the Blevins one night and met a boy who appeared to be very sweet. He danced with me all evening, and when it was time to go home, he asked if he could drive me. Betty Blevins said that would be fine, and since everyone supposedly knew each other, I agreed.

However, on the drive home, he turned off down a dirt road. The streetlights were suddenly gone. I felt so afraid because even though I didn't know my way around in Alabama, I was certain that this wasn't the right way home. I was still a virgin and quite terrified, but I suddenly remembered I carried a pair of Mother's scissors, which she used for sewing, in my purse. Very carefully I slipped the scissors from my purse, unnoticed.

After driving deep into the forest, he stopped without warning just as I had feared. He became nasty and aggressive toward me, demanding I have intercourse with him as he grabbed at my body. My hand was trembling as I grasped the scissors tightly. I raised my arm in the air and screamed at him, "If you don't take me home right now, I will rip your guts out!" I was scared to death by now, but when he saw the scissors in my hand, he quickly started the car and drove me home without hesitation.

During the short time we lived in Alabama, Mother took me to see the doctor because I had a kidney infection. I had never been examined by a doctor before because I was unwilling to take my clothes off; however, this time I agreed to a complete physical. The doctor was about sixty-five years old with a very large nurse standing behind him, so this helped me to endure the ordeal. Suddenly, he rose back on his stool and shook his head. I asked, "What's wrong?" He replied, "In all my years of practice, you are the oldest patient I have ever had that is still a virgin!" Knowing how my mother always treated me as though I wasn't a good girl, I quickly asked, "Will you write your words down on paper stating I'm a virgin?" He said he would be glad to. I proudly gave this legal document of proof of my virginity to my doubting mother. Yet, as I look back on it now, I realize I never should have been made to feel that I had to prove something so personal to her or anyone else. It was obvious that she was shocked to say the least—this same woman, my mother, who sat at my aunt Arleen's table and called me a whore when I was fourteen years old. The first opportunity she had, she passed around this paper to her sister, Addie, and my grandmother, and they were also shocked.

I met a young boy named Calvin Nash, whose father was the road commissioner and a close friend of Senator Goldwater. Calvin wanted to take me to Florida since I had never seen the ocean, so he arranged to have Mother and his aunt from Birmingham, Alabama, go along as chaperones. We all stayed in a beautiful house on the beach. Calvin told me he was in love with me, and he asked me to marry him.

When I refused to marry him, he still gave me a beautiful diamond engagement ring and asked me to wear it and just think about it for a while. Mother took my diamond engagement ring and pawned it for ten dollars. This ring had cost over $200. Everything Mother took from me to pawn was never picked up and returned to me.

One night when Mother had a little money, she loaded us kids up in the car and took us to the drive-in theater. That was the first time I ever saw *Gone with the Wind*. After we left the drive-in that night, Mother stopped in town (Gadsden, Alabama) and walked into a store to buy an Orange Crush soda pop.

While she was in the store, I guess there must have been a hundred men with long white robes and pointed, cone-shaped hats invading the streets of Alabama. It was around midnight, and, boy, was I scared. Here I had been raised in the Deep South, yet, until tonight, I had never before come face-to-face with the Ku Klux Klan. They were placing sheets of paper underneath the windshield wiper of every car along the streets. My numb body slumped in my seat as a KKK member walked up to our car window with only his scary eyes peering out from behind his white mask. When Mother returned to the car, she reassured me that since we were white, we had nothing to fear.

Mother always said she was not prejudiced, but each time I heard her make that statement, my mind would go racing back to the time when we were taking a train from Georgia to Indiana. I was ten years old at the time, and our train had a layover in Ohio. Mother had a brother, Bob, who lived in Hamilton, Ohio, whom we could have spent the night with, but Mother's sister Addie advised Mom not to go to Uncle Bob's since Mother had gained weight and she should be ashamed of her appearance.

My aunt Addie didn't want Mother having a close relationship with her own brother. She would rather have us sitting in those hard chairs all night in a cold, drafty train terminal, hundreds of miles from home, than to go to Uncle Bob's and sleep in a nice warm bed.

There was a black lady with her children and a small baby sitting next to us in the train depot. I thought that little baby was about the cutest little guy I had ever seen, so I asked politely if I could hold her baby. Mother quickly made me return the baby to his mother, and then she grabbed me by the arm and headed for the ladies' restroom. I was only ten, but I remember vividly her taking my brother's belt and lashing my back and legs while I begged her to stop. She told me I had better never pull a stunt like that again.

Between poke sallet and watercress, God made sure we didn't go hungry. Now we were completely out of money, as Mother, Josh, and I stood in the forest picking maybe six huge, black, plastic trash bags full of poke sallet. Suddenly Mother stopped and declared she was going to call Jacob to come for us.

Finally, when everything was so hopeless, my brother Jacob and my brother-in-law, Lance Mullins, drove from Kokomo, Indiana, to rescue us from this lonely place called Snead, Alabama.

37

Where Is Home

ONCE AGAIN, WE were headed for Indiana, and although I would have preferred heading for Dalton, Georgia, anything was better than staying where we were. When we arrived in Kokomo, Indiana, we stayed with my sister, Karen, and her husband, Lance, until we could rent a place ourselves. I applied for a job at Ray's Drive-In restaurant, and when I came home and asked Mother if I could work there, she slapped me in the face. Ray's Drive-In had carhops and Mother said girls that worked as carhops were whores.

I was hired at a canning factory, Libby, McNeil & Libby. I worked on a machine called a cooler. Water would spray down on the hot cans that arrived at my machine by cable. The cans were usually full of hot tomato juice after being filled and sealed in another area of the plant. The company supplied me with a raincoat and rubber boots, but the cannery was very warm inside because of the heat from the vats in the floor full of boiling juice, and the raincoat could get very hot so I usually chose not to wear it; however, I did wear the boots. I always ended up soaked to the skin, and since the cannery was hot and steamy, this was fine during the twelve-hour night shift I worked. When seven o'clock came, however, and I stepped outside and the cold morning Indiana air hit my wet clothing, I would begin to freeze until I got home.

When I did get home, the first thing I did was run very warm water in the bathtub and remove the cold, wet clothing from my skin, which had now turned red. I felt so grateful as I slid my freezing body into that warm blanket of water. I would moan aloud with pleasure and relief.

Mother took most of the money I earned from Libby's since she felt it was my place to contribute my earnings. Maybe it was, but I hated living in Kokomo and wanted to go home to Dalton. What money she didn't demand, she stole out of my personal bank in my bedroom. It was a black-and-white cow bank with a yellow butterfly sitting on a spring on its hip with pink flowers. Mother broke it to get my money out when I wasn't home. If she would have just removed the rubber cover on its belly and taken the large bills, she wouldn't have had to break my beautiful bank.

All my life Mother accused me of stealing, but I was never a thief even in my youth. However, for many years Mother had told us stories of her childhood and all the stuff she had stolen because they were so poor. The reality of Mother's accusations was that she was the one who was guilty of the things she accused me of. Mother was a good woman and she would have never stolen from anyone but me. She said it wasn't stealing because I was her daughter and in her mind that justified her actions.

Mother rented a house that, like many others in Kokomo, had withstood the Civil War. It was a two-story house with yellow roofing tiles on its sides and stood on the corner of Armstrong Street and Courtland Avenue.

It was 1973 when I met a woman at work by the name of Nora, who introduced me to her brother-in-law, Robert Logan. Robert was very quiet and shy and had very little to say, but it was obvious he liked me.

Since I didn't have a telephone, Robert gave me his telephone number and asked me to call him. There was a liquor store across the street from our house with a pay phone outside. When I entered the phone booth, all I wanted to do was call my aunt Arleen in Dalton and ask her to come and get me, but I knew I couldn't go home to Dalton, so I called Robert instead.

Mother's threat kept me in fear of being arrested and prosecuted for the unpaid bedroom suite and held me captive in a town I hated. So, I resigned myself to the fate she had chosen for me. I didn't want to live in Indiana, but if I had to stay, I had to find a way to get away from my mother with her approval since she held such a dominant control over me and my decisions.

I'd only known Robert two weeks when he proposed to me. He had kissed me but had not made any kind of sexual advances toward me. In my heart I still loved Chaney Stratton, and I knew I would never love anyone else, but Chaney had married Judy, so until the day when he could come and get me, I agreed to marry Robert. After all, I was almost twenty years old and still a virgin, and I wasn't getting any younger.

Deep inside my heart I was foolish enough to believe that one day my dreams would come true. I would spend my entire life going through the motions of living a life that I did not want and only causing my heart to ache even more. In later years I truly wished that I had never known Chaney Stratton. I had trusted him because of who he was, and that was my first mistake. In so many ways he destroyed my life. He left me believing he loved me and that he was suffering too— and that was the cruelest lie of all. Every decision I made in my life was with him in mind. Instead of embracing life, I was only existing, waiting for my true love to rescue me, a complete trusting fool.

Getting Married

I felt such sadness in my heart that cold December night when Robert drove my mother and me to Greentown, Indiana, to become his bride. The rain beat down on the windshield as tears streamed quietly down my cheeks. I wore a navy and dark-green dress my aunt

Mazy had given me two years prior to this dreary night. In my mind I pictured all the young girls at the Dalton church floating down the aisle in their white wedding gowns, marrying the men they loved. I was about to give a man I wasn't in love with something that I had cherished and guarded all my life. Knowing I would never be able to give myself to my true love in the way I had dreamed was tearing me apart. Robert drove the car up to a dismal little silver trailer displaying a sign that read "Justice of the Peace."

If things weren't bad enough, the justice of the peace was a woman. I never knew before that night that a woman could be a justice of the peace, and because of that, it just didn't seem legal to me. After all, I had been taught all my life that women were inferior to men and that even God loved them less. Once we married and headed toward Kokomo, Robert announced that Nora, Russell, and the kids were staying in town that night at Nora's mother's house so he and I could have their entire trailer to ourselves. I sat there in disbelief thinking he wasn't even taking me to a hotel.

I learned very quickly that life was not and would never be anything special for me. I know he didn't mean to hurt me; Robert was just raised differently than I was. So, things that were important to me were things he never gave a second thought. Nevertheless, it would have helped if I had been in love with him instead of having a desperate desire to get away from Mother.

Intercourse for me was extremely painful in the beginning of our marriage, so I decided to visit the doctor and find out why. During my examination, Dr. Vandenbark informed me that I was built extremely small and that it was not only because I had been a virgin. He said that my entire female structure was extraordinarily small and should I ever expect to have children, it would be necessary to admit me into the hospital now to dilate my insides; otherwise, I would never give birth normally. When you're green, you don't know you're green, so my first thought was "Yeah, Dr. Vandenbark will make things big." So, I declined his advice and went home.

Robert and I moved into a small, one-bedroom trailer on Washington Street. All the streets in town were named after presidents. Robert was very much a mama's boy in every sense of the word. He was extremely quiet and never failed to spend time with her every day. A part of me admired the closeness between him and his mother because that was something that never existed between Mother and me. Yet another part of me resented the fact that he couldn't seem to break the apron strings. Robert would visit his mother in the mornings before going into work and then stop there before coming home in the afternoons. Saturdays and Sundays were even worse.

I became pregnant three months into the marriage in March 1974. We stayed in the same trailer park but moved into a bigger trailer. It was around this time that I noticed my husband's drinking was somewhat serious. Prior to our marriage, I wasn't exposed to living around or with people who drank alcohol.

This particular night, Robert and I were invited to go to Martino's Italian restaurant for supper with Robert's eight brothers. Robert drank several Sloe Gin Fizzes. When we arrived home, he began to throw up on just about everything in the bathroom. Before we went out to dinner, I had just hung our new shower curtain, matching bath set, and towels, which was our wedding gift from coworkers. Getting drunk on Sloe Gin, which is very red, made a disgusting sight and, of course, I was the one who had to clean it all up. It was like scraping up bright-red mashed potatoes! There was so little moisture to this awful stuff that it made me squeamish. The whole ordeal stunned me, but then people have shocked me all of my life. There must have been something in my youth that caused me to expect more from people than I ever received.

Although Mother and I had our problems, she was exceptionally clean, decent, and demanded honesty. We were never exposed to bad habits, such as cigarettes, drugs, and alcohol in our home. Robert's entire family drank alcohol, and what a big family it was. Each time you saw a member of his family, their hand would be clinging to a can of beer.

One night, Robert and I went to visit some of his relatives. Robert became so intoxicated that I had to lead him to the restroom and hold his penis in the direction of the toilet bowl. He wore boots and kept slipping around as though he was going to fall on his face in his drunken state. Finally, he did fall between the toilet seat and the bathtub, causing urine to spray the bathroom wall. We had only been married a few months, and when you expect better than this from another person, all I can say is I was simply appalled. Robert, however, was so used to drinking and having everyone around him drinking that it wasn't embarrassing to him; it was simply his way of life. I know Robert loved me, but in many ways, he was still a little boy.

We were paying twenty-five dollars a month for life insurance for the first year of our marriage until one day I discovered his mother was the beneficiary. It was a struggle for us to make ends meet, and I strongly believed that if she was the beneficiary, she should be paying the monthly premiums, especially since we were expecting a child. His mother sent an old baby bed over for us to use when the baby came, but this was my first child, and I was determined to have a new baby bed for our little bundle of joy. I was so surprised and excited to receive a check from my aunt Mazy in the mail for $100.00 which covered the cost for a new baby bed.

I worked as long as I could at the cannery, and when I did go on maternity leave, I drew a weekly check until six weeks after little Hunter was born at which time I would return to work. I was convinced I would give birth to a son, so everything I purchased for the big event was for a boy. In the trailer, we had a middle bedroom that I turned into a nursery. Everything was Winnie the Pooh from the bedspread on the half bed to the little lamp with Winnie the Pooh holding a handful of balloons.

Winter seemed to last forever in Indiana, and they were so very cruel. It was now December, and I was eight and a half months pregnant. I carried my laundry basket on my hip up to the trailer door from the Laundromat. The wind was freezing cold and showed no mercy as it cut through my clothing as though I had nothing on. Once I put away the clean clothes and had all the cleaning done for the day, Robert arrived home from work.

Later, after supper, his brothers Roy and Gene and his sister Joyce came over to play cards with Robert and drink beer. Since I was only a couple of weeks away from giving birth, I began to grow tired some time before midnight. The card game and drinking were still going strong, so I finally gave up and went to bed. Since we had company, I decided to keep my street clothes on and just lie down across the covers. Around three o 'clock in the morning, I was abruptly awakened by sounds coming from the middle bedroom. Our bedroom was at the far end of the trailer just past the bathroom. I walked through the bathroom and into the middle bedroom I had decorated for the arrival of our new baby. There was a small window above the half bed with the light of the moon shining down on two naked bodies that were having sex on top of my brand-new Winnie the Pooh bedspread. I was barely awake and confused as the thoughts kept running through my mind, Who, was this? Was it Gene and some girlfriend? Although Gene and his brothers had not done anything like this before, what else was I to think? After all, they were the only ones here when I had gone to bed, and you never know what to expect when people are consumed with alcohol.

I walked into the living room to try to find my husband. Robert was passed out on the sofa, the television was turned over onto the floor, and the floor was covered with dead leaves where someone had obviously dragged someone else into the trailer through the front door, which was still standing wide open. I was scared to death, although I tried hard not to show it, as I tried to shake my husband's limp body into consciousness.

Here I was on the verge of having a baby with two strangers in my home I had never seen before. The couple walked into the living room after I sat my husband upright, half awake. The man was tall and slender, about twenty-eight years of age. The woman was medium built and about forty years of age. She wore a short, plaid wool skirt over off-black pantyhose with a large run up the side. Her hair was disheveled, and she glared at me viciously through smeared eye shadow as though she wanted to strike me when I announced I had called the police and they were on their way. The man began to plead with me, saying, "I'm a married man with six children, and I don't even know this woman. I picked her up in a bar tonight, and she said she lived here."

With no one to stop him, he ran out the door into the cold night, and the woman followed him. When the police arrived, they left quickly in pursuit of the intruders. Once daylight came, I called the police station, and they said they had picked up the woman but not the man. She was a hooker and apparently at one time had lived in the trailer we now occupied.

I went to the district attorney's office to find out what I could do about our uninvited guest, but each time I tried to contact him, he was out of his office. I was informed that it would be difficult to see him since it was during elections. I was left with a soiled Winnie the Pooh bedspread and sheets that I paid good money for, only to have to throw them in the trash. I felt violated with no one to defend me.

I later discovered how the intruders gained access to my home. After I had gone to bed, the drinking continued until everyone left for their homes. Apparently, Gene was the last to leave, and he was so intoxicated that he knocked our portable television set onto the floor while staggering out the door and losing his much-needed eyeglasses. Gene left our front door wide open just as the befuddled hooker and her customer came stumbling through the leaves. It was obvious that the two strangers had a difficult time supporting each other's inebriated bodies and staying on their feet from the leaves lying all over the floor. Even now, it still amazes me how the strange circumstances fell into place in order for such a weird situation to occur.

38

The Birth of Hunter Logan

IT WAS DECEMBER 21st and I was nine months pregnant. My husband Robert was drunk and unable to take me to the hospital for the birth of our firstborn child, so Mother drove me instead. During the past nine months, I hadn't informed my obstetricians that Dr. Vandenbark warned me of a complicated delivery should I ever get pregnant. I felt that if they were good doctors, they would already be aware of my situation, but my silence would prove to be a serious mistake on my part.

It was Friday night as I lay in the labor room waiting to give birth to my son. The contractions were so painful, but my body refused to dilate past two centimeters.

Finally, Robert showed up and sat in a chair across the room from my bed playing Solitaire. Neither Mother nor anyone else was allowed in my room, except for my husband. My doctor was not even at the hospital to care for me. Instead, he told the nurses to call him at home when I was ready to deliver. I assumed the reason for his absence was because it was almost Christmas Eve so he preferred to be at home with his family.

I had been in labor for what seemed like an eternity when once again the nurse put on a pair of rubber gloves to see if I had dilated any more. As she pulled the rubber gloves over her very long fingernails, she informed me that since the doctor was the only one who could use some kind of device to break my water, she would try to break it with her fingernail as she examined me. As she jabbed her rubber-covered fingernail into my vagina, it felt as though she was tearing my flesh from the walls within me. I knew she was only trying to help me give birth, but I couldn't help but cry out in pain. My husband quickly frowned at me and said, "Be quiet!"

It had been about thirty-six hours since the labor began, and up until then I was allowed to have a cup of crushed ice nearby to wet my dry mouth and lips. My heart sank when the nurse informed me that I could no longer have any ice. Mother kept sneaking up to my door to peek in and check on me, but she was run away by the hospital staff.

It had now been about forty-five hours of labor, and up until now the nurse would complete her job and then leave the room for a short time. Now the nurse pulled up a chair beside my bed and didn't leave me. She was so kind as she rubbed my face and dry mouth with a cold, damp cloth and talked to me. It was at that time I told her that Dr. Vandenbark had told me I would never be able to have a child normally without allowing him to do the necessary surgery he had recommended less than a year ago. I was so weak that I passed out after each contraction.

The nurse quickly left the room and called my doctor at his home. Shortly thereafter he arrived at the hospital. He was upset because the staff hadn't called him sooner. After he examined me, he informed Robert and my mother that I was too weak to give birth and that either I would die or my baby would die. With each contraction I had been having without the necessary dilation, little Hunter's head would be brutally thrust against the crossbones.

Once Mother was informed of how serious my delivery had become, she went to the basement of the hospital where the cafeteria was located. As she sat alone at a table quietly crying, a couple approached her and asked what was wrong. She told them about my pregnancy and how serious it had become. With tears in their eyes, they said they would pray for me too. Mother once again peeked into my room and asked me if I wanted her to call the church in Dalton and ask them to pray for me.

Although we were no longer members of the Church Assembly at that time, I could see that Mother really wanted to call them, so I said yes. I do recall, at that point I was so weak I felt as though the life was almost gone from me. I just wanted to close my eyes and not feel the pain anymore.

Regardless of all the unfair abuse my family and I had endured in the church by the Stratton's, that night God truly worked a miracle through the prayers of the church members. I had been in labor for 47½ hours and not dilated but two centimeters when, at the very time the members at the Dalton church were on their knees praying for me, the baby began to deliver so quickly that the doctors couldn't prepare me fast enough.

The delivery room was straight across the hall from the labor room where I had spent so many hours. The nurses put me on a cold metal table, and the doctors told me to bend my knees up to my chest and wrap my arms around my legs to try to keep the baby from coming out before they could give me a spinal block. I watched my precious little son being born. His poor tiny head was pointed from all the pain he too had suffered from trying to escape my body through the crossbones that had refused to release him. My grandmother was still living in Dalton and was at church when the prayer request was announced. She later told me that when the church members knelt and began to pray for me, she could hear my sweet Chaney crying and praying for me above everybody.

It was Christmas Eve, December 24, 1974, the morning after my little Hunter was born, when the nurse came into my room and placed him in my arms. It was by far the most wonderful, peaceful, and contented feeling I had ever experienced in my life. Up until then it seemed my mind was always going a hundred miles a minute, yet this morning it was as though all the bad feelings and memories simply floated out of my mind, replaced with the knowledge that nothing mattered except for this calm feeling of love for this precious gift from God in heaven. I don't believe any parent could ever gaze upon the face of their child and feel a deeper love than I did (and still do) for my little Hunter.

That night the nurse came to my room and asked me if I'd had a bowel movement, and I said no. So, she gave me a laxative before I fell asleep. The following morning, she returned to asked if I'd had a bowel movement, and I again said no. So, she returned with a suppository. Later, she returned and asked the same question again, and my answer was the same, so she brought me an enema. It was now Christmas morning, December 25, and I wanted to go home because tomorrow would be Robert's and my first anniversary. I remember my sister saying they wouldn't let me go home until I had a bowel movement, so when the nurse returned and asked again, this time I said I had, even though I hadn't.

When you're ignorant, you don't know it, so I thought eventually I would use the bathroom. The baby and I did go home, but I didn't have a bowel movement. During that week I took sixteen laxatives to no avail. Robert wasn't one to show any type of emotion or concern. Mother became alarmed when I couldn't move off the bed. It felt as though I was becoming paralyzed from my neck down my spine.

Finally, on New Year's Eve, Mother called my doctor and told him my symptoms and also that I had taken sixteen laxatives. He told her to get me to the hospital as quickly as possible. He said that many laxatives could be deadly. When I was being pushed on the stretcher into the emergency room, everyone began saying "Happy New Year" to one another. Because I was nursing my son, the doctor wouldn't give me anything for the pain they were about to inflict on me. I will not go into details about what they did to me, but, believe me, it was painful, especially since I already had stitches in that area.

Black and Blue

Mother and I decided to go to Kmart to do a little shopping. I left Hunter, who was about nine months old at the time, with his father. As we drove away, Mother said, "I have a bad feeling about you leaving Hunter at home." I replied, "Why? He's with his father; he'll be fine." Boy! Was I ever wrong. When we returned home, little Hunter was sleeping so I let him sleep. The next morning, I removed his clothing to give him his bath, and as I did, all I seemed to be able to do was scream. His little back and hips were a dark-blue color where he had been beaten. I took him to see his pediatrician, and the doctor said the beating had almost crushed his liver.

Robert had been drinking and watching TV while we were gone. Little Hunter kept crying, which got on his father's nerves, so Robert thought he would whip our baby to shut him up. Poor little Hunter had an ear infection and was too young to say he was in pain. Mother took the baby and me to Robert's mother's house, and Mother informed Lenore that we were going to have Robert arrested for child abuse. Mrs. Logan began to cry, and as she did, she said, "Chris (she called me Chris instead of Crusonda) was the best thing that ever happened to Robert because shortly before they met, we had discussed putting him in a mental institution." I believe she only said that to try to keep Robert out of jail.

I had married Robert after only knowing him a few weeks in order to get away from Mother, but that never worked because she moved in with us. She always needed to have control of my life, even when I was married. After Robert had beaten our baby boy so badly, I told Mother I was going to divorce Robert, but Mother said, "You'd better stay with him because no one else will have you." It seemed that no matter what she said, I took it to heart and believed it to be the law and gospel.

I always said that if my mother didn't make it to heaven, then no one else would be there. A part of me considered her a saint, and the other part hated her for what she had done to me. All my life I had made excuses for her hurting me because she had such a sad life and had truly suffered, but now I wonder if that is justification for her callousness and abuse, she inflicted on me emotionally. I wanted so desperately to feel that Mother loved me, and I am sure some part of her did, but it was obvious that she loved my siblings so much more than she ever did me.

Patty Bradford married my brother Jacob, but she had an affair with my sister's husband, Lance, before they met. Knowing this, Karen really hated Patty with a passion. During the time Mother was staying with me, Karen had said some bad things about Patty to Mother. Mother told Patty what had been said about her, but when Patty insisted on knowing who had said it, *Mother told her it was me!* Mother lied to protect my sister, Karen. To me, that was a perfect reflection of Mother's love for Karen and also how little Mother loved me.

I don't believe anyone could feel more love and admiration for their sibling than I did for my sister, even though it was never returned. I guess it was because I wanted so much for her to love me like Mother loved her. The qualities I loved most about Karen were her calmness and seemingly gentle nature. Nothing ever seemed to upset her though her life was anything but easy. I never thought of her as my stepsister, although in reality she was. I did whatever I could to try to gain her affection and approval. It was obvious that loving me was far too much to ask of her. I was slender, and she was very overweight, and she hated me for that. Her husband (Lance) had made passes at me ever since I was fifteen years old, and that never helped my relationship with her either.

When I was seventeen years old, I caught Lance with another woman, so I told Karen he was being unfaithful. When Lance came home, he and Karen had a terrible fight, and he began telling her I was just a troublemaker and that he was innocent. She loved him so much that she was willing to forgive him and accept that I was just trying to cause problems in her marriage. Shortly afterward, I was at the Kentucky Fried Chicken restaurant on South 41 Highway in Dalton, Ga. when I saw him ride past in a white Mustang with a blond-haired lady at the wheel. I went home and told Karen what I had seen, and once again they had a royal fight. I would always end up being referred to as the "troublemaker." Mother also played a major role in influencing my siblings against me with her disparaging remarks.

My brother Jacob was an extremely strong-willed individual who could talk anyone into anything. He showed up on my doorstep with his family late one night and never left. He moved his family into my home on more than one occasion, and when he did, he ruled the roost. I remember him taking possession of my husband's recliner when watching television, which was always tuned to what he wanted to watch. It was as though it was no longer my home, but my husband wouldn't say a darn word. It seemed that everyone was always afraid of Jacob.

Robert and I were working twelve hours a day, supporting our son and now supporting Jacob, his wife, and son too. We even bought their baby's diapers and their cigarettes, yet we received no kind of respect whatsoever. One day, as I sat at the kitchen table and looked at Jacob, I said, "You are going to have to find a job." Jacob immediately grabbed me by the neck of my blouse and twisted it in his one hand as he made a fist with his other hand and shouted in my face, "I will bust you in the f*@#ing mouth." He and his family were living in my home and taking over while his wife lay across the bed during the day reading *True Story* magazines.

Jacob started having the milkman come to my home and in my name without my knowledge. The first bill I had to pay was eighty-three dollars, which was huge in 1976. When Robert and I completely ran out of money, Jacob insisted I allow him to sell my bedroom suite because he said he knew someone who wanted it. He was relentless and such a bully, so he ended up getting his way just as he always did; however, when the time came for him to pay me for my bedroom suite, he didn't.

My siblings have always treated me with such blatant disrespect, and I know Mother was not slothful in teaching them by example. I just don't know why they found it impossible to love me. The only time my family ever had anything to do with me was when they wanted something from me. I was always willing and eager to help them, and they knew it.

39

The Blizzard of 1978

WORK SLOWED DOWN at Libby's and I was laid off for a while, so I decided to seek temporary employment elsewhere. I was hired at Fitz's Lounge and worked for the owner, Anne Fitz. Anne was in her late fifties, a stern-spoken lady who demanded perfection in whatever job you attempted for her. Most of her employees only pretended to have affection for her; however, she, for whatever reason, always held me in high regard. I worked hard in the kitchen, and Anne knew it. I loved Anne as though she was the mother I never had, and I could always talk to her about anything.

I was twenty-three years old and still naive in many ways. There was a small, probably 11-by-14-inch, glass window in the door that led into the dining room and another one in the opposite door leading into the lounge area. Once in a while I would look out that little window at the excitement and merriment taking place just on the other side of the door.

The restaurant was huge with three areas to entertain the public. Fitz's Lounge was the finest restaurant in Kokomo, Indiana. There was the main dining room that catered to Kokomo's elite and a middle area, separate from the dining room. This area was for sandwich-style eating with a bar for alcoholic beverages. The third area had a country-style band and its own bar. I remember watching everyone through that little glass window as they celebrated New Year's Eve, laughing, kissing and seeming so happy. As they sang to each other, my heart was crying inside because I felt so alone. Robert always spent his free time drinking or going deer hunting with his brothers; he never was one to take me to the movies, go out to eat, or send me flowers. I didn't seem to count when it came to someone doing something special for me. My wedding and honeymoon hadn't been anything special, and there was neither a wedding shower nor a baby shower when my son was born. I was legally married, but outside of my love for my son, I felt like the most alone person in the world.

The Storm Is Coming!

It was a cold wintry afternoon in January as I walked in the back door of the restaurant at Fitz's Lounge just as I did each day. Yet today would leave an indelible mark in my memory. It would be a day that I would never forget because I was totally unaware of what lay in store for me.

As I entered the kitchen, Dean, the chef—dressed from head to toe in his white uniform, with his tall white hat—smiled at me and said, "Hello!" Then he applied a match to a sizzling hot plate, causing it to burst into flames. I loved to watch him prepare what the restaurant called a "Flaming Sword" because as the waitress carried her tray into the dimly lit dining room, the fire would blaze from the meat and vegetables on the sword. It would light up the darkness, making it look so romantic. The waitresses, dressed in red dresses with black aprons, were running around quickly, preparing their stations with fresh condiments and filling pitchers with fresh water and iced tea.

Most of the waitresses had blond hair and were well groomed. Anne Fitz demanded perfection in all things, and she got it. Anne and I were close friends, and she always smiled as she told me I was the daughter she never had. Many nights when the dining area rush was over and that part of the restaurant was closed to the public, she and

I would sit alone and talk. Unlike my own mother, Anne really cared about what I thought and felt about everything.

As I would sit and look at her as she spoke, I was always asking myself, "Why does she care about me?" I was convinced that no one could love me once they got to know me because that's what Mother always taught me. Yet, here she was, and there was no doubt in my mind or anyone else's who worked at the restaurant of Anne's fondness for me. Anne and my mother had many things in common: they both had dark hair and were large framed, close to the same age, and perfectionists—Anne was born on September 1st and mother was born on September 3rd.

As the hours slipped away, it began to snow very hard. All the employees were sneaking to the back door at separate times to peek outside at the beautiful winter wonderland. However, many of the waitresses began to get worried when the snow drifts became so deep that it was difficult to push open the back door to even view the winter storm.

Suddenly, Anne entered the kitchen informing everyone that a hazardous blizzard had just been announced on her television upstairs. The announcer said that anyone who didn't have to be out should stay home. Anne said that she was going to allow a few of the waitresses to go home since it was a slow night due to the bad weather. Ollie, one of the waitresses, was adamant about going home because she lived so far out and especially since her daughter was pregnant. I quickly volunteered to stay since I only lived about a mile from the restaurant.

As the hours rolled away, the worse and more perilous it became for the employees to remain at work, so their numbers slowly dwindled as they left for home. Finally, there was no one left at the restaurant except for Anne, her husband Dwight, and me. Their office upstairs had the comfort and convenience of an apartment, so they decided to remain there for the duration of the snowstorm in case someone might need their help. Since they had plenty of food at the restaurant, they could better serve the public should anyone need shelter from the snowstorm.

It was now eleven o'clock at night and time for me to go home to Robert and little Hunter. When I walked out to my car, it was almost impossible to open the car door because of the deep snow. I did, however, manage to start the motor. As I attempted to drive away, the tires would only spin in an effort to pull out of the snow drift. The car did move but only enough to wedge it up against another car, making it impossible to move it without hitting the other car.

I just wanted to go home to my family, but it looked like that wasn't going to happen until a young man of about seventeen years of age began to beat on the back door of the restaurant about two hours after my attempt to leave. He said his snowmobile had stalled, and he would like to pull it into the breezeway and work on it in an effort to get it running again. The young man agreed to drive me home if he could get it started.

While he was dragging his snowmobile inside the restaurant, Anne and I looked out the back door to see how many inches of snow had accumulated. I was alarmed when I observed snow drifts as high as nine feet deep. You couldn't see much outside because the snow was blowing so hard it would sting your skin. Finally, the snowmobile started, and I prepared to leave for home.

Since I had only worn a sweater to work, Anne walked up and handed me a big pair of men's black rubber boots to cover my shoes. Then she draped a heavy leather coat over my shoulders and told me to put it on. While she was buttoning up the coat, which had been left by one of her male customers, I felt very special, as though I was her little girl, from the care she was taking to protect me from the harsh winds. She then took her own sheer headscarf and covered my face with it, tying it at the back of my head so the net would keep the blowing snow out of my face and allow me to breathe. As she prepared me to go outside, I had no idea how dangerous the blizzard had become.

Even though I was thrilled about going home to be with my little family, I felt my heart racing as I mounted the back of the snowmobile. Off we zoomed into the white darkness as the blizzard winds whipped our bodies so hard we could barely see the few inches of the snow-covered road underneath the beaming headlight in front of us. Just as we had made it to the street in front of the restaurant, the snowmobile stalled. I was so frightened when the young man informed me that I would have to dismount and return to the building. As I stepped off the snowmobile onto what was supposed to be a road underneath all that snow, I felt as though I was drowning. The blizzard winds were whipping so hard, it was a struggle to keep my balance in the deep snow. There just didn't seem to be a bottom to it. It was difficult to breathe with the stinging snow blowing down my throat. I was in tears by the time I was able to reach the door of the building.

Once I regained my composure, I was very upset because I couldn't go home. In a time of crisis, I think most people have a great need to be with the ones they love, and I was no exception to that rule. I kept trying to remember what there was in the pantry for my family to eat. I knew there was some food but not much. I felt sick inside because here I was with Anne, who was smiling and trying to comfort me by telling me we could have steak and eggs for breakfast, and I didn't know what my family had to eat.

Because Robert and I didn't have a telephone at our home, there was no way for me to contact him.

The next morning, I quickly ran to the back door to see what the blizzard had left behind in its fury. There was a heavy white blanket of snow as far as I could see, and along the wall at the back of the parking lot were snow drifts as high as fifteen feet deep. My heart sank as I realized there wasn't much hope of me getting home to my family. It was as though the world had stopped; the silence was amazing in comparison to the busy everyday sounds we were used to hearing in our little town of Kokomo. Our only connection with the outside world was Anne's radio.

The National Guard had been assembled to assist in the aftermath of the blizzard. A man with a heart condition was being transported to Indianapolis with two bulldozers in front of the ambulance to shovel away the deep snow. The entourage moved very slowly up the highway toward the hospital in Indianapolis fifty miles away. Local schools were designated shelters for people in need. Also, it was requested that anyone owning a four-wheel drive vehicle who could assist in taking milk, food, and other supplies to people in need should meet at the closest school in their area. Since my brother-in-law, Lance Mullins, worked for the City of Kokomo, he came to my rescue in a big white city truck. I was extremely grateful to say the least. The truck was so high off the ground that I could have used a stepladder to get inside.

As we pulled away from the restaurant, Lance said he had rescued a lady up the road in the Delco Electronics parking lot who was also stranded. She was about frozen when he arrived at Delco. On the way to her home, he had to let her out on the corner of her street, since the snow was too deep to drive the big truck down any side streets. When the lady had walked about ten feet from the city truck, she passed out and fell facedown into the deep snow. The blizzard was so strong that it took her breath away.

We arrived at the side street where I had to get out and walk the rest of the way home. We sat there for a few minutes, and Lance kept asking if I was sure I could make it. I said yes, although I inwardly struggled to get up my nerve to get out of the safety of the huge city truck.

We could see my home about two hundred feet away from where we were sitting, and just knowing my little boy was inside those walls, I knew I had to get to him. I had never been away from him this long, and he was the light of my life. He was so cute with blond hair that hung just above his eyebrows, and that innocent smile of his could make any sad heart sing.

As I stepped out of the big truck, I focused my eyes on the front door of my home. I would take a step forward, but the snow was so deep it was difficult to lift my legs high enough to take the next step. I tried so hard to move forward, but the strong freezing winds would pull me back.

When I made it to the front sidewalk of my home, with the door only a few feet away from me, my mouth was so dry from the brawny blowing wind down my throat that it was difficult to swallow. I tried to scream out my husband's name, but the words would not come. I was now in tears as I managed to get out one faint "R-o-b-e-r-t!" Suddenly my husband was at my side pulling me into the warmth of our home. I was never so glad to see them in all my life, and it was obvious little Hunter felt the same. He was all smiles when he called out, "Mommy!"

Robert wasn't concerned about food; however, he was furious that he was out of cigarettes.

The blizzard of 1978 was so devastating, and many people died. Some died unnecessarily because their electricity had been turned off due to nonpayment of electric bills. After the blizzard, however, a law was passed that never again would anyone be deprived of heat and electricity during Indiana's freezing winters.

As I sat in a chair in the living room with little Hunter on my lap, who was now four years old, I listened to the news reporter describing the circumstances that surrounded some of the deaths. One young girl and her baby, who lived in a rundown trailer park, were found frozen to death because the blizzard winds were so strong that it kept blowing out the pilot light to her little gas stove. An elderly man was found frozen to death because his electricity had been turned off for nonpayment. Ollie's daughter gave birth to her new baby at home because she was unable to get to the hospital.

As I held my little boy safely in my arms, I heard the reporter tell of a young couple who were unable to find their missing little boy who was also four years old. After the blizzard, they found his frozen body lying at the bottom of the steps in front of their home.

Regarded as the worst blizzard in Indiana history,
the 1978 storm dumped more than 20 inches of snow
at 50 mph for 31 hours on Kokomo, Indiana

40

Abused Abuser

MY HUSBAND, ROBERT, was an extremely quiet man unless, of course, he was drinking. Robert was a good man and a hard worker, but I always knew to keep a close eye on him when it came to our little boy. Even though I knew he loved little Hunter, he was emotionally unable to calmly teach him right from wrong. One day as I sat in the living room of Carl and Lenore Logan's (my in-laws) home, I was discussing with Lenore my concerns about Robert's way of reprimanding our son. I told her that I wouldn't allow him to spank little Hunter anymore because he was too rough with him.

Lenore began to cry, as she was reminded of how abusive Carl had been with their children. She was sixty-two years old, and her heart was still broken as she described the pain her husband had inflicted upon their little boys. Carl and Lenore had twelve children, three girls and nine boys. One little girl died at birth, so there were eleven children living. Lenore said that Carl would, on many occasions, put beer in her children's baby bottles instead of milk, simply out of meanness. As tears streamed down her faded cheeks, she told of how Carl would grab Robert and Gene by the hair on their heads and kick each little boy with his brogan boots into the air. Their bruised little bodies would go sailing across the room as though they were footballs.

Hearing my mother-in-law cry as she spoke of the beatings her children had to suffer at the cruel hand of their father helped me better understand my own husband's inability to be gentle with our son. I have heard that many times when you see a parent who is abusive with their children, in most cases the parent was also an abused child. Robert was a very quiet man and seemed to be incapable of expressing his feelings.

No Protector

One night when I was working at Fitz's Lounge, a waitress entered the kitchen and informed me that I had a visitor in the dining room waiting to speak with me. As I opened the door and entered the darkly lit room that was now closed to the public, someone grabbed me and kissed me on the lips. When I saw that it was my brother-in-law, I was furious inside. My brother Jacob was with him when Lance asked me to run away with him. Jacob said, yeah, If, you weren't my sister I'd ask you myself. The whole incident just disgusted me.

When I returned home that night from my job, I told my husband what had happened, but Robert never said a word to Lance.

Another time, when I was in the kitchen at Fitz's Lounge, the female bartender opened the door that led into the kitchen and informed me that there was someone at the bar asking to speak to me. When I walked into the lounge area, there was Roy Bushman, a longtime friend of my husband. I quickly asked, "Where is Robert?" He replied, "I don't know; I came to talk to you."

As we sat down for a short time at a table, I asked, "What's going on?" He then began to tell me that he had been in love with me for many years and asked me if I would run away with him. Both these men had wonderful wives and children, yet they were not smart enough to realize their attraction for me was just lust. They both drank a lot, but then so did the majority of the people we knew in Kokomo.

What hurt my faith in my husband the most, in regard to me, was his inability to defend my honor when I told him of the sexual advances these men had made toward me. I was twenty-three years old and very attractive, so someone was always trying to get me to go out with them, and it was so hurtful that my husband just stood by and never said a word to these men.

I worked very hard to be a good wife to Robert and a good mother to our little boy, but sadness lived in my heart and refused to leave. I grew up believing if I stayed a good girl/virgin, I would be happily married one day like the storybooks claimed. What a joke! Nothing about my life was anything I had envisioned.

41

Her Eyes Are Open, but No One Is Home
(Raped on My Birthday, July 9, 1978)

JULY 9, 1978, was my twenty-fourth birthday, but I still had to go into work.

There was nothing special going on; however, as the night wore on and I was cleaning up the kitchen, one of the waitresses came to the door and asked me to step out into the bar area for a minute. I never went into the bar area except for the time Roy Bushman showed up and asked to speak with me.

As soon as I came out of the revolving door, the bartenders and several of the waitresses began singing "Happy Birthday" to me. It felt so nice as they all began talking to me and insisting, I have a drink with them to celebrate. The manager was a very attractive man named Nick Hansen, who was in his late forties and a friend of the Fitz's. He was a huge gambler and made several trips to Las Vegas; you could say he was very much a man of the world. I agreed to have "one" drink with the girls, so Nick prepared it. I had never had an alcoholic drink without my husband, but I didn't think just one drink would hurt me. Two hours later I woke up in bed with Nick having sex with me. I was drugged and dazed and couldn't remember how I got there. I felt so groggy and confused while Nick buckled his pants and silently walked out of the dimly lit bedroom into the living room. I felt dizzy as I raised my head from the pillow, and my vision was blurred, but I could make out the face sitting in the living room chair; it was Dean. He called my name and asked if he could get into the bed with me, and I faintly said no. I couldn't talk as Nick drove me home; I just sat there. My head was spinning, and my mind was so foggy to what was happening around me.

Destruction of a Family

As I made my way to my front door, struggling to find my house key, the door burst open with my husband and my son, little Hunter, standing there smiling from ear to ear as they sang, "Happy Birthday." Robert held a birthday cake in his hands, and both had big smiles on their sweet faces.

I had never had sex with anyone but my husband, and I did not dare let him know anything was wrong. The shame was unbearable, but it would have been even worse if I had to say it out loud. It felt like something in my spirit had been crushed, like someone had sucked all the air out of my world and I couldn't breathe.

When I went back into work, Dean told me he was in love with me and asked me to move away with him. He said he had a job waiting for him at Callaway Gardens in Pine Mountain, Georgia, and he wanted me to go with him. Dean told me Nick had put some kind of drug in my drink. Dean said he wanted me, but he wouldn't touch me without my permission. It all made me sick to my stomach. Dean was in his mid-fifties, and I was barely twenty-four years old.

A seed of bitterness and distrust for men in general began to grow in my spirit, and my delusions of honorable men vanished like the faith I had in these two men who were old enough to be my fathers. I made excuses to keep my husband from touching me until I could see my doctor, which I did the following day. The doctor informed me there was a slight trace of a sexually transmitted disease and gave me a prescription for penicillin. I stopped at the pharmacy and bought the pills, and then I went to a local liquor store and bought my first bottle of whiskey.

I felt destroyed inside. I had gone from being a virtuous woman to feeling like dirt. The disgust and shame were unimaginable. Even though my grandmother had made me wash with alcohol when I was thirteen as if I was dirty and contaminated, even though Mother had called me a whore to my aunt Arleen (when I was a fourteen-year-old virgin), and even though Moreen Stratton didn't think I was good enough for her son, I had always known in my heart I was pure. Now I no longer had that confidence to lean on. I was contaminated and had forever lost my value as a virtuous woman. I kept asking myself, "What did I do to cause this to happen to me? It surely must be my fault."

Women are always in some way to blame when they're raped, according to society. Furthermore, I had listened to stories on a television special, from the husbands of women who had been raped, and their husbands would say they no longer wanted to touch their wives. I felt so lost and alone; there was no way to rewind yesterday and what had happened to me. There was no one, no mother or sister I could run to who would hold me, comfort me, and make me believe everything would be okay. I had to keep this ugly secret to myself because it only would have brought more shame to my broken heart if anyone knew.

Robert had never been a supportive husband and never defended my honor when relatives and friends made passes at me. His greatest joy seemed to be getting drunk with his brothers, and I just couldn't bring myself to tell him what had happened. I had to get away; I wanted to run, run as far away from this town as I could. I left everything behind—my furniture and personal belongings—except for the clothes I could get in my suitcase for little Hunter and me, and I headed home to Georgia.

42

Mother Won't Believe Me

I HAD HOPES of finding a place to live and getting a job to take care of little Hunter and me, but I would soon discover that Mother's controlling nature would never allow that to happen. When I arrived in Dalton, I had a little money to get a place to live, so I rented a newly built apartment on Wells Drive, and immediately Mother moved in to maintain control of me just as she always had.

I had a pretty decent income from Varsity Carpets, where I worked as a carpet inspector. During this time, I received a check from Robert in Indiana for thirty dollars, which was a state tax refund. All my life it seemed that the only time that Mother ever showed real affection toward me was when I was giving her money, so when the check came, I told Mother that she could have twenty dollars of it to buy some new shoes. Mother was paranoid about many things, and because of this, she said no to my offer and told me not to cash the check either. Mother said that Robert might, in some way, use me cashing the check to take little Hunter away from me. She always kept me frightened about everything.

When my grandfather, Daddy Joe, passed away, my sister, Karen, and her husband, Lance, came down from Indiana for the funeral. Robert came with them. Shortly before they left to return to Indiana, we all went to Six Flags Over Georgia. Once they headed back to

Indiana, Mother told me she wanted the check that I had received from Robert so she could buy those new shoes. Because she had made me afraid to cash the check, I had put it somewhere and forgotten about it. After looking in my bedroom drawers where I believed it to be, I told her I didn't know where the check was. She shouted, "You're a liar!" What I didn't realize at the time was the check was stuck in the front base of the drawer so when you opened the drawer you couldn't see it unless you used your hand and felt the inside of the front of the drawer.

Over and over Mother kept screaming at me, "You're a liar," at least seven times. She said, "I know what you've done; you spent that money at Six Flags Over Georgia!"

I felt so helpless with no way to prove or convince her that she was wrong. I was frantic as I desperately searched through my drawers hoping to find the check, knowing that was the only way I could stop her angry words.

When Mother looked at me with those stern piercing eyes of hers, I would totally wilt inside like a frightened rabbit that was about to have its heart cut out. I vividly remember the tears running down my face and dripping off my cheeks as I slowly walked back up the stairs to my room feeling defeated. I called out to her softly, "One of these days, that check will show up, and when it does, I hope you will remember how you talked to me today."

With that, there was nothing left for me to say except to hide my head in shame each time she looked at me. For days to come, I had a horrible guilt complex because Mother had preconditioned me to feel guilty about everything. I say this because anytime she accused me of something, I automatically felt shameful even though I wasn't guilty.

After discovering Mother had allowed Karen to charge her long-distant phone calls to my phone from Texas that ran over $1,000, I knew it was time for me to leave and go back to Indiana. There was definitely no possibility of staying separated from my husband and living in the South without her living with me and making me crazy, so I packed up Little Hunter's and my clothes and headed back to Indiana.

Once our plane landed in Indianapolis, Robert picked us up at the airport and drove us the fifty miles back to Kokomo. I remember it well because I cried all the way. I didn't want to come back, yet I couldn't bear to live with Mother either. As I look back on my life, I wish so much that I could have been emotionally confident enough to stop allowing Mother to control me with her belittling and degrading methods.

After being back in Kokomo for about two months, Mother began to move out of my apartment in Dalton since she couldn't afford to pay the rent without my income. I hadn't heard from her since I left, but then we were still on bad terms anyway.

One day the phone rang, and to my surprise, it was Mother. She was very friendly as though there were no problems between us, as she said, "I've been in the process of moving out of the apartment, so yesterday I was burning a lot of trash out back in that big barrel. As I was throwing papers into the flames, I happened to notice an envelope with your name on it on the ground by the barrel! I picked it up, and as I started to throw it into the flames, I thought that it might be something important, so I opened the envelope. Well, you will never guess what it was! It was that thirty- dollar check that Robert had sent you." Then Mother said, "Can I have it?"

After she had talked to me as though I was the worst, lowest human being who had ever walked and viciously called me a liar multiple times, she still had the nerve to ask me if she could keep the money. Her voice reflected no remorse, nor were there words of apology even though I had pleaded with her to believe me. Nevertheless, as always, I told her she could keep the money from the check.

43

Cash for Coons

ROBERT AND I lived at 417 North LaFountain Street in Kokomo. It was a gloomy area of town, but I tried to make the best of it. It wouldn't have been so bad if Robert would stay home at night, but he was gone a lot. He was either hunting deer, raccoons, or rabbits or at the Hoosier bar with his brothers. I hated being alone at night because I was frightened, which made it impossible to go to sleep.

I drove my sister, Karen, to the Indianapolis airport to pick up her husband, Lance. As we drove toward the airport, I suddenly spotted a huge, dead raccoon lying on the side of the road. I noticed that even though it was dead, it wasn't bloody, and I excitedly informed my older sister that Robert was paid as high as thirty-five dollars for their pelts when he would go hunting. During this time, money was scarce, so the thought of making thirty-five dollars had us both interested. I pulled over to the side of the road to further investigate the condition of the raccoon.

Karen and I stood at the back of my car with the trunk open just staring at the dead raccoon and wondering how we were going to get the coon in the trunk. Finally, I announced, "If you will pick it up and put it in the trunk, I promise I will give you half of the money for the sale of this raccoon." Karen looked at it grimly; however, her need was greater than her disgust, and she suddenly grabbed the coon by its tail and slung it into the trunk of my new car.

On we drove to Indianapolis, forgetting about the creature in the trunk. When we arrived at the airport, Lance opened the trunk and flung his huge piece of Samsonite luggage on top to the coon. Karen and I had totally forgotten about the coon; after all, that was many miles and several conversations ago. Lance was too busy talking about his trip to even notice we had a passenger in the trunk that had gone on to a better life. When we arrived in Kokomo, Lance suggested we play a game of cards. As the four of us sat at the dining room table playing poker, it suddenly hit me that I had forgotten about the dead coon in the trunk of my car.

I quickly announced to Robert that he was going to be so proud of me when he found out what I had. When I told him, I had found a beautiful coon—in mint condition—on the side of the highway, he looked shocked as he asked with a growl, "Where is the coon now?" I told him it was in the trunk of my car. He became alarmed and said to me, "Didn't you know that we could be arrested if we're found with a coon in our possession since it's not coon season?" The whole incident was hilariously funny to me, but Robert was never one to laugh about anything.

The Interview

Since there were so many people that we knew personally who were members of the Church Assembly, we were informed there was an investigation going on in Atlanta, Georgia, at a local television station. Ex-members of the church I had grown up in were trying to expose the church on live television, with their faces blocked out and their true voices protected. I was born into and grew up as a member of the church, lived on the Arizona church farm, had been engaged to Rev. Chaney Stratton, and had dated Rev. John Winston Stratton Jr., who now possessed absolute power and control of the Church Assembly, since the death of his father, John Stratton Sr., in 1974.

It came as no surprise when a reporter from that Atlanta television station called me in Kokomo, requesting I fly to Atlanta to be interviewed on public television. The reporter assured me that the television station would pay all my expenses should I agree to the interview; however, I declined the request. My only reason for not flying to Atlanta for the exposé was because I was still in love with Rev. Chaney Stratton. I didn't want him to suffer embarrassment from the information I could provide about the church.

44

Amanda, My Beautiful Baby Girl

It was 1979 and I had decided to have a second child. I didn't want little Hunter to grow up as an only child, and I really wanted a little girl after having my son. One thing about my children was they were both wanted children. Neither of them was an accident as I have heard many women say about their pregnancies.

When I was pregnant with Little Hunter, I was so certain that he would be a boy, I never bought anything for a girl. Now that I was pregnant with Amanda, everyone was declaring I would have another boy; however, every fiber of my being told me my unborn baby would be a little girl. I bought all girl clothes and some beautiful little dresses with lots of lace and cute little bows.

With Hunter, I had craved pickled okra, and now that I was pregnant with Amanda, I was craving it again. For some reason, the best brand of pickled okra was no longer available at our local grocery stores, so a friend of mine in Georgia shipped me a case of it. I was in hog heaven for a while, but then my cravings turned to chocolate. I couldn't get enough chocolate!

During March 1979, we had some very cold and icy weather. Most of our streets were solid sheets of ice, but I wanted some Hershey bars, and Robert refused to go to the store. There was never anything about Robert that was loving or thoughtful. I was determined to satisfy my chocolate craving as I zipped up my camel-colored, knee-high leather boots with the sheep fur at the top. Toward the bottom of the back of my right boot I noticed the threads pulling apart at the seam, making me well aware that I was even gaining weight in my legs. I was almost seven months pregnant as I waddled down the huge flight of stairs headed toward my car.

We lived in a gray two-story apartment in the city limits of Kokomo, so we were very close to everything. The apartment building was no less than one hundred years old. I cautiously drove my car over the ice-covered streets until I made it to Marsh's grocery store. I purchased the largest chocolate Hershey bar available, along with a tray of Reese's cups, and headed home.

During my pregnancy with Amanda, I increased my maternity clothing size three times. I was certain I could live on chocolate and nothing else, and it sure showed in my clothing. I remember my stomach being so big that I would hold my panties out in front of me and try to aim my foot in the direction of the hole to put them on. I would then lose my balance and fall on the bed, laughing at my extremely funny predicament.

When I went to the table to eat dinner, my stomach was out so far that I would have to set my plate on my stomach so I could better reach it. I used to lay a loaf of bread on my stomach and let my unborn baby kick it off. Everyone always laughed at how hard Amanda would kick. I told everyone Amanda was going to be a basketball player.

Living in Fear of Mother

Mother returned to Kokomo, Indiana, and moved in the house with us. I was still working at Libby's so Mother watched little Hunter while my husband and I worked. Mother charged me seventy-five dollars a week to care for my son, yet she never contributed anything to the groceries, rent, electric, telephone, etc. Seventy-five dollars a week was a great deal of money for a babysitter in 1979, even though we were working twelve hours a day. I wish that my husband would not have allowed people to always run over us, but he did. I don't know if that was because of his drinking or the abuse he had endured as a child at the hand of his father.

Mother was always taking money from me, and I was too emotionally weak to defy her. One day she told me she needed $150 to send to my brother in Kentucky. This time I refused and when I did she began quoting Bible scriptures to me that said something about shutting up the bowels of compassion. While I was at work, Mother even cut open my two-foot-tall, red dog plastic bank that I kept in the back of my closet where I was collecting old coins. Mother said it was not stealing since I was her daughter. She was always accusing me of things I wasn't guilty of, yet, she seemed so convinced of her accusations about me, it was very unnerving. Little Hunter was such a cute little boy, but he would pick up everything he heard. I don't know what caused him to start saying it, but one day while I was at work, he said to Mother, "Shoo, you stink!" When I arrived home, Mother was very angry with me. She looked at me sternly and said, "You went to Nora's house and told her that I stink." She spoke as though Nora had come and told her that I had said she smelled bad. Mother was always so cruel with her accusations. I told her I had not said anything about her to Nora, and I begged her to believe me. I even said, "Mother, if you did smell bad, I wouldn't tell anyone because I would be ashamed for anyone to know it." That seemed to calm her a little as she replied, "Then, why did little Hunter say that to me?" I tried to convince her that he was just a little boy, and he didn't really mean it. I was nervous just being around Mother for fear of the next time she was going to attack me for something.

Little Hunter became sick and had a very high fever, so I called his pediatrician to advise me on what I should do. Dr. Fields said I should place him in the bathtub and bathe him in cool water every twenty minutes to try to bring down his fever. Dr. Fields guided me through this dilemma, and I trusted him to know what was best for the health of my son. However, Mother absolutely hated the fact that she was not in control of the situation. She did not dare accept that I knew what I was doing; instead, she kept stressing that the way I was handling the situation was all wrong.

When she finally realized she wasn't going to be able to take control as she did in everything else, she went stomping through the house until she got right up in my face and, with righteous indignation, shouted at me. "I want you to know Vivian Long told me that you talked about me like I was a dog!" It was so obvious that she was trying to hurt me and put me on the defensive. I was already worried sick about little Hunter, and now Mother was screaming her vicious accusations at me.

Mother was relentless with her attack until she had me crying and begging her to believe me when I told her I had never said anything against her to my friend Vivian. Still, she wouldn't accept that I was telling the truth, but then she never did. I grew to hate her because I could never win her approval. I wanted so desperately for her to love me. The truth is I didn't really hate her. I needed her so much, but I just couldn't reach her heart. No matter how hard I tried, it just was not there.

Vivian Long was a lady who lived in Dalton, Georgia, whom I had not seen in seven years. Mother always attacked my relationships with people I really cared about. There were three women in my youth who were motherly figures for me, and their names were Frieda, Vivian, and Anne Fitz. On separate occasions, I was informed that my mother had called these women and attempted to malign my character to them. I never understood why Mother was always criticizing me to everyone I cared about. It was as though she didn't want anyone to love me or have a good opinion of me. Finally, Mother and I had one last battle before she moved out of my apartment and into Karen's house.

Amanda's Grand Entrance

Robert was in the living room watching *Vega$* on television, which had come on at 9:00 p.m. I walked into the kitchen, and as I did, I felt such a strong pain that I knew I was going into labor. I immediately felt pressure in the lower region and thought I needed to use the bathroom. When I went to the bathroom, I noticed a foreign substance passing from me, so when I came out of the restroom, I informed my husband that he needed to take me to the hospital, and he replied, "Oh, just go in yonder and lay down and it will go away." I did what I was told, but the contractions were very painful.

I called the hospital and made the necessary arrangements for my arrival. I walked into the living room once again, at which time I said, "Either you take me to the hospital now or I will call an ambulance!" *Vega$* was just ending as Robert hustled little Hunter, who was now five years old, and me down the steep flight of stairs. When I stepped out of our front door, there was an area of grass between our sidewalk and the street. I had such a strong contraction that I had to lie down on the grass until it subsided. Robert drove toward his mother's home, which was about two miles away. We stopped there to ask her to care for little Hunter while we were at the hospital. He lingered and chatted until the pain hit me once again, and I screamed at him, "Let's go!"

Robert was never one to get in a hurry about anything, and I was about to suffer the consequence of his dawdling personality. He must have stopped at every red light in town. Once we arrived at the hospital, Robert went downstairs to fill out the necessary papers while I was being hooked up to a monitor. The monitor would allow the medical staff to see how close I was to delivery.

Suddenly I began to throw up, which I had never done with my first pregnancy. I felt really bad about it, but I couldn't prevent it from happening. Robert had taken part in the Lamaze classes for expectant parents, so he would be permitted to participate in the delivery. Once the medical staff realized my little girl was about to make her grand entrance, they began to rush around my room like chickens with their heads cut off.

Because I had experienced Braxton Hicks contractions a few days prior to this event, Robert hadn't taken the labor pains seriously. He was standing calmly at the door of my room looking bewildered at the nurses running around in such a frenzy. "What's going on?" he asked.

One of the nurses threw a blue medical uniform in his face and said, "Put this on!" In her rush, the nurse had accidentally given him two pair of pants instead of a pair of pants and a shirt. I had never seen Robert look so shocked when he realized I really was in labor and the birth was just minutes away.

Amanda Caroline Logan was born June 20, 1979, at 11:20 on a Wednesday night, weighing eight pounds and nine ounces. She had olive-colored skin with a full head of beautiful dark hair. Little Hunter had straight blond hair, and Amanda had naturally curly hair that was almost black. She was a beautiful little girl who was born after only two hours and twenty minutes of labor. I was simply amazed!

I went into the hospital weighing 207 pounds and came home weighing 192 pounds. I breast-fed both of my children, so dieting was out for a while. I had never been so big in my life without being pregnant, and it was depressing. Robert showed me no mercy in criticizing me for my weight, but the most hurtful thing he ever said to me was when he called me "Fat Ass"! I felt my heart sink as he said those ugly words to me. It could not have hurt any less if he had just slapped my face.

45

Weight Watchers to the Rescue!

AMANDA WAS ONLY a few weeks old, so I felt Robert hadn't given me a chance to get back in shape. Still, I began to monitor my eating habits and did rather well on my own. I decided, however, that I needed a little direction in my efforts, so I joined Weight Watchers. I didn't want to take pills or follow some off-the-wall fad diet that I couldn't live with on a permanent basis. The night I joined Weight Watchers, I weighed in at 182 pounds. I was pleased with that, but I knew I had a long way to go.

I set my goal to lose forty pounds. I recall standing in line to be weighed that first night with two slender girls in front of me. I felt irritated as I looked at them and thought to myself, "Yeah, they're just here to make the rest of us feel bad." Wrong! I discovered during the meeting that both of these young girls had once been very heavy and were now about to reach their goal weight. I was ashamed for the resentment I had been feeling toward them, and now all I was feeling was shocked and very impressed!

There was one lady at the meeting I will never forget. She had initially weighed well over four hundred pounds and had lost 262½ pounds. To see the results and hear the other women's stories really gave me a boost of hope for my own success.

I had joined Weight Watchers in January 1980, and six months later I had not only reached my goal but I also had lost a total of sixty pounds. This was including the weight I had lost on my own after Amanda's birth. I was smaller than I had ever been in my life, and I felt wonderful. Robert would have to eat his words ("Fat Ass") for dinner. It was such a great feeling to try on clothes in a department store and not be ashamed to see myself in those dressing room mirrors that show no mercy, only precise reflections.

The most difficult thing for me was to have my thinking catch up with the reality of my smaller size. I kept gravitating toward the larger sizes in clothes that were good at hiding my figure. I slowly began to wear sweaters that would cling to the shape of my body.

Married to a Drunk

Robert continued to go out drinking with his brothers and leave me and the children alone until late at night, which I hated. He was always drunk, so I still felt as though I was alone. His brothers would deposit Robert on the floor inside the door downstairs, and I would have to guide his drunken carcass up the stairs, which was pretty rough on my back.

When my family bragged about how sweet and quiet my husband was, I didn't dare tell them he would get so drunk that he would urinate on himself, throw up, and slur his words. I was ashamed for anyone to know how disgusting it was to live with a man I had to strip down and care for like a helpless child. Mother had told me that no one else would have me, so I figured I should try to make the best of my unhappy life.

In the summer of 1980, I checked into the hospital and had my tubes tied. God had blessed me with two precious children, which was exactly what I had hoped for. When I came home from the hospital, I discovered my husband had invited another woman up to our apartment. I felt so betrayed, especially since it was in front of little Hunter, who was five years old, and Amanda was eleven months old. I later discovered this girl, Janey Grimes, was someone who patronized the local Hoosier Bar where Robert hung out.

46

Tears Flowed Like a River

I WAS BACK at work at Libby's canning factory, only this time I was operating a fill-and-close machine. As the noisy cans arrived on one side of my machine to be filled and sealed, they would slide through my machine and make their exit by cable. I stood there with tears quietly streaming down my face while the warm clouds of  steam hid me from my coworkers. I was alarmed that I couldn't seem to stop my tears from falling. It was as though a dam had broken inside of me, carrying away little pieces of my heart into a river of tears.

I made my first appointment with a psychologist in hopes that he could advise me on how to deal with my emotional state. I felt much better when I arrived home after our first session. When I walked in the door, Mother was sitting on the sofa by my younger brother, Josh. She quickly asked, "Well, what did the doctor say?"

Mother had accused me so often of lying when I wasn't guilty that it seemed to have caused me to be too honest, if that's possible. So, I softly replied, "He told me I should get as far away from you and Robert as humanly possible."

Mother responded, "Well, I'd just like to know what you said about me to him."

I uttered, "Mother, I'm not paying that man eight dollars an hour just so I can turn him against you." As I spoke those words, the telephone rang. It was my aunt Arleen in Dalton, Georgia, whom I dearly loved, but I panicked inside because I knew Mother hated her. After I hurriedly hung up the receiver, I smiled nervously and said, "Josh, Arleen wonders why you don't keep in touch with her." Mother angrily replied, "Because *he* loves *me*!" implying that I didn't.

I was so tired of being left home alone with the children, night after night, and the only big event that happened for me each week was going to K-mart, so I decided to make some changes. As Robert started for the door, I informed him that I was going too. When we arrived at the Hoosier Bar, I saw my sister-in-law standing behind the counter serving beer. I looked around at the dingy little bar with its one pool table and asked myself, "Why would anyone want to come to this crummy-looking place?"

The bar had a small band that performed country music. For some unknown reason, people in the north seem to crave the redneck life. The band asked my brother-in-law, Lance Mullins, to sing a couple of songs. When Lance finished the first song, he looked at me and asked me to sing with him. I had never in my life sung for the public, except in the church choir in Dalton and Arizona. However, Lance and I had sung gospel music many times together at home, so I agreed. I had made up my mind that any time Robert chose to go to the Hoosier, I was going to be right there on his heels come hell or high water, especially after he'd had another woman in my home when I was in the hospital!

Betrayed

Once again it was party time in Kokomo, so Robert and I went to the Hoosier bar. I was still carrying a lot of emotional grief due to Robert's indiscretion with Janey Grimes. I didn't believe Robert had sex with her because he drank so much, but then I could be wrong. Anyway, this particular night, she was standing at the bar talking to the bartender who was also my sister-in-law. As we sat at our table, I asked Robert if he would dance with me, and he said he didn't want to. He then walked up to the bar where Janey was standing and began talking to her. I was furious inside, so I pushed my chair away and headed for the bar where they were standing. I interrupted their conversation and asked, "Just what is going on?" Robert looked at me and said, "You're just jealous!" Here I was, this man's wife, the mother of his two children, and he tells me I'm just jealous! What kind of world did I live in? I felt so humiliated but I was determined to convince them I didn't care.

The boys in the band requested that I sing a song even though my brother-in-law wasn't there to sing with me. I marched up to the band with my head held high as though I owned the whole world. I knew in my heart that my in-laws knew of my husband's little fling with this woman. I felt rejected and embarrassed, but there was no way in hell I was going to allow them to know I was hurting. The first song I chose was one that I could put all my angry energy into singing. It was a Tanya Tucker song called "When I Die." I belted out that song with all the pain and fury I was feeling in my heart. When I finished singing, everyone was shouting, "More! More! More!" I began to sing a slow song by Anne Murray that I had always loved called "Could I Have This Dance."

Of course, I was thinking of Chaney. As I sang, I looked around the room smiling as though I was fine. Several of Robert's brothers and wives sat at our table, actually two tables pushed together. I noticed an attractive man I had never seen before, and he winked at me. I had no interest in this man, but I wanted to hurt my husband, so I smiled back at the stranger. After the music stopped, the man came over to me and introduced himself as Oscar Owens. Robert couldn't say a word after what he had done, so I smiled a lot and agreed to let this stranger sit and talk with me at my table.

47

Oscar

I HAD TOLD Robert I wanted a divorce after discovering he had been seeing another woman, yet I hadn't taken any legal action. Oscar pursued a relationship with me without hesitation. Although I had not been interested in him in the beginning, it felt nice to have someone show such interest in me and what made me happy. Oscar was a strong, determined man, and I had never had anyone like that before. First Chaney and then Robert who were both weak-minded individuals who couldn't seem to stand up without trying to cling to their mother's hand. I respected Oscar, and it felt good to have someone to really talk to who talked back.

Robert had never been one to express himself or hold a meaningful conversation with me. When I tried to express to him what I felt in my heart, it was as though I was talking to the wind. Robert had always been good at holding down a job and bringing his check home, but outside of that, there was nothing else to call it a relationship. The reason I had decided to have a second child with Robert was because I knew in my heart that I wanted two children with the same father, even if I had to raise them alone.

Oscar encouraged me to get a divorce as soon as possible because he wanted to marry me. Even though I was wrong for doing it, I maintained a relationship with Oscar, and I was so very happy. I had never had anyone be so kind and gentle with me before in my life. Oscar was divorced and lived in a beautiful house on McCain Street. Next to the house sat what he called his garage, but it was so big and tall you could have fit a small two-story house inside of it.

I guess I should have become suspicious, but I was so naive and never gave the strange-looking building a second thought. He drove a beautiful Cadillac Eldorado and appeared to be an upstanding citizen in the community.

Oscar had two boys and a little girl as a result of his marriage before we met. His daughter was twelve years old and such a sweet girl. So, I felt so sorry for her when she came home from school crying over the exposé about her father in the *Kokomo Tribune* newspaper.

Apparently, Oscar, this man I trusted, was in organized crime up to his earlobes. He had been involved in importing and exporting stolen property, such as Broncos, Jeeps, and other automobiles from Indiana, Illinois, Michigan, and Ohio. Many times, the vehicles would be transported by being hooked on the back of a wrecker, which allowed the vehicle to go unnoticed by police officers who might be patrolling the area. He had stolen merchandise from a company he had done business with worth a million dollars. Oscar also confessed to me that he even had a train derailed. He began to gradually lose everything he had acquired financially, and as he did, his personality changed too. On one trip to his attorney's office, he paid $5,000 to buy more time for himself. He was facing thirty years in prison for the crimes he had committed. He began to frequent the local bars on a regular basis. His casual drinking increased, only now he was drinking whiskey and Coke or gin and grapefruit juice.

48

When Dreams Turn into Nightmares

ONE EVENING OSCAR told me to get into his car; he said he wanted to take me for a drive in the country. As we drove toward Logansport, Indiana, which was about twenty-two miles from Kokomo, Oscar suddenly turned off the main highway onto a dirt road. Further and further into the woods he drove until we finally reached a secluded area surrounded by trees. His once calm demeanor toward me was now hostile. He said he would soon be going away to prison, and he was going to make certain that no SOB ever touched me. He pulled out a pistol from underneath his car seat and told me he was going to kill me.

I froze inside for a moment, but another part of me only felt numb. This always happened inside when something really bad was about to happen to me. I would just go numb and silent and wait for what was to happen next. Also, I guess a small part of me didn't believe that he was going to shoot me. I now believe that it may have made a difference that I didn't get hysterical like most women would have. I was so used to having people dump on me that I once again just waited there with no obvious expression.

As he raised the gun toward my face, he began to cry as though his heart was broken. He suddenly cried out, "I can't do it," and the gun dropped to his side. I should have feared this man much more than I did, but I believed he loved me and he had not yet taught me how vicious and dangerous he really was.

Libby, McNeil & Libby had announced to its employees that the company was going to close the Kokomo, Indiana, plant. Should anyone wish to relocate to Chicago, Illinois, the company would allot each employee $2,500 for the move. Employees who didn't wish to move to Illinois, such as Robert and me, still received money for severance pay, bonuses, paid-up insurance, etc. Even though Robert and I were divorced, Robert said he was willing to move to Georgia if I would take him back. I thought I loved Oscar, but I didn't trust him anymore, so I decided to go to Georgia and try to make a go of it with Robert. I knew if it didn't work out, I could leave. Still, for the children's sake, I wanted to try.

Our destination was Austell, Georgia, where my aunt Mazy lived. Between Robert and me, we had enough money left after paying our bills to get set up in Austell. Robert and I applied for jobs at Lockheed, Boxboard, and several other places. We rented a nice brick duplex and waited hopefully for the telephone to ring with the promise of a job. Robert and I both had excellent letters of recommendation from Libby, McNeil & Libby.

After a couple of months, Oscar called me. He had driven down from Indiana and wanted to see me. He said he was at a nearby restaurant and would wait for me there. I really didn't want to go, but I seemed to have a problem saying no. I was still afraid of him, so I went. After all, it would be in a public place. I told myself I would be fine, and he was such a bully that I didn't want him showing up at my home and starting a fight with Robert. He wanted me to ride back to Indiana with him on Friday and said he would fly me home to Georgia on Sunday. He wouldn't take no for an answer, and I reassured myself it would only be for two days. I was always afraid inside and always had a fear of making him, or anyone, mad.

Even though Robert and I weren't living together as husband and wife, I never should have gone with Oscar, even if it was out of fear and even if it was only for forty-eight hours. As I rode up the interstate with Oscar, Ricky Skaggs was on the radio singing, "Highway Forty Blues." I had always loved that song but this time my heart just ached inside and the sadness overwhelmed me because I was leaving without my kids. The further Oscar drove up I-75 north the more I felt like I couldn't breathe. I was sick to my stomach, wishing I could just jump out of the car and run back home.

After I left with Oscar, Robert got drunk and had a car wreck with the children inside. No one was hurt; however, my aunt Mazy decided I was the worst human being who ever lived for leaving with Oscar. I knew she was right, but I was young and scared, and I honestly thought the children would be safe with their dad for a short time. I would forever regret my decision to trust Robert with our kids and allow my fear of Oscar to control me. Robert was the father of both our babies and I really did believe he would act responsibly, knowing our children were depending on him.

When I returned to Austell, Aunt Mazy was furious with me. Robert left for Kokomo, Indiana, since that is where he really wanted to be anyway. Aunt Mazy had been the reason I had chosen to move to Austell to begin with because I loved her so much, and now she wouldn't come around me anymore.

The last day she came to my home, she had my aunt Addie with her. They told my seven-year-old little boy, Hunter, right in front of me what an awful mother I was for going to Indiana with Oscar. Even if they were justified in criticizing me for leaving the children with their dad, they were wrong in condemning me to my son. Still, I loved my aunt Mazy, and this would not change that in my heart; it only hurt. She had been my refuge growing up, and she gave me the love and acceptance I had never gotten at home.

Angels and Lions

The children and I were very much alone now with the food supply running out and no one to turn to. Hunter was in the first grade, and he brought home a form for me to fill out for free lunches. Robert was not sending any type of child support, so we were on the verge of going hungry. When I filled out the free lunch form, I was unable to list any income for the three of us because there simply wasn't any. A couple of days later, I received a letter from the principal of my son's school requesting he and I have a conference.

I had two dollars left to my name and a very heavy heart when I drove into the school parking lot. The principal greeted me when I entered his office, and he invited me to sit down. After asking several questions and discovering I had recently moved to Austell, Georgia, from Indiana, he asked if it would be all right with me if he allowed a local organization called the Lions Club to bring me and my two children a few groceries. My refrigerator was so bare that pride was not an issue. I felt so grateful in my heart to this stranger who genuinely cared. After thanking him for his concern, I stood up to leave. When I started for the door, he pleaded with me not to be offended as he took twenty dollars from his wallet and placed it in my hand. I cried all the way to the gas station. I truly appreciated the money, but the fact that he cared enough to give of himself in such a way touched my heart to its very core.

Although Aunt Mazy, whom I dearly loved lived just a few miles away but she wasn't speaking to me. I realize when a person is angry, it can close the heart to love but unfortunately, Danny was gone and

I hadn't lived there long enough to even know anyone or make any friends.

I thought about how alone I had felt with no way to feed my children as I stood in the doorway of my apartment watching several people carrying bags of groceries up to my door. People I didn't even know and who didn't know me smiled with the words "We care!" shining in their eyes.

Amanda was two years old at the time and Hunter was seven. They scrambled through the bags of food that the Lions Club members had left. We had cream cheese and Jell-O, which made for a nice dessert to go with the pinto beans and canned goods that had arrived. We were very appreciative of each and everything that God had blessed us with through the hearts of these people.

I had signed up for unemployment when I moved to Georgia; however, I never received the first check. In my despair I called Oscar, and he came for me and the kids to take us back to Indiana. I was worried about little Hunter missing so much school that year, so I registered him at the Pathway Christian Academy in Dalton in hopes that he would get a lot of private tutoring to make up for the many days he had missed until I could get settled in a permanent home for us.

Mother agreed to care for him if I would send her my entire child support check every week once I returned to Indiana and got it from Robert, so I agreed. I didn't want my son to suffer the consequences of my unsettled life. I owed Mother thirty-five dollars, so, even though I didn't have it, she demanded I pay her before I drove away. I took my treasured guitar and pawned it for the thirty-five dollars, and I would never get my guitar back again.

I went to the unemployment office to find out why I hadn't received a check when I returned to Indiana. I discovered the checks had been issued; however, they simply hadn't made their way to me. Finally, I received several checks and was able to rent a nice apartment in Kokomo.

Oscar had lost his home and was now laid off from work. He

moved in with me and Amanda but didn't offer a dime toward the rent or utilities. He claimed he had to send his entire unemployment check to his ex-wife for child support. I later discovered that was a lie; he had not been paying her a dime. He was always going to the local bars yet never offered any explanation about where he was going as he left.

I finally became so tired of being left at home I went out to dinner at a local steak house with a few girlfriends. As we pulled up to the Cimarron Steak House that night, Oscar flew into the parking lot with the tires of his Cadillac screeching to a halt. With the top down, he jumped out of his car and ran over to the van I was stepping out of. He grabbed the front of my blouse and twisted it with his fist as he stuck a pistol in my face. He was cursing and threatening me just as a customer in a three-piece suit opened the door of the restaurant and proceeded to his car. When the man saw Oscar with the pistol aimed at the center of my forehead, he became alarmed for my safety, and he shook his arms and pleaded with Oscar to let me go.

Oscar said to the customer, "You had better get the 'F' out of here or I will blow your head off." There were at least eight people in the parking lot now, nervously watching as Oscar dragged me to his car and forced me inside. This was the first time I truly believed Oscar would kill me. He took me home and beat me in my chest and face repeatedly with his fist.

If I was never afraid of him before, I was terrified of him now. He was not the same caring man I had fallen in love with. He was pushy, demanding, and constantly taking money from me. When he had sex with me that night, he was different from what he had ever been before. He made a fist as he began twisting my hair tightly and forced me to perform oral sex on him. I had never in my life gone down on a man before, so the sick feeling I had in my heart would be too difficult to describe. He cruelly laughed as he said, "One day, some man will appreciate what I am teaching you now." I was no longer in love. I was numb and sick at heart. I was terrified of Oscar. He would take my money, go whoring around, and then come home and find reasons to hit me.

Oscar wouldn't accept a steak that was prewrapped from the grocery store; I had to have the butcher special-cut it for him. On one particular day, I was unable to locate the butcher and scared of being late, so I hurriedly grabbed a steak that was prewrapped.

It wasn't nearly large enough to Oscar as he began cursing me at the sight of his steak. It didn't matter that I was the one paying for it. He grabbed my clothes and began slapping me in the face. He had hit me so many times, the pain seemed to not hurt as much as it once did.

Amanda was two years old at the time, and as she watched Oscar slapping me in the face, I realized how affected Amanda was by Oscar beating me. She took a butter knife while Oscar lay sleeping on the sofa and began hitting him in the chest with the butter knife. As young as she was, the knife was not angled on its side; it was angled straight up and down in the direction of his heart. It was obvious she was trying to stab him in the chest with the knife. He suddenly awoke, and for the first time, his face turned red with the look of guilt.

For many years I cried myself to sleep for putting little Hunter in the private Christian school because I realized all he could see was that his mommy left him behind.

My Darling Son
"If" is such a lonely word, with lessons hard to learn
And memories set long ago, a place I can't return
Our time is cruel and gives no slack
It takes the past, won't give it back
You long to fix and rearrange
Your choices made, you cannot change

I searched to fine my place in life
To make a home and be a wife
Yet while I searched, I did not see
You grew up quick, in front of me

Life can be cruel and seal your fate
I reach for you but it's too late
I wait alone, so old and flawed
With you not here to hear me call

The night has come I dream once more
To see you walk inside my door
You smile at me with love so real
Your warm embrace I finally feel
You have no wounds I have no shame
I have not failed, I'm not to blame
My hearts rejoice and full of joy
Come back to me, my little boy

Written & Composed by Yvette Lidy
12-23-2021

Recently, however, a friend, Clara Cross helped me to see that if little Hunter had been with me and saw Oscar beating me, he could have been hurt by Oscar for trying to protect me. Her wisdom removed such a weight of guilt off my shoulders that I had carried for many years. Forever replaced with a feeling of peace that it's difficult to describe and I will be forever grateful to her.

I had purchased a new living room suite and a washer and dryer from the money I had received when the plant closed. Now that Oscar had lost everything, he had to buy time before facing a jury, and he forced me to write hot checks on my checking account for his personal use. I was very afraid of him just like I had been afraid all my life, so I did what I was told. I was the responsible party since the account was in my name. I had to sell off my furniture, piece by piece, to cover the checks, so by the time Oscar finished with me, I had nothing left except the clothes on my back.

I couldn't go to my sister Karen's home because she had temporarily moved in with her sister-in-law, JoAnn. JoAnn's husband, Harry Short, had gone with Karen's husband, Lance, to find work in Missouri. That year, Indiana was the worst in the United States for unemployment, and Kokomo was the worst in Indiana. President Ronald Regan made a special appearance outside of the Kokomo Mall regarding unemployment with the promise that the crisis would indeed improve.

Robert had borrowed my car, gotten drunk, and totaled it. Knowing how Oscar beating me had affected my little girl, and even though I was so afraid, I knew for her sake that I had to get away from him. So, I filled my suitcase with a few clothes, placed Amanda on my left hip, and struck out on foot to find a safe place to stay and hide from Oscar until I could find a way back home to Georgia.

JoAnn had come to my home asking me for help not long before this because she had no money to buy milk for her new baby boy. She was an employee of Delco Electronics, but she had been laid off from work so long that the money had run out. I gave her money for milk and then made a special trip to the local Goodfellows and Salvation Army to guarantee her family would receive food along with Christmas gifts for her three children. They did receive gifts—nuts, fruit, a ham, lots of other food, and beautiful winter coats from JCPenney for her two girls, Allison and Laura. I believe that when you do something to help someone, you don't tell it; however, I have a special reason for bringing it to light.

When I came to JoAnn's door carrying Amanda and having no place to sleep, she never offered to let us sleep on her floor. I didn't ask if I could stay at her home for the night; nevertheless, she knew I had no place to go.

I later discovered that JoAnn, who was twenty-seven, was having a (short-lived) affair with my boyfriend, Oscar, and also with my niece Pamela's boyfriend, who was only seventeen. My sister walked outside with me with tears in her eyes and said, "I'm sorry. I don't know why she didn't invite you to spend the night." There was one last place I decided to go before settling on Amanda and me sleeping in Karen's car.

When I knocked on Oscar's mother's door, Dora welcomed me with open arms; however, we both knew Amanda and I couldn't stay at her house. Dora said her brother Ben had a house on North Bell Street where he seldom stayed. Ben was living with his girlfriend, so the house was almost always empty. After contacting Ben and telling him of my situation, Ben told Dora I was welcome to stay at his house until I decided what I was going to do. Ben's only request was that I clean it up for him.

Once I knew Amanda and I had a place to spend that night, I walked to town, which was several miles away. I would not have minded it so much, but it was chilly, and Amanda was feeling heavy on my hip. The discomfort would subside for a while by alternating Amanda from one side to the other. When my left hip began to hurt, I would place her on my right and vice versa.

I had always worked and had never received an emergency food voucher before in my life, but I was desperate and had to get something for us to eat. As I entered the dreary-looking building, I observed about thirty people standing along the windows in a, probably, 30-by-10-foot waiting room. I received a seventeen-dollar emergency food voucher, along with a separate voucher to buy some washing powders. It wasn't much, but it was a great deal to me. I was extremely grateful, and I thanked God for watching out for us as I walked toward Marsh's grocery store.

I talked to God all the time, but then I always have. Sometimes I wondered if He was really listening, considering the way I was taught in church, yet somewhere deep in my soul I knew He was.

Since I had always been nervous about being alone at night, Karen told me that she would let Pamela, my fifteen-year-old niece, spend the night with me at Ben's house. I worked hard putting a pretty shine to Ben's furniture and washing his bed linens in his ringer-type washing machine. Ben had two bedrooms; however, only one of those rooms had a bed in it. The other was used to store a bunch of men things. While I was cleaning Ben's bedroom, I came across a nice hunting knife with a sharp blade. The hunting knife was in a leather case on Ben's dresser. The living room featured a very long, big, and blue three-sectional couch, which Pamela, Amanda, and I would sleep on that night.

Late that evening, Ben who was in his late fifties, came home. He said that he and his girlfriend had had a fight, so he would have to sleep at his house. Ben was a pleasant, little, easygoing sort of man, so I felt comfortable and safe knowing he was in the room next to Pamela, Amanda, and me.

Of all nights for Ben to have a fight with his girlfriend, Oscar discovered where I was. Unbeknownst to me, Oscar was having an affair with our landlord's daughter in Peru, Indiana. Late that evening Oscar's nephew, Cody, went to see Oscar to collect on a car he had sold him, since Oscar had to sell the Cadillac. Cody said when he knocked on the door, the landlord's daughter thought it was me as she ran through the house naked and in a panic. As Cody was collecting the money from Oscar, without meaning to cause trouble for me, he mentioned that I was staying at Uncle Ben's house. Oscar was insanely jealous of any man being around me, even if it was his uncle.

We had all begun to fall asleep at Ben's house when suddenly someone began to beat loudly on the front door. Ben went to see who it was, and as he opened the front door, he saw it was Oscar. Luckily, there was a second door, a very heavy-duty screen door.

Oscar was cursing me like a sailor, vowing to beat the hell out of me once he got his hands on me. Ben quickly informed him he wouldn't let him in the house if his intentions were to harm me.

After a lot of cursing by Oscar, he realized he wasn't getting in, so he pretended to calm down. Oscar reassured Ben that he only wanted to talk to me. As Ben unlatched the screen and Oscar entered, he automatically shoved me into Ben's bedroom and began to beat me in my chest with his fist. He also slapped me in the face several times. Oscar always beat me in my chest so other people couldn't see my bruises.

By now Pamela and my baby girl, Amanda, were standing in the living room screaming hysterically. I desperately wanted to call out to Pamela to run next door and call the police, but I was terrified of Oscar, who had his hand twisted tightly around my clothing up to my neck almost choking me. I couldn't bring myself to speak the words. With each blow of his fist, my mind was racing. What could I do to stop him from hitting me?

Suddenly, I remembered the hunting knife on the dresser that was directly behind my back. If I could reach behind me and get the knife, I could stab this bastard to death, but I decided not to. It was as though a voice inside of me said, "If you kill him, you will go to prison and be separated from your children."

As I looked up at the man beating my chest, I thought, "That's all right, you SOB. One of these days I *will* get away from you." I guess I kind of felt like Scarlett in *Gone with the Wind* when she said, "Tomorrow's another day."

All of my life, no matter how bad things were, I always believed in my heart there was hope for tomorrow. That confidence came from my faith in God. The God of all creation that loved me regardless of what was happening to me in that moment in time. Finally, with a blow of his fist, the back of my head hit the windowsill and I blacked out. As I came to, Oscar was crying and begging me to forgive him. He would usually cry after the beatings and say, "Oh God, I love you."

The next morning, I knew exactly what I was going to do. In the recent past I had been forced to write hot checks for Oscar and never for me; however, this time would be different. I decided I would write a hot check for a plane ticket to Georgia for my baby girl and me. I knew if I could just get home to Georgia, I could figure out how to cover the bad check.

My sister, Karen, drove Amanda and me to the airport in Indianapolis and seemed relieved and pleased to help. Karen was such a gentle and loving person, although she and I hadn't been close, in the past. She had always had a weight problem and I was slender, so she later admitted that she had resented me because of my smaller size.

I used to take my entire paycheck when it was possible and buy Karen new clothes for two reasons. One was because she needed them so much, and two was because, subconsciously, I guess I was trying to buy her love. I loved her so much and needed Karen to love me in return, but it was too difficult for her to love me when she felt I had exactly what she desired. Boy, if she only knew the reality of that wish!

That day, as we drove to Indianapolis, I felt she really cared about me and even felt empathy for me. Karen was the mother of four children and was married for over twenty years to a man who abused her and made her life a living hell. As we rode down the highway together, not knowing what the future held for either of us and tears streaming down our faces, for a moment in time our hearts touched.

49

Fighting Back the Tears

WITH A HEAVY heart I boarded the huge Boeing 747 airliner, carrying Amanda in my arms as I listened to the song by Susan Raye playing in my head: "LA International Airport, where the big jet engines roar, LA International Airport, I won't see him anymore…Soaring high above the heavens in a 747, fighting back the tears that curse my eyes, Captain's voice so loud and clear amplifies into my ear, assuring me I'm flying friendly skies." I kept asking myself how I could have loved someone who was so mean to me. And as I questioned myself, I realized I wasn't in love with him; I was obsessed with him. He was a domineering and controlling person like my mother, and I had tried so hard to find acceptance and approval from them both.

As the huge aircraft began to ascend, I felt frightened as I always did when I had to fly, yet once again that same old scripture I kept tucked away in my memory began to surface to ease and comfort my fears: "**If I take the wings of the morning, and dwell in the uttermost parts of the sea, He is there" (Psalm 139:9 KJV).**

When I arrived in Dalton, I went to Mother's house since little Hunter was there. I was never so happy to see anyone in my life. My arms had ached so long to hold him again and see his precious face.

Caught

Mother walked into the house after going to church, looked at me, and said, "You'll never guess who was at church this morning, Vivian Long! She said she would really like to see you." I replied, "Well, I would really like to see her too." I immediately said I would be going to church that night and told Mother I was going to get Vivian right in front of her and demand she tell Mother just what I had ever said to her against my mother. Mother had obviously forgotten the time when little Hunter was very sick, and she had accused me of talking about her to Vivian.

Mother quickly said, "Oh, I wouldn't do that! I would just forget about that if I were you." Mother knew she was backed into a corner, so when she saw that I was determined to prove my innocence to her, she began to cry and admitted she had lied to me. Mother said, "I believed you were guilty, and I thought if I accused you of it, you would confess." Over the years, Mother had accused me of numerous things that I wasn't guilty of, and the emotional cruelty I had to endure was unimaginable.

Starting Over Again

The home my grandfather had built had a nice lake behind it and plenty of land around it to plant a garden. I dearly loved the idea of having a garden. My aunt Arleen told me I could live there with my children until I could financially get on my feet. However, there was one stipulation: I had to live there with Robert. My family wouldn't accept that I was divorced from him, and since they never knew his true character, they thought he was wonderful.

We moved into my grandfather's home, and I was truly grateful, considering the circumstances that had brought me here. I applied for a job at Queen Carpet. I presented an excellent letter of recommendation and was hired on the spot. I was a creeler on the evening shift from seven o'clock at night until seven o'clock the next morning.

When I went into work that first night. I was grateful to have an opportunity to start over. I would work very hard to regain all that I had lost, although I knew a part of me was lost forever.

My chest had hurt all evening, so when I went to the restroom on my break, I unbuttoned the white cotton blouse that I was wearing. There were four mirrors in the restroom, one above each sink, so it was easy to see my chest covered with bruises that had now turned green. Oscar was 452 miles away and could not hurt me anymore, but I still would have a constant reminder of him until the bruises healed and faded completely.

Right away I met a plain sort of girl named Barbara Duggan, who befriended me, and if anyone ever needed a friend, I did. She had naturally blond hair that hung down to her shoulders, she wore no makeup, and she was very much a tomboy. Barbara was twenty-six years old, and along with being a good Christian girl, she was also the creel boss. We began to do things together outside of work, such as shopping and going to church together. Barbara loved the outdoors, so we always had fun doing things. She took me and my two children camping, and up until that time, I had never been camping before.

One day when she came into work, she was upset because her niece and her niece's friend had run away from home. The girls had broken a window at Barbara's rental trailer trying to get in. So, the angry landlord informed Barbara she would have to move.

Since my grandfather's house was a two-story, I told Barbara she could live in my basement until she could decide what she wanted to do. Everything was great having my good friend around to do things with, and Robert didn't seem to mind either. I had bought a 1981 maroon Oldsmobile Cutlass Supreme from a guy who just wanted me to take over the payments, and Barbara had a small, cream-colored pickup. We washed our cars together, did things with my kids like going fishing, had barbecues, and enjoyed all-around fun times together. Life was peaceful, and oh, how wonderful that felt.

One day Barbara announced that she was finally ready to buy a new trailer to live in. She invited me to go along to help her choose the best one for what she was willing to invest. Once Barbara had bought her new home and had it set up at a trailer park on Cascade Drive, she invited me to bring my two children and move in with her. I was tickled pink to say the least. We both worked at Queen so riding together saved on gas. I was still trying to heal from the injuries Oscar had inflicted upon my heart and my soul. So, with pen in hand, I sat down at Barbara's kitchen table and began to write my first serious poem:

Dedicated to Oscar

You're a natural born brute beast,
you're an animal to say the least.
You're an evil mind, your heart is cold,
And I think it's time that you were told.

You say you're a man; you think you're so bad.
You brag all the time about the women you've had.
Well, look out, baby, it's judgment day.
Here comes a lady, gonna make you pay.

She's cool, she's calm, she's so polite,
but deep inside she's ready to fight.
She stood back and watched as you made your rounds.
There's blood in her eyes; she's gonna bring you down.

She'll take you in, she'll break your heart,
she'll sit back and laugh while you're falling apart.
She'll make you remember all the women you've used.
She won't feel your pain; she has nothing to lose.

She'll have the power in the palm of her hand.
You'll sit back and wonder if you're truly a man.
She'll make you cry you'll never be free.
What you don't know, baby, is that lady is me!

Written and composed by Yvette Lidy 1984

After I had lived with Barbara for a few months, a guy who lived a few doors up from us tried to tell me that Barbara was a lesbian. I angrily came to my friend's defense as I retorted, "That's just not true, and furthermore, that is a terrible thing to say about anyone!" My own thoughts quickly reassured me of her innocence because she had never said anything inappropriate to me. She never tried to come in the bathroom when I was bathing, and she had shown no interest in me in that way. She never wore makeup or used a perm in her hair, but that was because she had psoriasis.

One night Robert was driving drunk and ran into a fence on a country road. He already had several DUIs against his record, so I hurried over to where the accident had occurred. Luckily, the police hadn't arrived yet since this location was close to where I lived. I knew that Robert would probably have to serve some jail time since the law enforcement community had become very strict regarding drunk drivers because there had been so many deaths. I had spent my entire life rescuing everyone around me from their problems, and this would be no different.

When the police officer arrived, I quickly confessed to driving the vehicle. He looked at me firmly as he said, "Do you realize you could go to jail for falsifying your statement on my police report?" He then smiled at me pleasantly and walked away.

Shortly after that, Robert earned another DUI and was facing a prison sentence because he had received so many within six months' time. I wouldn't be able to get him out of this one. After getting him out of jail, I spoke with an attorney about what I should do to keep Robert from going to prison.

The attorney said that as long as I paid his fines, Robert should leave the state and return to Indiana, and no one would come looking for him. However, if Robert left the state before his court hearing without paying the fines, the law would definitely track him down and return him to Georgia. I borrowed the money to pay Robert's fines, which were somewhere in the neighborhood of $1,200, and he eagerly returned home to his mother in Indiana. My, marriage to Robert would be the only marriage that I considered even being a marriage. It's true I wasn't in love with him when I married him but he was my first, we had children together and that in itself builds a bond between two people or at least it did me. I have no doubt if he had been protective of me and gave up the alcohol, we would still be together because I was committed to making our marriage work. I would have never been tagging along with Robert to a bar and therefore, never met Oscar. I never wanted my children to grow up without their father like I did. Those wounds are too deep and they last a lifetime.

50

Someone to Love Me

AFTER LIVING AT Barbara's for a while, I met a man by the name of Jim Brown, who was about forty-eight years old. Jim was much older than me, but he was the closest thing to perfection in a man I had ever known. He was tall and handsome, and oh, how very safe I felt in his arms. He was sweeter and kinder to me than anyone I had ever known. He listened to what I said and how I felt about things, and it mattered to him. I had never had that before; he was my "Gentleman Jim." Jim was divorced and he lived alone while his son was in college. So, on many nights when I got off from work at J&J Carpet Mill's I would drive to Jim's house. The house he owned was between the carpet mills and Barbara's trailer. When I arrived at Jim's home, I would be covered with lint and fuzz from the spinning machines I operated at work. Jim would lead me, sweaty and extremely tired, to the bathroom where he had drawn a warm bubble bath for me. Everywhere I looked there were candles burning from the front door to the bathroom, including around the tub. I slid into the warmth of the bubbles, and Jim then brought me a wonderful mixed drink with a colorful little parasol hanging over the top.

After the bubble bath, Jim would kiss me affectionately while he dried me with a downy soft towel and dressed me in the beautiful lilac teddy he had bought for me. We then went into the den where he had placed logs on the fire, and they were ablaze.

The den was also decorated with flaming candles. It was the only truly romantic time in my life I'd ever experienced. I never knew a man who could or would take care of a woman like he did me. I can't even write these words without smiling. Jim began to serenade me as he played his guitar, and I would sing along with him. The song that says, "The sweetest thing I've ever known is loving you" could never be anyone but my sweet Jim Brown.

He loved to hear me sing and was always recording me. He rented a house on the river in Gatlinburg, Tennessee, and we sat out in the backyard talking as we listened to the river flow down the mountain. When the weekends rolled around, he would invite me over for dinner. When I arrived, he would have prime-cut steaks grilling that he had marinated in different wines, and they tasted heavenly. He made his own dressing for our salads. The nights we didn't eat at his house, he took me to The Cellar restaurant in Dalton, and then we would dance the night away with him holding me in his arms.

Jim gave me a nickname, and it made me feel so special because no one had ever done that. He called me "Casey." He told me that when I became a great singing star, he wanted me to remember that he was the one who gave me my new name. I never before or since have met a man like Jim Brown, and I will always remember him and smile.

I took a job singing for extra income at a local family restaurant called PC's, which stood for Paul and Carol's Deli. I loved to sing and had big dreams of one day becoming a famous country music singer. In order to do this, I knew I needed to be heard, so that too was in the back of my mind when I took the job.

I had a friend named Samantha who would go with me when I sang. I felt nervous and uneasy being out at night alone, so I always tried to have someone with me. I never allowed any man to take me out on a date that came into the restaurant. Jim Brown was the only man in my life and the only man I wanted in my life. Nevertheless, there was always someone trying to pick me up.

51

You Can't Pet a Rattlesnake

THROUGH SOME MUTUAL friends I met a man by the name of Jasper Lewis, who owned a local carpet mill. He was pleasant as he invited the kids and me out to dinner for pizza. I had no personal interest in Jasper other than being his friend, and I even told him I was seeing someone. He insisted he just wanted us to be friends, and I must say it felt nice having a man not only invite me out to dinner but also invite my children. I was very impressed by this since Jim didn't seem to want any part of small children. When Jasper took me home that evening, he tried to kiss me. I turned away and once again told him where I stood, reiterating that I was in a serious relationship. I said, "I think it's best we don't see each other anymore." Jasper pleaded with me to continue our friendship, reminding me he had invited my children to join a group of children he was taking to Holly Creek for an outing.

Jasper was wonderful with kids, but he was very aggressive with me. One night he called and asked me if I would go with Billy, Debbie, and him to the Governor's Lounge in Chattanooga. He said it was his birthday, so I agreed to go along.

When his birthday rolled around, I completely forgot about it and stood him up. Late that night, when he returned to Dalton, he called me, sounding very hurt. I felt bad about what had happened but tried to explain that I had forgotten. He sadly asked me if I would come over and talk to him since he was so depressed. I hated the idea of driving alone at night, yet my sympathy for him overpowered my fears.

I arrived at Jasper's home, and after talking to me for a short while, he began to try to kiss me, and I pushed him away. He had been drinking brandy and continued to grab at me. I shouted, "Why can't you just try to treat me like your friend, like you treat Billy for example?" He angrily retorted, "Why can't you act like a g*ddamn woman!" Then he cursed me and accused me of being frigid.

At this point, I knew it was time to get out of there. I quickly headed for my car and nervously drove home, promising myself I would never be around him again. I prayed all the way home that God would let me make it safely inside the doors of Barbara's trailer, and He did. The next day, when I had calmed down from the ugly altercation with Jasper, he called and apologized for his outburst. He said it was the brandy that caused him to act so nasty to me. I said I would, yet, in the back of my mind, I knew I needed to keep my distance from this man.

52

So, This Is What "Happy" Feels Like

LIFE WAS SO nice at Barbara's, and we seemed to get along great. One day she announced that she would like all of us to go to Disney World in Orlando and then on to Daytona Beach, Florida. I was so excited at the prospect of going to see the ocean again, since I had only been there once with Calvin Nash in Alabama when I was eighteen years old. I thought to myself that this trip would be different because Mother wouldn't be there, and we could be free to enjoy the sights and make our own decisions.

I went to my brother Jacob's home and requested that he allow Valerie, my niece, to come with us. I then went to my sister, Karen, and asked if Carlie could go, and she said yes. The other nieces and nephews were being treated for head lice, since there was a huge outbreak in Dalton, and that's why the other kids didn't get to go. I knew we would have a great time, and I loved the idea of showing the children how much fun we could all have together.

My nieces had been deprived of experiencing the joys that life offers, and I wanted to be there to see their faces when they saw the ocean for the first time. I don't know if I can express the thrill I felt in my heart as Barbara, Little Hunter, Amanda, Carlie, Valerie, and I headed toward Florida that warm sunny day in Barbara's new, light blue Toyota. All of the children were under nine years of age, so they would drink up the joys of Disney World and the ocean with a special enthusiasm that grown-ups seem to lose with age— except for me, of course, because I was the biggest kid of all.

I eagerly looked forward to being partly responsible for the expression I knew would cover my little boy and girl's faces when they discovered what was in store for them. However, I didn't realize that even I was in for the time of my life and a vacation I would never forget as long as I live. Outside of giving birth to my two children, there were three events that had taken place in my life that I truly enjoyed, and this would be the third. The first was my visit to Las Vegas and the sights I saw there. (However, some of my joy was dampened when Oscar kept taking the money, I had won away from me.) The second joy in my life was the tenderness and kindness I was shown by Jim Brown. The third was the best of all: this trip with my children to Florida.

When we arrived at Disney World in Orlando, we boarded a huge steamboat that took us across to the other side of the river and stopped at the entrance. I was in awe of the beautiful landscape and the gorgeous flowers that surrounded the banks of the river. Suddenly, we saw the big castle, and we knew we were in Disney World.

The kids were ecstatic as they pointed from one unique observation to another. They all were screaming excitedly, "Look here, look at this, look at that!" We were holding hands and happy as we could ever expect to be while we eagerly walked off the steamboat. I think my favorite ride was the one where the little voices sang "It's a Small World." I guess there was no bigger kid there than me, and for a moment in time, I could believe and feel in my heart that life was really decent and good.

We spent one night in a motel in Orlando, Florida; however, we took Barbara's tent along planning to sleep at Daytona Beach to save money. When we arrived at the campgrounds, I was surprised to discover they offered restrooms and showers. Since I had never stayed at a campground before, this was all new to me.

I was like an excited little kid who had been locked away in the dark from all the wondrous joys in life until someone suddenly opened the doors to set me free. I wanted to see, feel, and experience this wonderful fantasy world in case I was never permitted to return. I was in a dream world, my very own fairy-tale land where dreams do come true, if only for a day.

There was a man set up next door to our tent who had watermelons on the back of his truck. He was very generous in sharing his melons with us, and we shared our hotdogs with him. It was great being outside and roughing it until the announcer on the man's portable radio warned the public to expect a possible hurricane that night.

As the winds picked up, we quickly began to gather all our equipment and prepare for the upcoming storm. The winds became stronger and stronger and began to whistle in the darkness as they took me back in time. I was twelve years old again, back in Arizona, where I slept in that little shack that was almost like sleeping outside too. Luckily, Barbara's tent was a top-of-the-line, heavy-duty tent, so when the rains began to beat against it, it held together well.

From so many trips to the bathroom, the zipper on the tent had become stuck and wouldn't zip all the way up, so when the rain started beating down hard, Barbara began to work with the zipper to close the tent completely. Suddenly, the zipper broke, and we were all exposed to the rain. The blankets we were sleeping on got soaked and covered with sand. Barbara was very resourceful, telling us to blow up our water mattresses. She said we could sleep on the floats to keep from sleeping on the wet ground, and I was impressed with her ingenuity. Although the experience was a little scary, it was also kind of thrilling to me.

After this very nasty night, we were covered with mud and grit, yet grateful to have survived the storm. When morning came, we headed for the nearest Laundromat to wash our clothes and blankets. The kids were eager to head to the beach, so I bought the kids a tray of Reese's cups to snack on while we waited for our clothes to dry. All in all, we still had a fantastic time in Florida.

The Daytona Beach 500 races were going on, and President Ronald Reagan was in town for the festivities. It was July 4, 1984, Independence Day, and we all sat around on our blankets beside a huge lake. The children and I were so happy as we watched the spectacular fireworks shooting up into the sky and exploding into brilliant lights that seemed to rain from heaven. The reflection of the fireworks on the water was so romantic, and my heart ached just a little as I thought of Chaney Stratton.

Disillusioned

That everlasting hill my feet just cannot climb,
That everlasting torment that lingers in my mind,

Those everlasting memories of you I still can see,
The boy who cried tomorrow, my love will wait for thee.

But morrow's now, my precious one, who for me you sang your song,
And words grew weak you once did speak,
and you did wait too long.

So sad heart cease your weeping and never more to care.
His heart knew only lies to speak, and love was never there.

Written and composed by Yvette Lidy

It was Friday when we arrived home in Dalton, Georgia, and all the children were covered with blistered, yet happy faces as they modeled their new blue-, green-, and white-striped Daytona Beach shirts with fringe hanging down to their shorts. They also had big blue floats that said "Daytona" on them with a big white seagull on the front and ropes hanging off the sides. I had a wonderful time, yet I was glad to be home again, especially since I had a birthday coming up that Sunday, July 9, 1984.

53

I'll Cry Tomorrow
(History Repeats Itself! July 9, 1984)

ON SATURDAY, I received a call from Jasper with an invitation to go to Six Flags Over Georgia and attend a Jimmy Buffett concert with him. I had only been fortunate enough to attend two concerts so far in my life: "The Donnie and Marie Osmond Show" and "The Loretta Lynn Show," back in the late 1970s in Indianapolis, Indiana—so the thought of going to hear Jimmy Buffett in concert sounded great; however, because of the mistrust I had for Jasper, I declined his invitation. He persisted, pleading that his daughter was visiting him from Texas, and she and her boyfriend would be going along too. With this reassurance, I knew I wouldn't be alone with him, so I agreed to go. I didn't trust Jasper very much because he was always so pushy.

When I told Barbara of my plans to go to Six Flags with Jasper, she became very angry and tried to convince me not to go. It wasn't as though she was worried about me going with him. Instead, she had begun to be very possessive of my time. When she saw that I was determined to have my own way, she rebelled by jumping into her car. She angrily declared that she was going to her mother's house in Tennessee and wouldn't return until Monday.

As soon as we arrived at Six Flags, we began to walk around the park looking at the sights before the concert, which was a couple of hours away. Jasper and I were walking several feet behind his daughter when he began to make vulgar remarks about her large breasts. His words didn't sound like the words of a father speaking about his daughter, and I would come to learn that there was nothing about Jasper Lewis that remotely resembled a true father.

When the concert was over, it was very late as we headed back to Dalton. Jasper suddenly decided that we should stop for breakfast at the Waffle House at the Fairmount exit in Calhoun, Georgia. It was around one-thirty in the morning, and I was having ham and eggs with hash browns and toast. When we got back to Jasper's, it was around three o'clock in the morning, and I was nervous about driving home alone in the dark, especially since I knew no one would be there when I arrived.

Since Jasper already knew I didn't trust him, he assured me that if I wanted to stay, he wouldn't bother me. Also, I felt I would be safe with Jasper's daughter in the house. I was convinced that he wouldn't try anything with her there. I was so very wrong.

As I lay in bed, falling asleep on my stomach, Jasper was suddenly on my back, shoving my face into the pillows. He viciously attacked me from behind, holding down my body with the weight of his own while he tied my hands crossed behind my back. I cried and pleaded with him to stop but to no avail. I tried to scream that I was going to throw up, but the sound of my voice was garbled by the pillows pushing into my mouth.

Jasper seemed completely void of conscience for what he was doing to me. When the humiliating violation of my body and spirit was over, I sat silently bewildered on the edge of the bed covered with a blanket. I held my head down to hide my shame.

I realize now I was in a state of shock as I tried to regain my thoughts. I felt numb as I stared at the floor. I was faintly shaking my head no as I asked myself, "Why?" During the rape, I never once saw his face because he assaulted me from behind, making it impossible to fight back. I don't believe this rape was only a perverted need within this man for sexual gratification because men can always find a willing participant for that purpose. I do believe it was to conquer me, control me, and steal a piece of my spirit, which he did.

My first thoughts were that I would send this bastard to prison for what he had done to me. And then the fear kicked in, and I thought about how it is always the woman who is made to feel that it's her own fault. I thought of Chaney, what he would think, and the shame of him knowing I had been raped. I began to think about how it would look—the fact that I had willingly spent the night there. What would I say? Tell them I was afraid to drive home in the dark alone? Yeah, right! They would probably say I was lying about this pillar of the community, since he was a successful businessman who owned his own company.

There really wasn't anyone I could turn to and no one to stand up for me. I had a family, and yet I didn't. They had never been there for me before, so why would now be any different? The main thought that stood out in my mind was how it would look if I turned him in, having spent the night there. I felt so helpless inside because once again I realized that I didn't count. I was just blood, flesh, and bones that anyone could kick around for their pleasure.

Suddenly, without warning, someone was beating on the door downstairs as though they were going to bust it down. Jasper had no choice but to answer the door. While I still sat there feeling sick inside and ashamed, someone loudly called out my name. "Casey! Are you okay?"

I called out softly, "Yes!" Although I didn't recognize the voice that was calling out to me, whoever it was obviously knew who I was and that I was there. Nevertheless, the rape was over, so what could they do to save me now? Casey was the name I used when singing at PC's restaurant. I was so ashamed for anyone to know what had happened to me, but now as I look back on that dreadful night, I should have realized these men who came to the door were already aware of my presence. It just didn't register at that moment. It would be months later before I would discover why these two men were at Jasper's home shouting my name in such an uproar.

I never talked to anyone about that night because I had learned very early in life that even though people sometimes acted concerned, there was no evidence to believe I could trust anyone. Six years earlier I had been raped on my birthday in Indiana, and now I had been raped again on my birthday in Georgia. It felt like an internal waterfall of tears flowed into my heart, making the heaviness almost too much to bear, but I worked diligently to smile outwardly to the world. With each new day, I stuffed the hurt inside with all of the other memories I didn't know how to cope with as I took another step and another step and another step forward.

54

Men Are Like the Tin Man, They Have No Heart

MY TWO-WEEK VACATION was over, and I had to return to work at J&J Carpet Mills on the second shift. With a heavy heart, I stood silently operating the spinning machines. As I stared down at the yarn wrapping around and around the spools at lightning speed, I wanted to scream out in agony for the world to just stop and let me off. I didn't want to be around people, much less talk to them.

I stayed to myself, and even though I appeared silent, my mind was constantly racing through the tormented memories of my life. When my coworkers went to the break room, I was pleased because I could be alone for twenty full minutes and sit quietly on a bench by my work area. To find soothing relief for a short while from my thoughts, I would sing gospel songs such as "It's Me Again, Lord," and many times I would begin to cry.

As the tears rolled down my cheeks, I would keep watch for my coworkers to return to their workstations. I talked to God on a regular basis, and although I don't know if he was always listening, many times I believed he was. There were times when I would be singing to him and I would feel the hair on my arms stand on end while little goose bumps covered my flesh. At that moment I would feel a rush of tears covering my face, and I wanted to lift my arms up toward heaven and worship the Lord and ask him to take me home because I knew he loved me and understood my pain.

I realize now, much more than I did then, that I was extremely attractive and very slender but that was not a good thing. Men are attracted to the visual and their affections have nothing to do with their heart, if, they do indeed, have one. I was in no way conceited; I just wanted to be left alone with my thoughts. Yet, as I sat on the little bench in my work area, some of the young men realized I never took my breaks with everyone else. They began to harass and aggravate me to no end. Three boys started standing close to where I was sitting and flip each other with their white work towels. Eventually, I got up and started to walk away, but as I did, one of the boys popped me on my hip with a towel and it hurt. He was the supervisor's younger brother, so I decided to keep my mouth shut and find another place to avoid their unwanted attentions. I began to sit in the well-lit office that had windows all the way around it in my department. It was always empty during breaks, and I had access to the telephone to call home and talk to my kids. The boys began to come into the office also and sit on the supervisor's desk.

One of the boys kept insisting I go out with him, and when I refused, he and the other boys began talking filthy. They stood between me and the door, and as I stood up to push my way through, they shoved an opened nude magazine in front of my face and made some dirty remark about the naked woman in the picture, comparing her to me. I returned to my workstation very upset.

When I got into my car to drive home from work, I noticed a car behind me. It was one of the pushy young men from work. He had followed me all the way to my front door, which made me extremely nervous.

This was shortly after Jasper had raped me. I was very nervous and scared, knowing this guy knew where I lived, and because of this

I didn't go in to work the next afternoon.

I knew I had to do something to keep him away from me. I decided to talk to Clint the manager of my department. When I told him that I was being sexually harassed on my job, he seemed concerned until I told him who was harassing me. His entire demeanor changed toward me, and he suddenly complained that I had missed too much work that year, so he decided to let me go. I had come to him for protection and he fired me!

I had never in my life been fired from a job, and I was crushed and devastated by his words. I had missed work for female problems that eventually caused me to have a hysterectomy, and I didn't feel this was a fair and reasonable justification for his decision. I decided I was going to write the owner of the company a letter.

I did write him a letter and intended to send it; however, with my pre-disposed awareness that I always ended up on the short end of the stick, I finally dismissed the thought of trying to fight for my rights. I was so broken and defeated inside with no faith that things would work out for me, even if I did try to defend myself.

55

Jasper's Plan Exposed

BARBARA BECAME MORE and more possessive of my time, which took all the joy out of our friendship. It was obvious that Barbara really cared about me, but it was to the point that she was smothering me. She didn't want me hanging around my friend Sam, who was nineteen years old and looked like a model. Sam (Samantha) dated Jim Brown's son, and we were great friends. Barbara didn't want me seeing Jim either.

Finally, it got so bad that she didn't want me being around anyone, even my family. One day, as I sat on the sofa, Barbara came bouncing through the front door and pitched a letter at me as she headed for the bedroom. As I sat there quietly, I opened the letter and began to read. My stomach began to feel like it was tying itself up into one great big knot as I read the words, "I love you more than I have ever loved anyone." Her affection for me seemed to take on an entirely different light.

Barbara had been married once in her life for about six months to a man named Mitch. I shouldn't have been bothered by her telling me she loved me because I would have assumed she meant it as a friend. However, in this letter, it said, "I love you more than I ever thought about loving Mitch." To compare me with the kind of love she had felt for a man really disturbed me, especially after what the neighbors had been telling me. I had never met a lesbian before and been aware of it.

I knew of a man named Roger who lived in the same trailer court. He had offered me his help should I ever need to get away from Barbara. I interrupted little Hunter and his friend Jamie, who were playing in the yard, and asked Hunter to come inside for a minute; I needed to talk to him. When Hunter walked in the trailer door, I asked him to go get Roger, and he quickly responded.

Barbara overheard my conversation with my son, so, as soon as he ran out the door, she stepped into the living room and said, "Come in the bedroom; I want to talk to you." I was very upset as I replied, "I'm not going anywhere with you, and furthermore, I am getting out of here tonight!" Barbara warned me that should I decide to leave, she was going to keep my stuff. This threat made me furious; after all, I had lost everything with Oscar, and now all I owned, outside of the children's and my clothing, was a television set, a record player, and a bed.

Suddenly she was standing in front of me as I sat on the sofa. "I'll drag your ass in there!" she said. I was shocked at the sound of this once meek Christian friend using such profanity. I replied, "You're not dragging me anywhere!" At this point, she reached out to grab me up from the sofa; however, I caught each one of her hands with my own and bent them back. She turned and ran back into the bedroom. I had bronchitis and was very weak; I didn't need to be physically fighting with her.

Little Hunter was coming in the front door with Roger on his heels. Roger asked, "Casey, are you okay?"

I replied, "Yes, but I've got to get out of here!" It was now dark, raining and sleeting outside as Roger, little Hunter, and his little friend Jamie loaded the back of Roger's open-bed pickup truck with our clothes, television set, record player, and bed. I had Amanda, who was four years old, on my lap in the passenger seat surrounded by more of our belongings.

Before we knew it, the small truck was loaded, and I suddenly realized there wasn't enough room in the cab for the boys. Little Hunter and Jamie eagerly volunteered to ride on the back of the truck. It tore my heart apart as I turned and watched the boys, who were both nine years old at the time, standing with their little feet planted firmly on the back bumper of the truck and their little hands clutched tightly to the sides, while the sleet and rain ran down their faces. It was so cold outside, but Roger kept reassuring me that the boys would be fine until we could drive to the other end of the trailer park. Still, I couldn't hold back the tears at the sound of my sweet boy's voice calling out to me, "Mommy, I'm okay; really I am!"

Roger was basically a stranger to me, yet I felt I had no other recourse but to accept his offer of help. Roger would soon be moving into his cabin in the mountains once the electricity was installed, but for now we would make the best of a bad situation. He would sleep on the sofa, and my two children and I would sleep in the bedroom.

That night we sat and talked about many things when he admitted that he was one of the men who had come to Jasper's the night I was raped. Finally, one year later, all the blank spaces were about to be filled in regarding one of the worst nights of my life.

Roger said that he and the other man worked for the carpet mill that Jasper owned. For months and months, Jasper grumbled to these men about how he had tried to get me into his bed to no avail. Jasper even went as far as to ask their advice on how to get me to submit to him.

Finally, Jasper decided he was going to rape me and actually admitted his intentions to these two men and how he intended to carry out his plan. The very night Jasper planned to rape me these two employees knew about it. They had initially intended to mind their own business, keep their mouths shut, and retain their jobs. However, Jasper's plan must have bothered their conscience more than they realized.

Both men had a drink together that night, and of course, I was the topic of conversation. They admitted to each other that from seeing me and watching my behavior when I sang at the restaurant, I was a decent woman who didn't deserve what was about to happen to her. They had never seen me even leave with a man from the restaurant. As the night wore on, they drank heavier and heavier with the dark cloud of guilt lingering over their heads. The more they drank, the angrier they became, and finally they made their decision and agreed they would kill Jasper if he hurt me.

With both men now drunk, they headed toward Jasper's house. As one of the men beat on the door, the other man held an ax in his hand. It was at this point that Roger shouted out my name. "Casey, are you alright?"

My own shame and knowing the damage had already been done, I replied yes. If I had only known then what I knew now, I would have taken pleasure in watching those two men kill the bastard and not blinked an eye. Nevertheless, if these men had harmed Jasper, they would have gone to prison, and I most likely would have blamed myself for being in the wrong place at the wrong time. My emotions were way too fragile to carry that kind of guilt.

I do believe it was the Lord's will that these two men didn't succeed in harming Jasper, yet I still believe the day will come when God will take vengeance on my behalf without my desiring it. I don't believe you can mistreat a child of God without having to someday answer for it. Above all else, I know I am a child of God!

The final information Roger related to me was that Jasper had intercourse with his own fifteen-year-old daughter, and she heard her father raping me, yet she remained silent. If I had only known these two men were aware of what was going on, I would have pressed charges against Jasper and had witnesses to testify on my behalf in court. For the first time in my life, I would have had someone to stand up for me.

56

I Will Not Die Today

THE INTERIOR OF Roger's trailer was very much like the tacky trailer I had to live in back in 1974 when I was pregnant with little Hunter, yet my mind went to work right away as to what I could do to make it more pleasing to the eye.

Barbara's trailer was new, so this was definitely a step down from my and the children's recent living conditions. Still, Roger had welcomed us to stay in his rental trailer, so I wasn't about to complain. Soon after we moved in, electricity finally extended out to the area where Roger's cabin was located, so he was able to head to the mountains.

One day, as I was walking outside of the trailer, I heard a faint voice crying in the distance, and I began to walk in the direction of the whimpering. To my shock and disbelief, I found a hole in the ground just big enough for the little boy, about four years old, who was barely hanging on by his little fingertips as he cried out for help. He was completely underground inside the drainage pipe, so I bent down and reached inside, grabbed his little hands, and pulled him out. He couldn't speak English, but what an amazing blessing to know I had literally saved someone's life because I have no doubt, he would not have been able to hold on much longer. God is so good!

Every day I desperately swept at the nasty carpet that looked thirty years old, yet when I opened the door to sweep out the dust, I could see millions of small dust particles floating in the air, which made me feel I had been defeated in my efforts. There was no vacuum cleaner, so I did the best I could with a broom.

The nasty bathroom carpet was three different pieces of carpet covering the floor. As I swept it, one of the squares of carpet flipped back, and I discovered a magazine peeking out from underneath the filthy carpet. I reached down to retrieve the book since it didn't look very old. It was a dirty magazine but nothing like I had ever seen in my entire life. It was no wonder it displayed a price on the front cover of thirty-five dollars. I disposed of the book because the pictures were so offensive; it was nauseating.

I went to apply for unemployment but was informed that I couldn't draw it because I had been fired from my job at J&J Carpet Mills. When the lady told me I couldn't draw unemployment, she never mentioned it was only temporary. The pantry was now bare, and I had no idea what we were going to eat. I thought I was being punished for being fired from my job, so I foolishly never even considered that I could get welfare.

I sat on the sofa feeling like the loneliest person in the world when someone knocked at the door. It was my wonderful, precious younger brother, Josh, standing there with a little white bag in his hand, smiling as he said, "I bet you can't guess what this is." As he walked in the door, he handed me the little bag, and I realized it was cake mix. I quickly informed him that I didn't have any eggs. He grinned as he replied, "You just add water." He said it was called "generic" cake mix and that it only cost eighteen cents.

I was so grateful for the many cakes Josh continued to bring to the trailer that week but very embarrassed when little Hunter bragged to his friends at school that we had eaten seven cakes in one week.

Just when I thought things couldn't get any worse, Amanda, my four-year-old, became very sick. I had to take her to the hospital emergency room because she had been scratched in the face by the neighbor's cat, and the scratch had become infected, along with the fact that she was running a high fever.

The doctor said she had impetigo and scarlet fever. They gave me prescriptions for her, but I didn't have the money to have them filled. That night I knew I had to do something to help my little girl get well. So, I finally decided to call my aunt Arleen. When I called, my cousin Janet informed me that Arleen was not at home. I had nervously driven, in the dark, four miles to a pay telephone to call my aunt, only to discover she was at church.

As I headed back down the dark country road to the dismal trailer, I felt such hopelessness in my heart that I didn't want to go on. The woods hovered around me with no sign of lights anywhere, except for the headlights on the front of my car. As I watched my car lights bouncing off the trees, I was aware that there were deep trenches on each side of the road used as drainage for the well-known rainy nights of Georgia.

All of a sudden, I had an extremely strong desire to propel my foot on the gas pedal and take my life. Nevertheless, I knew I couldn't go through with it for two reasons. I couldn't be so cruel to my precious little Hunter and Amanda, who depended on me so completely, and I didn't want to go to hell for committing suicide. So, with tears streaming down my face, I drove home. When I got there, I held my babies in my arms and cried, and they cried with me. This place was so nasty, and I knew it contributed to Amanda being sick. Still, I would keep on fighting for my babies, and I would not die today.

57

Moving from Pillar to Post

FORTUNATELY, I WAS hired at West Point Pepperell, and this was about the best news in the world for me. I immediately began searching for a decent place for me and the kids to live. I drove by a duplex located on Pine Street, and as I peered into the house, I saw that someone was there. I stopped and went inside.

A man was painting and identified himself as the landlord. He struck up a conversation with me and told me he was a deacon at Welcome Valley Baptist Church. I informed him that I had attended vacation Bible school there when I was seven years old with a little girl named Carol Hammons, who lived in my neighborhood. He seemed interested in renting to me as I assured him that I was extremely clean and would take good care of his property. I returned home with high hopes while I continually prayed, "Dear Lord, please, if it be your will, help me to get my children out of this dump."

The next day I drove back by the duplex and the next day and the next day. It seemed I was just living for the moment when I might get to live in this clean house. I would daydream about where I would set my few pieces of furniture and pretend it was already our home. When I looked at the little yard, I would picture my children playing in this nice clean yard, instead of the trashy trailer park where we lived now.

The very next week when I was driving by the duplex, the landlord was once again inside, so I stopped and walked up to the door. I know that God had answered my prayers because right away the landlord said that I could rent his property, I felt such a rush of joy in my soul that I almost couldn't contain myself. It was clean, freshly painted, and furnished with a brand-new stove and refrigerator. It only had one bedroom, a small kitchen, a living room, and a little bathroom, but it was clean, oh, so clean.

I worked very hard at West Point creeling on third shift, since I had not worked there long enough to be on the day shift. It was difficult for me to adjust to working at night. I'm not a night person and never have been. I found it almost impossible to try to sleep during the daytime, and I kept a continual cold.

I liked my job creeling simply because I didn't have to mingle very much with people. I didn't trust anyone and felt if I stayed to myself, I wouldn't have to worry about anyone hurting me anymore.

My coworkers thought I was stuck-up because I would only speak if there was no way around it. One young girl told me I was a bitch, which felt like she stabbed me in the heart with her words. She didn't know me at all and had never had a conversation with me, but because I didn't socialize, she thought I felt I was better than anyone else. They had no idea my heart was grieving.

I was always grateful to the Lord for His blessings on me, but I still carried such torment in my soul that would not heal. When my thoughts would go wandering back into the past of lost dreams, degradation, and disappointments, I would verbally reprimand myself by whispering aloud,

"Shame on you. You should be grateful for what you have now, a roof over your head and two sweet, healthy children."

One day when little Hunter got off the school bus, a neighbor lady was shouting that there was a big snake on her porch in front of her screen door. Little Hunter quickly ran over to her rescue and picked up the huge king snake. Little Hunter seemed to have a special understanding of all creatures great and small.

I had an opened bag of potting soil outside, laying by the house, only to discover it was full of baby copperheads. Without my knowledge, Hunter put the snakes in a fruit jar as pets. I was so shocked to see the poisonous baby snakes in the jars, wondering how this was possible without my son being bitten.

Then I recalled that when little Hunter was five years old in Indiana, my mother-in-law had bought him a screened cricket cage to catch lightning bugs. Little Hunter, however, used it for the yellow jackets he had caught with his bare hands. He filled the cage with several bees, not one time getting stung. There was something different about little Hunter that's difficult to explain, other than he just seemed very special. He was so kind and good-natured that I felt not only blessed but honored to call him my son.

I was able to maintain my rental home until the hospital began to sue me for medical bills. A few were covered by insurance, but the insurance company was very slow in paying. I went to the local collection agency to make arrangements to pay the debts.

Up until that time I had always thought that a collection agency would have to accept whatever you could afford to pay as long as you were making an effort to pay the debts. Wrong! I wanted to pay them twenty dollars a week, but they wanted three times that much. They were very cold but not nearly as cold as the nasty letters they sent me. The letter said I must not be an honest person because an honest person would pay their debts. I took it all to heart and cried like a baby, not realizing this was a form letter that they sent to anyone. I finally received a check from the insurance company and paid the entire $300 that week to the hospital. That very next week, after paying the $300 on the hospital bill they started proceedings once again to garnish my wages on a different hospital bill. I was informed at work that should I be garnisheed again I would lose my job.

That evening, while I lay on my bed sobbing, not knowing how I was going to pay my rent, a friend called from work. When I told her what was going on, she suggested I file bankruptcy, which I soon discovered cost $700.

The landlord came by soon after I hung up, and when he saw my tears, he insisted I tell him what was wrong. After hearing I had already used my rent money to pay my medical bills to keep from being garnished a second time, he suggested a way to maintain the apartment without having to pay any rent. He said his last tenant was a very attractive girl like me, and she never paid rent. You would think by now, nothing would surprise me. However, I was surprised and disappointed to discover he was just like everyone else, only he wore the title of a deacon at Welcome Valley Baptist Church.

I was out of groceries because I had paid every nickel, I had to the collection agency. I remembered a story I had once heard about a woman who was out of food, so she not only prayed but she also placed her Bible in her empty refrigerator. I thought to myself, "What could it hurt?" and I opened the door to my refrigerator and placed one of my Bibles inside.

Amazing as it sounds, that same day, a friend of mine came by and placed eighty dollars in my hand with no conditions. Furthermore, I was offered a place to live by a man whom I worked with, who was also my friend. When I say friend, I mean just that; we were never at any time sweethearts.

58

Little Hunter Catches the Big Fish

JOHN SAID THAT the kids and I could live at his house since he was never home. It was a rundown farmhouse, but the kids loved it, especially little Hunter. There was a fishing pond close by, and my son could catch huge fish better than any adult I had ever been around. I was stunned the day he came dragging those monsters up to the house; they were almost as big as he was.

I had a Rubbermaid trash can that came up to my waist, and Hunter had caught four catfish so large that my new trash can could barely hold them. I will always regret that we never had a camera to take pictures of these fish because their size was amazing, and he was so proud of them.

Little Hunter Catches the Ole Granddaddy

There was one other time when my sweet little man made the catch of the day. It was when we lived in my grandfather's house, and little Hunter asked Mr. Richmond, who lived next door, if he could fish in his lake. Little Hunter was only eight years old, so Mr. Richmond laughed and said, "Sure, just don't catch the ole granddaddy of them all. I'm saving that one for myself." My friend Susan walked out to the lake where Hunter was fishing and sat down on the ground to watch him.

Suddenly, he had a bite, but the fish was pulling so hard on his pole that it was about to pull little Hunter into the lake. Susan grabbed him around his waist and pulled him back, while he reeled in his big fish. The catfish was so enormous that we put it in the bathtub and covered it with water. The catfish weighed twelve pounds. For my little Hunter and all who had witnessed it, this was truly a memory of a lifetime, never to be forgotten.

The house where we lived was on Marla Drive. It probably wasn't over ten miles from work, but after staying up all night it was dangerous for me to be driving. I would get off work, pick up the children at the sitter's, drive home, and then drive little Hunter about five more miles to school in Cohutta. On this particular morning, I found it almost impossible to stay awake.

As I drove up Cleveland Highway, I rolled down the window because I was dozing off at the wheel. The air was very chilly but not cold enough to keep my eyes open. I finally told little Hunter to slap me in the face continuously, and he complied. I began to say, "Harder, harder," because I was on the verge of simply passing out.

We were just past Gobblers Knob and almost home when suddenly I fell asleep at the wheel. It was only for an instant but not before I had run a lady off the road who also had a small child in her white car. No one was hurt or hit, but I was scared out of my wits to think I could've hurt little Hunter or been responsible for someone's injury or even death. I knew I couldn't continue to live so far out, but I didn't know where I could find a decent and safe place to live, with rent being so high.

When I had lived at Roger's trailer, I had filled out an application for a government apartment that I would be able to afford because the rent would be based on my income; however, I hadn't heard anything and didn't expect to because the waiting lists were so long that it could be years before I got a favorable response.

One night at work, as I was taking my break, a little guy named Doug Bennett sat and talked with me. Doug was so small, he didn't look like he weighed one hundred pounds soaking wet, but he was pleasant to talk to. We began talking a lot at work and eventually he learned more about what was going on with me.

One night, out of the blue, he suggested a solution to both our problems. His situation was entirely different from mine, but the solution for both of us was the same. We each needed a place to live that we could afford.

When Doug suggested we rent a place together and split the bills, I was agreeable, especially since I was in no way afraid of him. He was much too small to physically hurt me should the plan lead to violence. Doug and I did rent an apartment together, and it was one of the best things I had ever done in my life. He was so nice and very easy to get along with. He never tried to control me or push himself on me; he was simply my good friend.

Doug and I were very clean people so that helped a great deal too. My children and I had a nice comfortable home to live in, and Doug could bring his two children there on the weekends. The arrangement was a wonderful setup for both of us.

59

Battered and Bruised

THINGS WERE LOOKING up for me, except when I would see Mother. She was constantly pushing me to sell cakes at work for her and wouldn't take no for an answer. I didn't want to ask people at work if they wanted to buy a cake. I just wanted to be left alone with my thoughts, but Mother was always bullying me into submission.

Finally, I sold a birthday cake to a girl named Connie Martin, who was also a member of the Church Assembly. The night I brought the cake into work, I had made it very clear to Connie that she would need to return the cake plate to me since Mother was out of the disposable kind, and Connie said she would. Each night after that when I would go to work, Connie would be there but without the cake plate.

The days turned into weeks and then a month. Mother was continually screaming at me for not getting that cake plate back. I felt sick inside and just wanted the attacks to stop. I hadn't wanted to sell cakes at work to begin with, but my fear of making Mother mad was stronger. After all, what I wanted didn't matter.

After Mother had screamed at me and made me a nervous wreck, I went into work determined to get the cake plate back. I approached Connie and demanded the cake plate, and she laughed at me. I firmly said, "If you don't bring that cake plate tomorrow when you come into work, I'm going to whip your ass!" Remember that I said in an argument I could start out strong with all the words I needed to demand respect, but I couldn't follow through with it? Well, this was no different. Here I stood outside after work, at five feet, four inches, looking up at this, probably, five-foot, seven-inch girl about to fight.

My intention had only been to look at her really mean and frighten her into bringing back Mother's cake plate. Obviously, it backfired on me. I stood defiant until she threw me down on the concrete and sat on my stomach. She then grabbed my hair and constantly beat my head against the pavement several times and blacked both of my eyes. I would have been better off if she would have kicked me in the stomach or hurt some other part of my body. She had a reputation for starting fights, but up until this moment I was unaware of it. One of the few times I tried to fight for my rights and look where it got me.

When I went in to work that night, I was the joke for everyone to laugh at even though I had covered my bruised face with makeup. In their eyes, Connie was the winner, and I was just a loser like I had been all my life. I talked very little to people at work; nevertheless, I was well aware that Connie laughed as she bragged to everyone how she had "whooped my ass."

In a carpet mill, winning a fight was something to really be proud of, so it was just another place where I knew I didn't fit in with the crowd. I felt so sad as I stood alone in the huge frames of the creel racks with the sweat rolling down my back and face. As I worked, I talked to God. I felt like the most alone person in the world, yet I knew in my heart I wasn't alone. He was there with me. A scripture came to mind that felt like it applied to me: "Blessed are the poor in spirit for they shall see God." That sounded like I must be important to Him.

60

Rags and Hand-Me-Downs

ALTHOUGH I WAS grateful for having the apartment with Doug, it was still a struggle to pay the bills. Robert never sent child support even though he was supposed to. The few times I could even reach him in Indiana, he would say he wasn't working but that he never worried about the children because he knew I would take good care of them, as if that was supposed to make me feel better. I would later discover that he was lying when he said he wasn't working. I told him I would get out and pump gas to take care of our kids, and I didn't understand why his concern wasn't the same as mine.

When Christmas came that year, we were surprised to receive a box from Robert in the mail. The kids were so excited as they rushed to see what was inside of the box from their daddy. When little Hunter and Amanda began pulling out its contents, I couldn't help but cry as I looked at the disappointment on their faces.

Robert had sent used clothing from a yard sale. The pants were weird colors like purple and red with the knees worn out. If that wasn't bad enough, they were the wrong sizes. Why couldn't he just have sent them ten dollars each? At least they could have gone to McDonalds and still had enough left over to buy something to play with from Kmart.

61

When Heaven Opens a Window

OUTSIDE OF MY love for my children, I felt very little joy in living. Life was only a struggle from one paycheck to the next. One day, when I went to check the mail, I was so happy to see a letter from the Government Housing Authority. I became very excited because I assumed by getting this letter to come to their office, it meant I would be getting an apartment based on my income. Wrong!

When I arrived for my appointment with Mrs. Rogers, I was so disappointed to discover the reason for my being there was simply to update my application. During the interview, Mrs. Rogers began asking questions regarding my circumstances. When she discovered my two children and I had to sleep in the same bed, she agreed to rent me an apartment. Mrs. Rogers then handed me a key and suggested I go to take a look at my new home and then return to her.

When I returned to Mrs. Rogers's office and she asked how I liked it, I told her I was extremely grateful to her for the apartment; however, I admitted I felt uneasy about its location since it was in a slum area of town. She admitted to me that the man who lived in the house next door to the apartments was a convicted pedophile. She hesitated for a moment and then said, "I have another apartment across town that a lady was supposed to rent but never returned to pick up the key, and it is in a very nice area of town." She then smiled and asked, "Why don't you drive over and take a look at it?"

When I realized where the apartment was, I became so excited. It was close to Dalton High School on Cascade Drive. I took the key and unlocked the door to a very clean and freshly painted, three-bedroom apartment. Little Hunter, Amanda, and I would each have a bedroom of our own. The back bedroom had a big picture window that overlooked the forest, and I felt so excited because this room would be mine. The tears filled my eyes as I said, "Thank you, Jesus."

A person can't fully appreciate the good things in life if they come too easily for them. Unless you have walked in the shoes of a parent with no hope of obtaining the bare necessities of life to care for their little ones, you don't know how it feels to struggle to keep your head above water and, even then, feel yourself drowning with no one to lend you a hand. You couldn't possibly understand the joy I felt as I walked through the rooms of this apartment that would be my home. To know with all certainty that no one would push me around anymore, or that I'd have to worry about moving again and again and again, sent such a rush of pure joy through my soul. I wanted to laugh, holler, and cry all at the same time.

I stood at the back door and looked at the little clothesline where I knew I would soon be hanging my clothes, and it felt wonderful. Everywhere I looked I could visualize having my curtains hanging at the window or my can goods in the now-empty pantry. The rent would be based on my income, so maybe now life would get a little easier for me to survive and I would no longer have to move from pillar to post.

As I drove back to Mrs. Rogers's office to sign the necessary papers, I recall driving over the hill on Waugh Street, and with no one in the car to see the tears of joy streaming down my face, I shouted aloud, "Thank you, Jesus; thank you, Jesus; thank you, Jesus." I didn't have enough furniture, yet I felt like the luckiest woman alive because we had a home, our very own home.

My brother Jacob gave me some scrap pieces of carpet he had left over from installation jobs he had done, which really helped keep our bare feet off the cold cement floors. I tried to place the strips of carpet where I knew our feet would be, especially in the hall and bathroom on those many nighttime trips to the restroom. Cement floors hold the cold so much that your feet ache and feel numb if you stand on them very long. For the first time in so many years I was happy and even felt hope for the future. I could afford the rent, and I didn't have to depend on a man. It doesn't get better than that.

62

Dumpster Décor

ONE DAY AS I took the trash out to the dumpster, I noticed a love seat that had been discarded by a neighbor. I was pleased because even though it had several rips in the cloth, it was in pretty good condition. As my mind began to race with ideas, I knew I could place a spread across it to cover it up, and it would do nicely for us to sit on. After all, it was much better than sitting on the floor.

I had bought a portable television set at Walmart and placed it on a kitchen chair in the living room. I was tickled pink one day when I noticed in the dumpster a very old coffee table that had been discarded by another neighbor. It would be perfect to set the television on; after all, we needed that chair in the kitchen. I had bought a used metal table with four chairs at a yard sale, but soon after I had brought them home, I noticed one of the chairs began to wobble and bend if you sat on it.

One day my neighbor, Ms. Mary, came by to visit and as she stood in my living room talking with me, she noticed her old coffee table with my portable television sitting on it. I told her I had gotten it out of the trash, and I planned to refinish it since it was an antique. Ms. Mary immediately said she had thrown it away, but she now wanted it back. My heart sank, but I didn't argue. I just took my television off the coffee table and watched as she took the table back to her apartment.

I don't believe I was ever more at peace in my life than I was in my little apartment on Cascade Drive. After living there, a couple of years, I would still walk through the apartment and look around as I said, "Thank you, Lord, for my home."

I had no interest in dating anymore, so when other parents decided they wanted to party on the weekend, they would drop their children off at my apartment. We had a great time together, and one thing the children seemed to enjoy so much was when I would make up little poems for them.

One particular Saturday stands out in my mind as being very special. As I sat in the living room with about six children, it was raining outside, and oh, how I loved the rain. When it rained, it always made me feel as if God was wrapping His arms around me, and I felt so safe. The more the thunder roared, the calmer I felt in my spirit. Oh, how I loved God, and oh, how I loved His heavenly rain. It truly was a wonderful day as each child gave me a little information about what kind of story, they wanted me to write. They all seemed so thrilled at the funny poems I made up and personalized for them. In my heart, I felt proud and pleased to know I had brought so much joy to their little hearts with something that came so easily for me.

The Little Worm

As I sat out in the yard, finding rest from playing hard,
Something crawled across my foot; my eyes moved quick to take a look.
It was a worm upon my toe. He smiled at me and said hello.
"I know you're tired and I am too, so I thought I'd stop and talk to you."
I screamed at him, "You cannot speak. I'll crush your head beneath my feet."
And then he cried so sad and hurt, as he crawled back beneath the dirt.

"I'm so ashamed for what I said. I won't hurt you or crush your head. So please come back and try again. I truly want to be your friend.

I'll be so careful when I walk. I just did not know that worms can talk." So, now you know that worms can speak, watch where you step and put your feet.

Written and composed by Yvette Lidy

63

The Payback Possum

I'M SO SERIOUS about everything, and I think that personality trait is a reflection of a life of heartaches and broken dreams. I have experienced very little joy in my life, so it takes something really special to make me laugh.

Late one afternoon as I walked to my back door, I noticed a small possum had climbed into my blue Rubbermaid trash can that was sitting outside. My backyard faced the woods, so it was no surprise that the creature had come from that direction. I think possums are so ugly that I can't even bear to look at them, so I felt very squeamish when I saw it. The deep trash can was empty except for maybe a gallon of rainwater that had collected inside.

I called out to my son Hunter and my nephew Bradley to please come outside. They were both about twelve years old, so when they asked what I wanted them to do with the possum, I told them to dump it in the dumpster. I didn't want them to just dump it on the ground because I thought it might bite one of us. It was so ignorant on my part, but I just didn't consider what might happen.

As night fell, Ms. Mary walked to the dumpster to dispose of her trash, and as she did, I heard a horrifying scream. Everyone came running out of their apartments as she described the bizarre occurrence that had just taken place. White as a ghost and trembling in fear, she told her sad tale of the monster that leaped across her shoulder and brushed her cheek as she attempted to throw her trash into the dumpster.

For days and even years to come, I would be driving down the road alone and burst out laughing at the thought of what had happened that night, and I did not dare ever tell her I was responsible for the possum being in the dumpster. Ms. Mary was the lady who had taken her coffee table back, and she was also the lady who told my Hunter to never bring his collection of Garbage Pail Kids cards into her house again because she said the cards were witchcraft!

Hunter was such a sweet-natured boy and desperately needed a father, and for her to be so unkind to him was unforgivable. The cards were the same as Cabbage Patch Kids, only the dolls had pimples and ugly faces. The cards were made for boys to collect like baseball cards. There wasn't anything about them that was offensive.

64

Deceived

I WAS NOW thirty-three years old, a very slender and attractive single woman who, many assumed, had it all together. However, my life would begin to unravel due to numerous changes, which were never determined by confidence and peace of mind. Instead, they were entirely based on past experiences and the tormented fears that still dwelled inside the mind of a frightened little girl.

At work, I stayed to myself with the obvious impression that I didn't want to talk to anyone. Every important person in my life I had ever loved and trusted had made me feel as though I didn't matter. My fellow employees would have been shocked if they had only known how frightened I was of them.

At times I did try to fit in, but I just couldn't laugh at their jokes or bring myself to take part in their after-work parties. It wasn't just them I couldn't seem to relate to; it was everybody. I was so serious about everything that I felt no laughter in my heart, so I didn't blame anyone for feeling I was no fun to be around. I felt safest when I was alone because no one could hurt me if I didn't allow them to get close to me. It is never an enemy that hurts a person; it's someone you trust—someone you allow to get to know you and your thoughts, who can, and will, one day use that information to destroy you.

I met a girl named Marsha at work who seemed genuinely

interested in being my friend. When she discovered that outside of work, I wasn't socializing like most people our age, she remarked that everyone at work wouldn't believe it if they knew I didn't date anyone and only spent my time at home with my children.

I have found that, in life, people are not only quick to judge you by what you have, but they are also quick to assume many things about you simply from physical appearance or their own dirty minds. Marsha insisted I go out with her because there was someone, she wanted to introduce me to. I was thirty-three years old and still naive enough to believe a person was decent if you met them through a mutual friend or church. That proved to be a huge flaw in my character to trust anyone at face value, especially a man. I had foolishly believed if I were good to people, they would in turn be good to me, which couldn't be further from the truth.

It was the second week of July 1988 (a few days before my thirty-fourth birthday) when Marsha introduced me to Lucas Bolin at a local nightclub. He was tall and seemed like a very nice person, so we talked for hours. I learned that he wasn't only an electrician, but he also worked as a carpenter alongside a member of Mother's church, making me feel even more at ease with him.

After listening to me and my own interests, such as being a good mother, I related to him how I desired to go to church somewhere and take my children. It was important to me that they know the Lord and learn about His ways, but I didn't want to go back to the Church Assembly. Lucas seemed very pleased and began telling me how he had secretly wanted to start his own church. He talked to me outside of my apartment, while sitting in his van, until the wee hours of the morning. We only talked; however, he did kiss me goodnight. Lucas said all the right things to a woman who was very lonely and emotionally needy. Although I wasn't going to church, I had been trying very hard to live a life I believed the Lord would be pleased with. I knew it was a sin to sleep with a man if you weren't married to him, and although I hadn't always respected that rule, it had been several years since a man had held me in his arms and made love to me.

Lucas said he would love to take my son fishing. Knowing how much Hunter loved to fish, I felt so happy inside at the thought of this man taking an interest in my son. Hunter was such a good and easygoing kid, but he was very lonely for the love and companionship a boy can only receive from a father.

To look back on my life now, it is so hard to believe I could have possibly agreed to marry a man after only knowing him for five days, and I was always ashamed for anyone to know. Unfortunately, men can be so convincing when they see something they want. Men will tell you whatever they know you want to hear, even using God as an instrument of their deception. I wanted so much to believe that Lucas was a good man and that we could be a family, but once again I would be harshly awakened to the cold hard facts of my life.

The following week, after marrying Lucas, I begin to discover he was nothing like I had expected. We were standing in the kitchen, and he was talking against my children's father for not paying child support. I have never understood why; however, when Hunter walked into the kitchen, Lucas suddenly said, "Robert is a mother f #^*@r! And Hunter is just like his dad!" Shocked and confused about why he would talk this way, I asked him to leave our home.

Lucas began to laugh and said he didn't have to leave because this was now his home too. I angrily retorted, "I'll call the police and they'll make you leave!" Still laughing at me, he said, "I could break every window out of this apartment, and there isn't a damn thing you can do about it because I'm your husband."

I then picked up the telephone and started to dial the police, at which point Lucas took the telephone out of my hand and hung it up. I had no idea that Lucas took drugs when I married him. However, I would soon learn there were many more things I didn't know about this man I had foolishly chosen to share my life with.

A short while later, Lucas went into the living room, sat down, and began talking on the telephone to his sister. I felt so angry because he was sitting in my home where he hadn't lived long enough to even help on the rent or electric bill, yet he was in total control of everything. I couldn't verbally fight with him, yet without warning, I reached up and unplugged the telephone cord from its outlet as I said to myself, "If I can't use my own telephone, then you can't either!" When I disconnected the conversation between Lucas and his sister, he grabbed the cord and began twisting it around his knees. He pulled the cord as tight as he could and it snapped, making me think he had broken the telephone cord.

Suddenly, someone was knocking on the front door. It was Mother, and the first thing she did was head for the bathroom. While she was out of the room, Lucas, with a mean look on his face, said, "If your mother hadn't walked in when she did, I was going to break your god*#&n neck!"

When Friday came, I used my rent money to file for divorce. I was amazed to discover I was Lucas's seventh wife. He came into my attorney's office, and as he sat there, Dianne asked if I would need a restraining order. Before I could respond, Lucas quickly said, "No, I won't bother her," so, as always, I remained silent.

Later that evening, Marsha came by my home and asked if I would go to see an Elvis Presley impersonator with her at the Heritage Inn, and I reluctantly agreed. The Elvis impersonator wasn't very good, so we left and drove to the Waffle House on Walnut Avenue to get something to eat. When we walked in, the first thing I noticed was Lucas sitting in a booth with another woman. I immediately walked out and headed for the car, and we drove to the Waffle House at the Rocky Face exit.

I didn't want to be out very late because I had to work the next morning—on a Saturday, meaning overtime pay—and I certainly didn't want any trouble with Lucas now that I had learned how mean he could get. Shortly after Marsha and I had placed our order, Lucas walked into the restaurant and up to our table. He told me to come with him, and when I refused, he grabbed me by the shoulder of my blouse and began twisting it, my slip, my bra strap, and my gold necklace in his angry clutches.

Lucas dragged me out of the restaurant by my clothes while digging his fingernails into my flesh until I bled. He was so forceful in pulling me out of the restaurant, he broke my bra strap, slip strap, and the gold chain I was wearing. There were other customers in the restaurant, yet not one person attempted to help me. Lucas had a pistol, and I thought to myself, "Oh my God, it's Oscar all over again."

Lucas cursed me with every breath as he drove up the dark highway. My mind was racing as I contemplated jumping out of the speeding van. After driving for several miles, we reached a deserted house off Cleveland Highway, and the van came to an abrupt stop. As we sat in the van, he screamed that he hated me at one moment and the next moment he was professing his undying love for me. He began grabbing at me and trying to kiss me, but I folded my lips tightly inside my teeth. Still, he continued to try to force his affections on me. He insisted I go into the deserted house with him so we could talk, but I knew once he got me in that house, he would try to get me to have sex with him. I firmly rejected his request. I felt relieved that he was not going to rape me, but I had no doubt, after observing his violent temper, he was definitely capable of hurting me physically.

I kept telling him I needed to go to the bathroom, and he used that to try to get me to go into the house. Eventually, he did allow me to relieve myself outside of the van while he stood guard in the dark. Finally, after just sitting there for a couple of hours, his anger softened, and he continued to try to persuade me to take him back. I realized the only way he would let me go was if I convinced him that I would forgive him and try to work things out.

I began to agree with his ideas for a future relationship and told him I still loved him too. He said he wanted me to go somewhere with him so we could be together. I told him I would go with him if he would take me to my apartment and let me check on my kids. He suggested we just call them on a telephone. Luckily, I reminded him that I had forgotten my purse when he dragged me from the restaurant, so I would need to stop and pick it up. I assured him that was the only way I would go with him, peacefully.

Once I walked into the door of my apartment, after being held captive by Lucas for four hours, I called the police and reported Lucas for what he had done. They didn't even pick him up. They said because we were married and there was not a restraining order against him, it would have to be handled in the divorce hearing. I had only lived with Lucas for two weeks before filing for divorce, so it was now August 1988.

50

Rings and Wrong Choices

I DON'T BELIEVE anyone could have ever loved to sing as much as I did, even as far back as when I was in the second grade. I vividly recall walking home from East Morris Street School and singing my heart out as loud as I wanted to. My favorite song was "Once a Day," and I never missed a word. Even as a child I felt lonely, and singing made me feel so happy inside because it would drown out the sadness in my heart.

When I felt the most defeated is when I would sing songs that seemed to relate to my particular circumstances. One song I loved to sing was by Connie Francis, not only because of the words but also because I had heard that she recorded it after being raped. It was called "Who's Sorry Now." It said, "You had your way, now you must pay. I'm glad that you're sorry now."

I had sung at a local television station the week of my thirty-fourth birthday, and a boy by the name of Ken Dawson saw me singing on television. After discovering that his aunt, Emma Dawson, worked with me at Shaw, he asked her if she would introduce his dad to me. Emma Dawson had worked for Shaw, formerly known as West Point Pepperell, for fifteen years. She was very sweet and well respected by all who knew her. When Emma invited me to her home to sing country music with several other guests, I declined her invitation. She was very insistent, although I gave her many reasons why I'd rather not. I finally told her I didn't own a car, and she said, "That's no problem. I will pick you and your children up in mine."

At no time did Emma mention her plans for introducing me to her brother-in-law. My children and I did go to Emma's home that evening and had a nice time. She introduced her brother-in-law Albert Dawson to me, but he didn't make any sort of impression on me. I politely said hello and thought that was the end of it.

However, when the evening came to an end, Emma looked at me and said, "If you don't mind, since Albert lives in Dalton too, he'll drop you and your children off at home, and I won't have to drive back into town." I was in the middle of my divorce from Lucas and didn't have the slightest bit of interest in this or any other man.

Albert turned off the interstate onto Walnut Avenue and suggested we stop at McDonald's because he wanted to get the kids a Happy Meal. I saw no real harm in it, and eating out was something that was a treat for my children. Even a hamburger and fries from a restaurant was something they ordinarily didn't get to enjoy, so I agreed. Once we arrived at my apartment, Albert asked if he could come in and talk for a while. The kids were awake, so I said yes. Albert was eleven years older than me, and it hadn't even entered my mind what he was about to suggest.

After sitting at my kitchen table for a couple of hours, telling me his life story and asking me every question in the book, Albert admitted that since his boys were now grown, he was very much alone and longed for the companionship of another person. He believed my children and I needed someone to take care of us, and in his opinion, he could be the one to do it. I had just met him a few hours ago, and already this man was proposing marriage to me. I responded with "I don't even know you." He insistently declared that he only wanted companionship. He stressed that if I would marry him, I would not have to have sex with him.

I told him no, yet he seemed like he cared about what was going on with me and the kids. In the past, men only seemed interested in showing me off as though I was some prize, they had won. I remember getting off work in the early mornings at West Point Pepperell and standing out in the cold winter months scraping the ice off the windshield of my car. I would then head to the sitter to pick up my kids, and I would say to myself, "No one is ever around when I really need someone to care for me or just scrape the ice off my windshield."

Even Jim Brown was selfish. He proudly walked me into many places during our relationship with his head held high. As much as I cared about him, I knew it was a self-indulgent ego trip for him to be my date, especially since he was about twenty years my senior. One night after dinner at the Cellar restaurant, when Jim and I were dancing, he told me he loved me and wanted to marry me. He said he would love for us to spend our lives together and travel *if* I didn't have children. It was as though he was asking me to give up my kids.

How can a man say he loves you but doesn't want your children? But that is exactly what he did. This was just another affirmation of the true character of men.

There was nothing about Albert that I could possibly find appealing to me, even though I had tried so hard to convince myself that marrying him would resolve so many problems for me and the kids. If I had followed my own heart, I would have never married Albert; however, circumstances assured me that I had no other choice. My love for my kids far surpassed the desires of my heart, and besides, I had lost all hope and faith in believing God had a special someone who would truly love me.

No matter how hard I tried, the medical bills exceeded my income. I worked on the first shift now, creeling at Shaw. The heat in the upstairs creel racks was so intense, I would almost pass out. I would go to the restroom, and my entire body would be so wet with perspiration that it was almost impossible to push my blue jeans down to my knees. Then I would literally peel my panties down as I realized there wasn't a dry area on my entire body.

My goal each week was to get my forty hours in as soon as possible so I could work on the second shift for at least another four hours a day. I had an excellent record of being one of the fastest creelers in the plant, so the supervisors were pleased to have me creeling as much as I wanted to. Still, there wasn't enough money to keep the financial wolves away from my door. I had several medical bills, plus I had used my rent money to file for divorce from Lucas. Everything together totaled close to $800.

Albert came by my apartment one day and insisted on giving me a check for exactly $800 and told me to go pay my bills. I didn't want to take it, but I couldn't afford to lose my job over being garnished again. I was a young, attractive, thirty-four-year-old woman in a desperate situation, and Albert being much older, with his own plan for my life, insisted I sign his name to the check that was made out to him.

As hard as I had tried to convince myself I could handle it, I just couldn't bring myself to marry Albert, no matter how much he pushed. Then one day when I was at work, he called my home. Amanda, who was eight years old, told Albert she was hungry and there wasn't anything to eat. This was the clincher that helped make my decision to marry a man who completely disgusted me. I believed if I married Albert my kids would have a much better life. I wanted them to have the security that comes with having a real home and not one spent living in the Projects.

My whole life was already wrapped up in fear of people, so I always expected the worst—this coupled with the knowledge that I had no value anyway and no one would love me, as Mother had told me years earlier. I knew no matter how grossly offensive the thought of marrying Albert was to me I would survive as I had so many times before. After all, I had been honest with him and made it clear I wasn't in love with him

The one big fear that lingered in the back of my mind was the fact that I had signed his name to a check he had given me, even though I had his permission. I was afraid if I backed out of his marriage proposal, he would be angry enough to have me arrested for signing it. I had learned early in life that you can't really trust anyone, especially a man. Fear was always the driving force in all of my decision-making.

When I went for my hearing with Lucas, my attorney stood before the judge and verbalized the fact that though there were twenty-six customers at the Waffle House the night Lucas abducted me, not one person attempted to help me. Lucas was forced to pay me $800 for his vicious attack and tearing my clothing. How ironic, that was just what I had needed when I had signed Albert's name to his check. If only I had received this money sooner. My divorce from Lucas became final on October 21, 1988, and I reluctantly married Albert two days later.

Albert had promised me that I wouldn't be expected to have sex with him, but I knew that promise wouldn't last forever. Nevertheless, I was safe for the moment. The first night of our marriage, we didn't have sex. I wore some beautiful green flannel and satin pajamas. Right away I went out and bought Albert some pajamas because I wanted as much clothing between us a humanly possible. I encouraged him to sleep with his back to me, saying that I wanted to snuggle up to his back. Even then, my nose would be close to his smelly toupee. If it had just been me I would have run like the wind but I had such a desire to give my son and little girl a better life and Albert had made big promises that I knew he was capable of keeping. I wanted my kids out of the Projects and in their on yard and I knew I couldn't do it alone. I knew I would be faithful and do my best to be good to him, yet, I still wondered if I could endure living with a man who disgusted me with his vulgar mouth and his offensive bad habits. In the beginning he related to me that Zoey was a bad housekeeper but I soon discovered he was the one that couldn't seem to throw anything away, not even trash. I quickly learned he was more of a junky sort of person in that he took no pride in his surroundings. His car was knee-deep with trash from restaurants, envelopes, and junk mail he had accumulated. I cleaned his house from top to bottom before I would even consider bringing my children to live in it. I may have been poor as a church mouse, but I was extremely clean, and now I had married a hoarder. To see the man, I married speaks volumes to my pathetic self-esteem.

I painted the house and stripped and padded the floors before the carpet was laid. I had learned how to do this from working at a construction company in Indiana, when my regular job was slow. It was a nasty mess, but knowing what the end result of my efforts would be kept me going. I had the house looking pretty good, but the problem with the sewage in the bathroom was intolerable. I pleaded with Albert to have it fixed, but he seemed unconcerned. I would take a large, deep, stainless steel cooking pot and place it upside down in the bathtub. Since I was little, I could stand on it while I took a shower because the sewage kept flowing up through the drain.

Here I thought life was going to be better. It wasn't as though Albert didn't have any money; he owned valuable property and rented homes. Yet the thought of spending a dime on anything made him very unhappy.

One of the many offensive things I learned about Albert was his nasty mouth. I had met several ruthless people in my lifetime but never one with such a vulgar mouth as my new husband. I started to leave the house one morning to go shopping for a sweater, and Albert said, "If Zoey (his old girlfriend) wanted a new sweater, she would give me a b*@# job!" I was appalled at the sound of his ugly words. I responded, "I thought you said you and Zoey only had intercourse once a month." He replied, "That's true, but she gave me a blow J on a regular basis." I had thought because I was attractive, kind, faithful, a good cook and a good housekeeper, Albert would be proud of me enough to respect my feelings and be kind. I have learned that physical appearance does not prevent a man from being depraved, cold-blooded, brutal, and sadistic.

I walked away wondering if there were people anywhere in the world who looked at life the way I did.

Even now, after all I had been through in my life, I couldn't understand why he couldn't see how offensive his ugly words were. I guess someday I might realize that I just don't fit in with the people who have surrounded my world, but how could I escape my own environment outside of taking my own life? After all, I had signed away my inheritance because of my aunts' greed, the Stratton's got my deceased father's life insurance money, and when I think of all my mother contributed to making the Stratton's life better it only reminds me of what we were deprived of in the process.

66

Missing Chaney

I **DECIDED TO** visit the Church Assembly because I missed Chaney. I had not been there since I was seventeen years old, back in 1971, but I had carried his memory close to my heart all those years. The love of my life was just a few miles down the road and even though I had accepted long ago that we would never be together; I just needed a glimpse of his sweet face before his memory faded completed into my world of broken dreams.

As I sat on the church pew that Sunday morning in November 1988, I remembered that I had promised the Lord back in December 1974 that if I ever had the opportunity to visit this church again, I would thank the members for praying for me when little Hunter was born.

I looked up at Rev. John Stratton Jr. in the pulpit and requested permission to address the church. In a friendly tone, he replied yes. I looked around at the possibly four hundred members in attendance and began to explain the details of how God had blessed me with a miracle when my baby boy and I were given up to die in childbirth. That very moment, when the members of this church were down on their knees praying for me here in Dalton, Georgia, my baby was finally and quickly delivered into this world in Kokomo, Indiana. I knew God had given me a miracle, and although it happened thirteen years ago, I wanted to keep my promise to God that I would give him praise for what he had done for me and my baby boy through the prayers of these people.

Even though I had no confidence in the Stratton's, who ruled the church, I did have confidence in the sincerity of its members. After I sat down, Brother John W. Stratton Jr. rose to his feet and said many nice things in regard to me keeping my promise to the Lord, although I don't recall exactly what he said.

I knew many of the members of the church because I had grown up in it, and since Chaney wasn't at that particular service, I decided to return the following Sunday morning after being invited by several of the church members.

When I walked in the doors that following Sunday, I immediately spotted Chaney sitting on the rostrum watching me walk down the aisle. I gasped excitedly as my stomach was joyfully doing somersaults with each shaky step I took. I knew he was staring at me as I bubbled over with joy inside my soul. I kept asking myself if anything was out of place. Was my slip showing? No! Was my hair out of place? I was suddenly seventeen again, and for a moment, all my bad memories disappeared, and I was overwhelmed with happiness. It was as though there was an electric current flowing from his heart to my own, and we were both undeniably aware of it.

A Dove Mourning for Its Mate!

Since the church planned in advance who would officiate at each service, Chaney was scheduled to conduct this service, so there was nothing Sister Moreen could do about it now that she knew I was present.

When Chaney began to speak, I could tell it was difficult for him since I was there. He kept preaching on why it was necessary for a church member to marry another church member, hinting that I had left the church. In the middle of his preaching, I went to the altar to pray. No one was at the altar but me, and Chaney suddenly stopped preaching in midstream. He placed one hand on each side of the podium, bowed his head, and began to sob as though his heart was broken. In the midst of his sobbing, he spoke, and the microphone carried his anguished words across the room for all to hear. "My heart is crying like a dove mourning for its mate." I always knew in my heart that Chaney loved me when we parted fourteen years ago, and this only reaffirmed that he still did.

Even though I knew I wouldn't do anything to try to come between his and Judy's marriage, especially, since they had children, it meant the world to me to know that he still loved me. I was convinced that we would be together in heaven. When Sister Moreen had stepped between the love Chaney and I shared, I was still a virgin. I wouldn't pursue Chaney now even if he wasn't married because I didn't feel I was worthy of him anymore, considering the direction my life had taken me and the men I had slept with.

67

Karen

THANKSGIVING ROLLED AROUND and my sister, Karen, began having her annual holiday dinners. She always invited my mother and my two brothers but never me and my children. I tried to get used to the rejection, but it was heartbreaking to see my kids hurt. Amanda looked up at me with tears in her eyes and asked, "Mommy, why won't Aunt Karen let us come to Thanksgiving dinner?" I didn't know what to say because I knew I hadn't done anything unkind to cause Karen to exclude us.

I knew at that moment I would be willing to stay in the background and encourage a close relationship between Karen's children and my own. I wanted my children to be able to visit and play with their cousins, and if that meant me staying out of the picture, that's exactly what I would do. Karen had a different father from mine, so she was short and obese. I couldn't have loved her more, but she couldn't have hated me less.

Nevertheless, there were many times that I took my entire paycheck and spent it on her. I bought her a beautiful leather coat during the cold, harsh winters in Indiana. I loved her so dearly, but there was nothing I could do to make her accept me. After she had moved to Georgia, her husband, Lance, was drinking almost all the time and chasing women. For an entire year, when I got my paycheck on Fridays, I would give Karen enough money to pay for her children's lunches each week. She was nice to me during that time but still couldn't find it in her heart to love me. She thought because I was slender and attractive, I had a wonderful life. One day in a harsh and angry voice, just out of the blue she said, I don't understand "why" your life is so perfect and mine is so awful!

68

The Cries No One Hears

EVEN THOUGH ALBERT was my husband, I felt so ashamed of myself for sleeping with him. I didn't love him, and oh, how he disgusted me. The Bible says, "What God joins together, let no man put asunder," and I knew God hadn't joined Albert and me in holy wedlock. God is love, and love did not join me to this man. It was only fear and need, and that's not the same. I never in my life was fortunate enough to marry a man I loved or even attracted to and that was my horrible reality. This marriage was a complete nightmare.

After going to church, I felt even sicker about the marriage in which I had trapped myself. I kept trying to justify it by saying lots of women married men they didn't love in earlier times because the marriages were arranged by their parents. Still, I felt so ashamed of what was happening to my heart, body, and soul. I never had intercourse with Albert without first drinking enough wine so I couldn't feel the pain and heartache. Only God knows how I hated Albert touching my skin. Only God knows how many tears flowed silently down my face and into my hair as I lay in bed underneath this man.

I wanted desperately to please the Lord, and I knew in my heart that the Lord wasn't pleased with me sleeping with this man who possessed no concept of common decency and self-respect.

One evening, as Albert sat on the sofa in the den with my eight-year-old daughter, he brought to her attention a water fountain on the television screen. It was a statue of a nude young man with water spraying from his penis. He was so insistent that she look at the man. Some people might think I was being overprotective, but I felt his actions toward my little girl were totally inappropriate and unacceptable. I had several dirty-minded relatives who would have had sex with me when I was very young if their plans had succeeded. So, I was not about to put undeserved trust in any man where my daughter was concerned. No one, not my mother or anyone else, had protected me and supported me emotionally, but by George, I would be there for my baby girl, and no son of a bitch would harm her.

I wanted so much for my children to have the necessities of life and feel the security that is so important in raising a well-adjusted child with the knowledge that they have a home and belong somewhere. However, the emotional torture I was subjecting myself to, in order to provide my children with that security, was on the verge of pushing me over the edge.

I continued to drink the wine until I could numb my heart and soul from what I had to endure with this man touching me. I hated him touching me more than anything I had ever experienced in my life. Even when I was raped, there was an end to it, but this situation was an unending nightmare that was destroying me in a way that I could not describe.

Albert's Controlling Nature

When Albert took us out for hamburgers, he made it very clear that the children and I didn't need to choose what we wanted on our hamburgers. It didn't matter if we didn't like ketchup; we had to eat them the way he ordered them or do without.

Sometimes at night Amanda would cry for me because she was afraid of the dark. She wasn't used to sleeping in a room alone; she was used to sleeping with her mommy. Albert demanded all the lights be turned out. It was tearing me apart as I lay in his bed next to his smelly carcass, with tears running down my cheeks, to listen to my little girl crying out from the next room. I kept asking him if it would be okay if I slept with her just long enough for her to fall asleep. He firmly said no!

Finally, I couldn't stand it any longer. I jumped out of his bed and ran in my little girl's room with no concern for his demands or what he might do. Amanda clung to me as I wrapped my arms around her and assured her that I wouldn't leave her alone in the dark. Suddenly, Albert was standing in the doorway shouting for me to get in his bed. I shouted back my refusal because I no longer cared if he was mad at me or not. That was a huge step for me because I was always so afraid of making people mad.

The relationship was doomed from the beginning but not because I wasn't willing to try. It was because I did not trust Albert around my little girl. One day I watched out of our bedroom window as Albert gave Amanda a new bicycle and discussed our marital relationship with her. I remembered my stepfather talking so nice to me when I was seventeen. He said he would buy me my first car, and it was all an attempt to sleep with me. Albert had no business discussing grown-up things with my eight-year-old daughter, and that's when I made up my mind to plan my getaway.

As I drove toward the housing authority office, I remembered I had bought Mrs. Rogers (who was the manager of the apartments) a dozen roses along with a card when I had moved out. It expressed how much I had appreciated her giving my children and me a place to live when we had no home of our own. I would go to her now and pray that she would help us again, so we could get away from this living hell on earth.

Breaking Free

After living with Albert from October 1988 through March 1989, I went to see Mrs. Rogers. I prayed all the way there that God would touch her heart and she would help me because she was my only hope.

When I walked into the housing authority office, Mrs. Rogers's daughter was at the front desk, and she asked me if I was Yvette Lidy. I replied yes. She immediately expressed how much she appreciated me sending her mother the roses. She said it was a very nice gesture that other tenants never made, and she thanked me for being so thoughtful. It made me feel good inside to know I had made someone smile as I listened closely to her words of gratitude. I was so used to doing things for people that I had forgotten about sending the roses, but I was so glad I did.

When I was permitted to see Mrs. Rogers, she was eager to help me, and I could have cried for joy right in her face but held it in. I felt as if the heavens had burst open for me and were raining down such joy in my spirit that I could have leaped off my seat when she said, "I have a two-bedroom apartment over where your other apartment was located." She said she would let me have my old three-bedroom apartment back once it became available. I was so excited and relieved as I drove back to Albert's house. I didn't know for sure that Albert would molest my little girl, but I wasn't about to take any chances. The one thing I did know for sure was I didn't trust him with her.

I had initially believed that Albert would be true to me because I was attractive, much younger than him, and good to him. I was very clean and could cook about anything his heart could possibly desire. Still, he thought he could have me and secretly continue his relationship with his former girlfriend, Zoey. I discovered he had never ended his relationship with her.

I didn't want to fight with him; I just wanted to get away from him. So, I planned to move out while he was at work. Once Albert realized I was gone, he began searching for me and eventually began stalking me when he discovered where I lived. Right away, he was on my doorstep pleading with me to take him back and saying things would be different if I would. I was confused about how he discovered where I was living, but it wouldn't have surprised me if my mother had told him. Albert made me feel like I was his property and I would never be free of him.

Later that evening, I talked to Emma Dawson, Albert's sister-in-law. She informed me that Zoey was at Albert's place that same day, lying out in the sun half naked, while Albert mowed the grass. I also discovered that Albert had taken Zoey to my mother's home. I never felt loved by my mother, and allowing my husband to bring his girlfriend to her home only intensified my feelings of resentment toward her.

Her disloyalty was humiliating. It was as though she was verbally admitting to my husband and his mistress that she had no respect for me or any regard for my feelings. She had pushed me to marry Albert in the first place, and I knew it was because she felt it would benefit her and never because she loved me.

When Lucas had kidnapped me at gunpoint and held me against my will, Mother had said, "Oh, how romantic!" Mother also hired Lucas to rewire her house after we divorced. How dare she say she loved me!

69

Snapped!

AFTER LEARNING ALBERT had taken his girlfriend to my mother's house, I felt such overwhelming anger and a sense of betrayal. I called Albert and calmly asked him to come over to see me since I was not feeling well. I knew Albert would never come if he knew I was angry, but he would make a beeline to my apartment if he thought I might take him back. I slid a pair of scissors into the back pocket of my blue jeans in preparation to see him, and I filled my glass with ice water since I had no iced tea. Albert had always made fun of and joked about how he had thrown a glass of iced tea in his ex-wife's face when she informed him that she was leaving him after sixteen years of marriage. It had always offended me the way Albert disparaged the mother of his two boys, and tonight I would display a little vengeance on her behalf, as well as my own.

When I married this man, I wasn't in love with him, yet I had committed myself to him. I had promised to be faithful and be good to him. He wasn't at all attractive and looked as though he were thirty years older than me, instead of only eleven. To think he had betrayed me in the presence of my own mother, and she had allowed it, was more than I could stand. People had been stepping on my heart all my life, and now Albert was doing the same.

When he had taken me to the grocery store in times past, I would quickly say, "I just need to pick up something that won't take but a minute," and then I would jump out of the truck and run inside. I would hurry as much as possible because I was ashamed for anyone to see him with me since he took no pride in his appearance. Now, even someone who disgusted me so much because he possessed no self-respect was betraying me too. I also knew if anyone from the Church Assembly would see me with him, they would talk about me from one state to the other since they had so many churches. They were the world's worst for criticizing and judging people. The more negative gossip to share, the better they liked it.

I had always loved to sing, but Albert took no interest in my singing. He always demanded I turn off the music if I had Christian music playing on the radio. I couldn't even go to church without catching hell from Albert when I got home.

That evening, when Albert arrived at my apartment, I walked out into the yard and suggested we sit in his car and talk. When we sat down in his car, I asked him to turn on the radio. I secretly planned to get his keys so he couldn't escape my wrath. I didn't plan to stab him with the scissors, but I sure as hell planned to make him think I was going to. He had no sooner turned on the radio than I reached over and turned it off again and collected the keys. I said, "Oh, I really don't think I want to listen to the radio after all." I said, "Why don't we get out of the car and walk."

It was very dark as we stood on the hill next to Boundary Street. I looked at Albert and asked him if he was seeing Zoey. He said no! I then reminded him that he had joked about throwing iced tea in Sara Jo's face. I said, "This one's for her," as I threw the ice water on him. I called him everything in the book and told him I knew he had been to my mother's home with Zoey.

It may have been dark, but the streetlights were working fine. Albert could see the shiny silver scissors in my hand as I pulled them from my back pocket. I viciously screamed at him, "I'm going to cut your F-ing heart out!" The look of sheer terror covered his face because he knew he had no keys to drive his car. I began coming toward him with the scissors held above my right shoulder and clutched in my fist. He ran down the street as I chased after him with the scissors, screaming what a sorry bastard he was.

After running down the hill after Albert, I suddenly stopped in the middle of the street. I realized I really wanted to stab him, not only for his indiscretion but also on behalf of everyone who had wronged me and caused my heart to ache—Nick Hansen, Oscar, Jasper Lewis, Connie Martin, Lucas, Sister Moreen Stratton, and the list goes on. My hands were trembling as I looked down at the scissors and asked myself, "What am I doing?"

My heart was racing so rapidly, and my mouth was dry. I knew I had to pull myself together because I felt as though something inside of me was about to snap. I felt so weak and depleted of my strength as I silently made my way back to my apartment without saying another word. I did, however, drop the keys in the street so he could find them and leave.

70

Nowhere to Run

I FILED FOR divorce from Albert, but something was going on inside of me that was frightening. It was as though the world was closing in on me, and I could hardly breathe. My nerves were tied up in knots inside my stomach as I tried desperately to understand what was wrong with me. Why had my life ended up this way? I was decent, I was a hard worker, and I wasn't a bad person, but something must be wrong with me that made everyone want to control me and own my very soul. Everyone around me seemed to have a great need to tear me down, and I just wanted to know why! I was a servant for everyone and couldn't seem to say no to their requests for money or whatever help they needed. They always knew who to call on, yet they were always disrespectful and unkind to me.

Even though I had only known Albert five months, he had not been faithful to our marriage vows. Still, he was treating me like I was his property. After a few months of fighting with him I began to see a very nice Christian man named Larry Mason. Larry was close to my age and such a nice person; it looked like things were going to get better in my life. Larry and I went to visit the Baptist church he and his parents attended. On one particular Sunday, Larry renewed his covenant with the Lord. After church he took me to his parents' home for Sunday dinner, and I had such a nice time being around what I considered "normal people."

Although I was in the middle of my divorce, Albert still wouldn't leave me alone and was doing everything in his power to prevent it from becoming final. Even though he knew I was aware of his continued relationship with Zoey, he was determined to keep me as his possession. He followed me continuously and harassed me constantly, especially when he discovered I was seeing someone too.

One evening he knocked on my front door and informed me that he was aware of every move I made. He said he had once worked for the police department in Los Angeles and had experience in running a check on license plates. He said he knew who I was seeing and where he lived. I felt he had a lot of nerve since he was the one who had broken our marriage vows. For some unknown reason, men have the attitude that it's okay for them, but it's not okay for a woman to exercise those same liberties.

Larry and I took the children to Indiana to share a two-week visit with their father since they had not seen him in several years. We would, however, return in two weeks to bring the children back home to Dalton, Georgia. On our return trip home, as we drove through Nashville, Tennessee, my heart began to race. I felt as though I couldn't breathe, so Larry drove me to a local hospital. I was still very confused about what was happening to me, but I was given a mild sedative to calm my nerves.

When Larry and I returned home from Indiana, he asked me to marry him. I thought, finally my life was about to change. Larry was my age, extremely good-looking, and was so kind and gentle with me. In my eyes he looked like Chaney, and that made me like him even more. It was so obvious that he was very much in love with me. He bought me a beautiful new car and a marquise diamond engagement ring. He was always sending me flowers, and the most precious of all his gifts were the special cards that spoke of all the love he felt for me in his heart. We would marry as soon as the divorce was final, and we began to look at houses and discuss exactly where we would live.

This would be the first time I would marry someone whom I wanted to marry. I would not be trying to please everyone else. I was finally happy; nevertheless, I should have realized that fate still had me by the throat and had only let up for a moment to secure a tighter grip.

After the July 4th vacation week, I returned to work and was asked to operate the spinning machines since they were short of help in that department. I didn't mind doing something different at work for a change, so I accepted the request. However, my back had been hurting so badly all week long that I had to do something to try to relieve the pain. My co-worker Doug had some pain pills the dentist had prescribed for his toothache, so I took one, thinking it would relieve the pain in my back. Ordinarily, I didn't take pills of any kind, but I was in so much pain I had to do something to continue to work. I took one of the pain pills about seven thirty that morning, and around ten o'clock the pain was still present, so I took another one with a cup of Coke. I usually drank about thirty-five small paper cups of Coke a week at work because it was so terribly hot inside the carpet mill.

Shortly after taking the second pill, as I stood in front of the spinning machine, my heart began to beat so fast I felt as if it would burst right out of my chest! I thought I was having some kind of bad reaction to the pills. Without waiting to grab my purse, I ran toward the front office to the nurse's station to see Wanda Sizemore. She was the company nurse and a personal friend. I quickly suggested she drive me to the hospital without hesitation because something was very wrong with me.

By the time we arrived at the hospital, I was covered with a red rash on my chest. The doctor gave me a shot and told me to go home and rest. He also suggested I shouldn't have any stimulants because of the type of medicine he had injected in me. When I arrived at home, I drank two Pepsis (not realizing they were stimulants) before falling to sleep. I lay on my bed for a very short while before my heart began beating so fast it felt like it would burst out of my chest once again, just as it had at work. I had never had a heart attack, but this surely must be what was happening to me. I was in such a panic that I ran down the hill to my friend Joyce Owens' home.

A short while later, an ambulance arrived and the EMTs requested I lie down on the gurney so they could do a little testing before taking me to the hospital. I listened as the driver called the hospital and informed the staff of my condition. My symptoms sounded disconcerting, causing me to feel even more alarmed. I was convinced that I was going to die right then and there. The attendants decided it would be unwise for them to take me to the hospital. They called the paramedics who were better equipped to treat a heart attack situation. Their concern and response toward my condition only frightened me even more.

I decided if they were afraid, I might not survive the ride to the hospital, which was only three blocks away, I surely must be dying. As I lay on the gurney with the oxygen mask over my face and nose, I waited for the moment I was certain was about to take place.

I was convinced that any second, I was going to witness the angry face of Jesus. I was totally horrified by the possibility that He would send me straight to hell. I had left the Church Assembly, so there was no hope for me. I was raised on hell, fire, and brimstone tactics while being taught very little about a loving God, so I was expecting the worst.

Once I arrived at the hospital, my symptoms began to subside and I was suddenly drained of all my strength. I had used up all my energy in my distraught and panicky response to my overwhelming fears. The doctor assured me I wasn't having a heart attack, and I later discovered this was the beginning of the many full-blown panic attacks I would have to live with on a regular basis.

71

Drowning in Fear

IN THE DAYS to come, I would get in my car to drive somewhere, any-where, when suddenly I would begin to feel like I was smothering. I would have many symptoms, but the worst was an overwhelming fear that I was going to die and, of course, go to hell. I would quickly return to my apartment, and as I walked in the door, the symptoms would quickly fade away. I couldn't understand what was going on with me, so how could I expect anyone else to? I had been informed by the attending physician in the emergency room that I may have been having what he called anxiety attacks. Anxiety attacks? That didn't sound like anything serious, so I must be okay. I had heard that word all my life, and I never thought of anxiety as being any big deal.

I had visited the Church Assembly a few times in the recent past to see old friends and, of course, Chaney. Now, with the constant fear of dying looming over my head, I decided to start going to the church I was raised in so I wouldn't go to hell if I suddenly died. My own conscience was always discouraging me to go back to this church, but having no confidence in myself, I didn't trust my own inner voice. It was all the voices and the sermons I still carried in my head as far back as I could remember. This church was the gateway to heaven, and if I didn't follow its path, I would go to hell. The church's belief was "my deep-seeded truth," and I couldn't escape my reality no matter how hard I tried to break free. I had been taught all my life that this was the only way to heaven and everyone else was going to hell. My grandparents were members of the church, and both of my parents were raised in this church, so who was I to say they were wrong?

In my eyes, I had been a failure at life, so maybe if I couldn't be happy in this life, maybe I could be in the next. I stopped wearing makeup, threw out my cherished blue jeans, stopped cutting and perming my hair, didn't curse, and constantly prayed. I pleaded with God to forgive me for thinking the wrong thoughts, or just anything that would cause Him to reject me, while I fearfully waited to die.

I had to take a leave of absence from work since I was having such a difficult time leaving my apartment, and emotionally I was tied up in knots.

Since I was raised to believe that thinking the wrong thoughts was a sin, that covered all of the bases. It was just a matter of time before I fearfully gazed upon the angry and accusing face of God. I went to see Dr. Poehlman, a cardiologist, and he ran several tests to discover what might be wrong with my heart since I was having palpitations. I was convinced that I must have some terrible heart condition that would take my life.

After completing a whole series of tests, Dr. Poehlman called me in his office to discuss the results. He reassured me there was no abnormality affecting my heart's performance, and he began to ask me personal questions regarding my private life. Always in the past, I had kept my emotions well-guarded from anyone, but suddenly the tears began to fall. There was no stopping the pain I had kept hidden deep inside my soul. His kind words were so soothing as he suggested that all the problems I was having were related to my emotions and not my physical state.

72

Psychiatric Hospital

DR. POEHLMAN SAID that most people have bad things happen to them, and then they have a period of healing before the next crisis strikes their life. My cardiologist said, all your life you have had one bad thing right after the other happen to you with no time of healing. So, now your body is reacting to all this pain the only way it knows how. He said, "I know it will be difficult for you, but I feel the best thing you could do to help yourself would be to admit yourself into the psychiatric hospital for a while."

I was willing to do anything to get better and make the panic attacks go away, but the thought of being in a psychiatric hospital sent all kinds of concerns through my mind. Would there be a bunch of crazy people sitting around pulling their hair out? I didn't know, but I had to do something to get well. The panic attacks had become more and more frequent, and I didn't know how to make them stop.

Although Dr. Poehlman suggested I admit myself into the psychiatric hospital, he failed to mention there was one only three blocks from my apartment connected to Hamilton Medical Center. I looked in the telephone book to find one, and I saw the name Greenleaf. I called the number and discovered it was located in Fort Oglethorpe, Georgia. Now, how in the world could I go to Fort Oglethorpe when I couldn't even drive across town without having a panic attack?

The panic attacks kept getting worse and more frequent to the point that it seemed the only place I felt safe was in my bedroom. If I tried to walk outside to the mailbox, it would happen, and many times just walking into the living room started my heart beating so fast that I was terrified I was going to die.

I finally discovered the Westcott Psychiatric Hospital, a part of Hamilton Medical Center. I didn't hesitate to pack my clothes and head for this place, which might help in the healing of my broken spirit. I needed so desperately to learn how to live with the tormenting memories of my life.

Happily, "Never" After

To have been raised in a world with the fairly-tale movies that always ended with "and they lived happily ever after" was a very misleading concept of my reality. I needed to find a way to accept that dreams really don't come true for everybody, even though I had stayed a virgin until I was twenty and married. My true love would never come looking for me, I would never be a famous country or gospel singer, I would never own my very own home, and I would never have some good Christian man to love me, to be good to me, and to take me for his bride. I think the worst thing that finally happened to me was I had stopped believing things would get better. I lost the hope I had always carried inside my heart that no matter what bad and ugly things were happening to me and around me at that particular moment, things would be better tomorrow.

I had foolishly believed Scarlett O'Hara when she said, "Tomorrow's another day," insinuating there's always hope and a better day coming. I dreamed of what a relief it would be to go to sleep and never wake up again, to never feel this pain anymore. I would just have to live as close to what was perfect as I could, so I wouldn't go to hell. The light at the end of the tunnel had finally gone out, and I was left alone, alone in the dark.

I checked into the Westcott psychiatric hospital late that evening and sat on the sofa waiting to be taken to my room. Two men dressed in white uniforms came down the quiet, empty hallway with the clicking of their shoes echoing their footsteps. Suddenly, I heard the doors click as they were being locked from the inside. The nurse walked in the room and looked at me with a sweet, reassuring smile and said, "Yvette, we're not locking the doors to keep you in; we're locking the doors to keep out all the bad people who have hurt you." For me that felt profound because I knew there were a lot of them outside those locked doors.

I made it clear to my friend Doug Bennett to not let Mother or anyone know where I was. Mother was always coming around to take money from me. Eventually she had to be told because she was making Doug's life miserable from all her insistent badgering as to my whereabouts. When she did discover where I was, she never hesitated to call the psychiatric hospital and ask to speak to my doctor to put in her two cents regarding me. Dr. Green assured my mother that she wasn't the slightest bit interested in anything Mother had to say against me. Mother quickly suggested, "Well, talk to her husband; he'll tell you!"

Mother came to visit me once when I was finally allowed visitors, and right away she wanted to borrow some money. I gave her what I had. However, Dr. Green discovered Mother had borrowed money from me and was agitated with Mother for her lack of concern for what was in my best interest. Dr. Green verbally reprimanded my mother for coming to the psychiatric hospital to take my money.

During my stay at the hospital, I was informed of all the facilities that were available to me for my needs and comfort. One of these was called the Blue Room, where you could go to release any anger or frustration you might be feeling without hurting yourself or anyone else. If you wanted to scream or beat on the walls and floor, then so be it because the doctor said it would help to get out all of the pain I had been stuffing inside for years. The room was padded from the floors and walls to the ceiling.

Right away I went to work on healing all the other patients and assuring them everything was going to be all right with their lives. However, soon after my doctor discovered I was helping everyone else, she suggested I deal with what was going on inside of me instead. It had always been easier for me to help other people than to deal with the pain and anguish within my own heart.

There was an art room, where you could express your creativity. It was here where the instructor asked each individual at which time in their lives, they felt the most at peace. I had never been asked this question, but now that I had, my answer was, without hesitation, when I was in Florida lying on the beach in my lawn chair and listening to the ocean. I have never before or since felt such tranquility throughout my soul. To my surprise, every one of the other patients agreed that it was at the ocean where they too had felt the most at peace with the world. The instructor smiled as she admitted it was a proven fact that there was some sort of hypnotic substance in the seaweed located at the ocean's shores.

73

Crumbling Beneath the Weight

MY CHILDREN WERE in Indiana with their father while I was in the hospital. I had to send seventy dollars each week to Indiana to feed them, even though Robert hadn't sent any child support to me for several years. After being in the hospital for a couple of weeks, I was permitted to go home on the weekend to spend the night, with the understanding I would return to the psychiatric hospital at a designated time the following day. When I arrived at home, Larry told me he wanted out of the relationship. He asked for the engagement ring that he had given me before I had gone into the hospital. It was strange the way things ended, considering how crazy he had been about me all along.

After the breakup, I never saw him again, but I always wondered what made him change his mind about me. I later discovered that Albert had taken down Larry's license plate numbers and ran a check on his car. He was able to obtain an address and the telephone number of Larry's parents' home. Albert bragged to me that he had called Larry's parents in an effort to place horrifying doubts in their minds regarding my character. Albert had called me every dirty name there was to destroy my relationship with Larry. I wished Larry would have been man enough to stand up for me, but, honestly, I'd never met a "real man" before anyway. I don't know why it took me so long to realize I could never trust any man with my heart.

Albert gloated to me about what he had done to cause Larry to break up with me. Now, Albert was waiting in the shadows to once again take control of me and my life.

Finally, I had to figure out a way to bring my children home from Indiana, since I was no longer emotionally strong enough to make the trip and didn't own a car. I couldn't bear the thought of having anything to do with Albert; nevertheless, he was the only person I could count on to be there for me. He eagerly drove to Indiana to pick up the kids and waited for me to leave the hospital so he could take control of my life once again. I wouldn't be able to function on my own with the simplest of tasks, such as driving myself to the grocery store, so Albert would have me just where he wanted me. For his help, I would pay a price no woman should ever have to endure.

When it was time for me to be released from the psychiatric hospital, Dr. Green said it was necessary for my mother to come for a meeting to try to work out the problems between us. Dr. Green said this was a procedure that each patient was required to go through before leaving the hospital. The day that Mother came for the meeting, I felt like I would die inside, knowing I had to confront her with all the pain she had inflicted on my mind, body, and spirit growing up. I was terrified of her and almost collapsed when she walked into the room.

If a person could imagine the most frightening feeling, they could possibly experience, that is the way I felt knowing I had to confront her. She had such a stern, piercing look of disapproval when she looked at me that I felt as though I was smothering at the very thought of her coming to that meeting. Minutes before she arrived, I was covered with an ugly red rash. I had broken out like this before when I was nervous but never to this degree. My entire body, including my face, was covered with this rash.

Dr. Green talked to my mother to try to help her understand why this meeting was necessary for my recovery. With encouragement from my doctor, I began to talk to my mother about the many things that she had done to me, and I asked her why. Mother just brushed me off and directed her attention to the doctor. She told the doctor that I wasn't telling the truth when, suddenly, without realizing what I was doing, I screamed at her from the top of my lungs, "You're a f#@ king liar!" and then I collapsed. Later, when I realized I had spoken such an ugly word to my mother, I was stunned. I had never in my life used a word like that in her presence, and now I had not only cursed her but I also had used the worst possible word I knew. What was just as shocking was I didn't even realize what I was saying until after I had said it.

Mother seemed nervous now, and she admitted there were many times that she had accused me of things without knowing I was guilty. She told my doctor that she believed if she accused me of all those things and told me she knew I was lying, I would confess. The problem was I hadn't been guilty in the first place. Further on into the meeting, there were so many ugly things Mother had subjected me to in my youth that she finally stood up, walked out of the hospital, and went home.

Dr. Green said ordinarily they never advise patients to separate themselves from their family members. She said their goal was to try to help them work things out; however, in my situation she said her advice would be, for my own mental health, to stay completely away from my mother. Dr. Green said that in this stage of Mother's life, she didn't believe Mother would ever change.

74

Agoraphobia

ONCE I WAS released from the hospital and went home, it was more apparent that Larry was truly gone from my life. However, I was so numb from the drug therapy, it didn't matter that much. People had let me down all my life, and this would be no different.

Dr. Sandvi prescribed Buspirone and Xanax for my medication. I had assumed that once I was out of the hospital, I would regain my life. Unfortunately, I would soon discover I would lose myself in a way that was too horrible to imagine. The panic attacks continued on a regular basis, and I was so screwed up about religion that I stayed obsessed with death.

Albert lived on the other side of town with his old girlfriend, Zoey. He knew I had no way of knowing because I couldn't drive anywhere, so he began his double life. He would come almost every day and take me places that I needed to go to, such as the grocery store or the Laundromat to dry my clothes. I had a washing machine but no dryer.

One day, when he took me to the laundry, I had just put the wet clothes into the dryers and turned the knob when suddenly I panicked. I felt as though I couldn't breathe and experienced an overwhelming fear of impending doom. I quickly grabbed my wet clothes out of the dryers, threw them into my laundry baskets, and insisted that Albert drive me home as quickly as possible. Once I walked in the front door of my apartment, all the bad feelings disappeared and I was okay.

The panic attacks overwhelmed me each time I would leave the house until, finally, I couldn't go anywhere. Dr. Sandvi said I had what is medically termed "agoraphobia," which is the worst of all phobias. This phobia can even cause you to have other kinds of phobias. My safe place, as the doctors called it, was my apartment. My safe place continued to close in on me to the point that it was difficult to walk out to the mailbox.

My Safe Place

Always holding back and not being me,
No longer trusting in things I can't see,
I push people away, not letting them near
for feeling loves pain. It's my greatest fear,
Fear of pain that I know all too well,
I sometimes feel I'm living in hell.
Scared to move on, I'm stuck in one place,
with a painted smile across my face,
Afraid to feel what I've felt before,
As my broken heart crashed to the floor.
So, I'll just look in from the outside
Because I feel safe whenever I hide.
Safe from feeling anything at all,
keeping my distance, all alone,
Just me and my wall.

Written and composed by Laura M. Cross

My Two Feathered Friends

I felt safest in my bedroom, so that's where I stayed, day in and day out, for the next two years. I would stand at my bedroom window facing the woods and sing to a beautiful little blue bird and red cardinal that always seemed to find their way into the trees in my backyard. They both would fly down to the ground and stand there outside my window as though they came to visit me and hear me sing each day.

The little blue bird was my favorite, and I felt a little joy inside my soul each day when he would return to visit me. I felt so envious of him as he swooped down among the leaves and landed in my yard. Just knowing he could fly up into the clouds toward heaven with no fears of any kind seemed like the most wonderful thing in the world to me, and I knew God wouldn't send that little blue bird to hell.

75

I'll Sing Until Heaven Hears Me

AFTER ABOUT THE first year of being confined to my bedroom, I wondered if I would eventually lose my mind because the anxiety and fear were so intense. But God had given me a voice to sing, and I believed as long as I could sing, I would keep my sanity. I had a karaoke machine and, on the wall, a picture of a beautiful lighthouse that I bought at a yard sale for a dollar. Many days I would cry and stare at that picture and sing a gospel song I knew called "The Lighthouse." Then I would look out the window and see my little feathered friends had returned, so I would sing to them.

I had heard as a child that singing drives evil spirits away. So, I sang at the top of my lungs, hoping God was listening and would someday free me from this horrible prison that was keeping my spirit and mind captive. I would always sleep with my Bible clutched to my chest believing it would somehow keep me safe. I was afraid of people because they would only hurt me; I was afraid to go outside because that's where "they" were. I was afraid of the God I learned about in church because I knew, at the slightest provocation, He would send me to hell. I used to pray to God to help me drive around the block alone—for me that would have been a miracle.

I seldom ventured out of my apartment, but when I did it was in the company of Albert. He would have to hold my hand because I was so frightened to be outside. I was an adult, thirty-four years old, yet I was totally dependent upon him emotionally, and he was taking full advantage of me. Many times, we would get a half block from my apartment, and I would panic and insist that he turn the car around and quickly drive me back home. There was no one on God's earth who was there for me except Albert, so I had no choice but to accept his help. I despised him with every fiber of my being and had to remain silent. He deliberately tormented me to no end and took pleasure in making fun of me. He would laugh as he told me my family didn't care anything about me, and I knew it was true, which made it hurt all the more.

It was as though he was trying to push me over the edge, but Albert didn't have the commonsense God gave a Billy goat! In exchange for driving me to buy food and short trips around town, I was subjected to his perverted mind and sexual desires. I would cringe at the touch of his hand. He showed no compassion or sensitivity for my feelings, only a demand for his just reward for not deserting me. I was very much a frightened little girl in my mind, and I knew if I didn't do what he commanded, he would leave me alone, and that terrified me. When he crawled on top of my body, I lay there sick to the very depths of my soul with the constant fantasy of holding a knife in my hand and stabbing him repeatedly in his side. I was silently screaming, but no one could hear me, no one but God.

Regardless of how I despised his hands on my body, I knew I had to keep those feelings hidden. So, I would travel somewhere else in my mind like the ocean. I loved the ocean because it was such a peaceful place to me. I learned to separate my spirit from my body at least to the degree of surviving the ordeal. I would drink wine to try to dull the pain, but eventually I stopped for fear of becoming an alcoholic like my children's father.

There was a whole world of feelings and expressions that I needed to find a way of releasing. I realized that even though I couldn't express myself openly to anyone, I could write exactly how I felt in ink. I could recapture and preserve my sanity by writing down my feelings, so I began to write poems again and the story of my life. I enjoyed writing and I enjoyed singing, so—although the doctor said statistics suggested that someone with agoraphobia to the degree I had it was likely to commit suicide—I was determined, with God's help, to survive.

My children's father never paid child support, and it took three years for the Social Security disability to begin. There was very little money that flowed through the doors of my home. Albert had an excellent income and would help out a little financially, but only in his demented way. I never could understand why he seemed to have a great desire to destroy my identity, yet it always seemed to be his goal. We were still legally married, but his method of giving me money was so degrading. He would put the money in his undershorts and grin as he told me to fetch it as if I were a dog.

76

Waiting for "Someday"

WHEN I WAS in the psychiatric hospital, I had been asked, "What is the one thing you wish you had that would make you happy?" Without hesitation I responded, "A high school diploma." I was a strong believer that knowledge is power, and with that knowledge and with that power comes self-confidence. An adult learning center was two blocks from where I lived, and I was determined to go there no matter how difficult it was for me. Even though I couldn't go alone, I would make it if Albert would go with me, so he agreed.

The class lasted for one hour, and Albert would sit outside in the car and read the paper while he waited for me. There was no way he could drive away and leave me there without me coming unglued. I would sit by the window in the classroom because I had to be able to see him and know that he wouldn't leave me.

When he took me to the grocery store, I would take the car keys in the store with me because I was so afraid, he would leave me. If the store was very big, I couldn't go to the back, so whatever I needed to buy had to be close to the front door or I'd just do without it. If I knew exactly where something was located, such as milk from the back area of Kroger's, I would almost run to the back of the store, grab the milk, and rush to the front before my breathing became too labored and the panic too intense. My mouth would go dry, my heart would beat as though it would burst out of my chest, and I felt as though I would faint.

There were many other sensations, but the worst was a terrified certainty that I would die and go to hell. Being raised in the church had convinced me there was an angry God in heaven just waiting to send me to hell. It was a very slow process, but with faith and determination, I began to ease out of my safe place.

When Albert was finally able to take me to Belk's department store, he had to wait in the car at the front door while I hurriedly picked up what I came for. He began to park in the parking lot. Every few minutes I would rush to the door and check to see if he was there, and if I wasn't able to see him, I would become extremely panicky and upset. I started taking the car keys inside the store with me because I didn't trust Albert to keep his word and stay close to the door. He enjoyed making fun of me and even hiding from me in the parking lot before I started keeping the keys. He laughed one day as he said to me, "I hope you never get over this agoraphobia!" I asked why he would say such a cruel thing, and he responded, "I know if you get over this agoraphobia, you will tell me to hit the road."

I don't understand how someone can say they love you and be so insensitive, but I always knew Albert was only looking out for his own interest. He said he loved me, but I knew I was just his trophy. I began to feel more at ease doing the driving instead of Albert, even though he had to be with me. I needed to feel in control of something in my life, and I know that's why I preferred to drive.

Albert would sit on the passenger's side of the car and reach over to grab at my breast while the car was in motion. I would have to fight him off with my right hand while I held the car on the road with my left. I pleaded with him to stop, that he would make us have a car wreck, but he was totally unconcerned. This wasn't something that seldom happened; this was something that happened every time I was in the car with him. He would grab and yank at the nipples on my right breast so hard (through my clothing) they felt like they would bleed.

Albert had the sharpest and hardest fingernails I have ever seen on a man. They were shaped like a womans except they were much stronger. One day when I was fighting him off with my right hand, his fingernail dug into my wrist so deep I needed stitches, but he never took me to the hospital. I carry a noticeable scar on my wrist as a reminder that will be there for the rest of my life.

77

Searching for the Beauty in My Ashes

IT WAS 1990, and I had to find a way to function by myself and heal my broken spirit. I longed for the day when I could get Albert out of my life and function on my own. I attended outpatient classes called "Emotions Anonymous" at the Westcott Psychiatric Hospital. I desperately wanted to get well, so between the medications, therapy/classes, and most of all the self-help books, I began to gradually improve. I done breathing exercises and techniques to calm down the anxiety. I read many, many books on anxiety/panic attack disorders, low self-esteem, and people-pleasers to try to help myself get better. I read *Toxic Parents*, *Churches That Abuse*, and most of Joyce Meyer's books. I also listened to her tapes. *Beauty for Ashes* and *Battlefield of the Mind* were instrumental in my healing.

I still slept with my Bible in my arms or in the bed close beside me with my hand on its black leather cover. When I read the Bible, I would only read the scriptures that said God loved me and not the ones where He was going to punish me and send me to hell for what I might be thinking. I tried to keep that pushed out of my mind because I had heard it enough at the Church Assembly. I knew His love came with conditions, but so did anyone's who had ever touched my life.

I spoke good things over my life because I knew if I were to survive and be spiritually whole again in my mind, it would be from fighting for my sanity. I had already experienced way too much fear and violence in church, performed in the name of God. So, I chose to cling to the God of love, the one I had been talking to ever since I was a little girl. I felt His presence no matter how bad things got or what hell I was walking through. He was right there beside me every step of the way. I would sing to Him day after day as I watched the blue bird and the red cardinal outside my bedroom window, He was there, and His sweet love would flow over my body so strongly, I felt I could reach out with my hand and touch His precious face. He was in another realm, however, and I could only see Him with my heart. Since, I couldn't leave my home I would make gospel tapes in my bedroom for Eleventh Ave. Baptist church. They would send someone by to pick them up and they played them on their gospel radio program. A radio announcer took my tape to Nashville and a well-known figure in the music industry wanted me to come to Nashville for a meeting. I couldn't make the trip because of my agoraphobia and I was devastated. I still have the letter. It felt as though the deck was stacked against me from the time I was born. Nevertheless, God had His own plan for my life.

Battered Women

I was invited to a candlelight vigil for battered women to be held on the steps of the Dalton Courthouse, and I was asked to sing a song. So, I wrote the words to this song for the event:

(First verse)
There's a home in Whitfield County,
and its door is open wide,
for the brokenhearted spirit,

it's a place where you can hide,
for the battered women everywhere,
who may think no one really cares,
their hand is reaching out, you'll see,
because it once reached out for me,
this family is for me.
(Chorus)
This family is for me,
the spirit here is pure as gold,
a pleasant rest for my weary soul,
this family is for me,
a far cry from a life in doubt,
that the flame within had faded out,
but your love has made the spark,
and saved me from the dark,
this family is for me.
(Second verse)
I've walked the road of desperation,
the tears I cried, I cried alone,
when I reached out for a friend who'd care,
no one ever was at home,
all the love in life I thought I'd found
seemed to find me just to tear me down,
but today I'll make a start,
for you've saved me from the dark,
this family is for me.

Written and composed by Yvette Lidy

78

Losing My Safe Place

WHILE I WAITED for my disability payments to begin, my children and I enjoyed making out a grocery list of the food I would be able to buy. Canned goods, tuna, snacks, detergent, dish soap, personal hygiene products, desserts (ice cream, chocolates, brownies), etc. were listed in columns with lines drawn to separate each one. I had a pantry for my groceries, and I would walk by the empty shelves in my kitchen and dream of the day when it would be full of food. To be able to afford going into a grocery store and buying anything we wanted to eat was, for us, like winning the lottery. We would get so excited just planning the trip. Albert gave me the coupons from his newspaper, and for months I cut them out and separated them into categories. The kids would help me choose which coupon we would use; it was so much fun dreaming while we waited.I was now able to drive a few miles from home but not very far. When I did go somewhere, such as to the grocery store, I would take the same street each time and never a new direction. Many times, I would start out and not get a block down the street before I would panic, quickly turn around, and go back home to my safe place. Once I walked in the door, all the fear would leave and I would be okay.

It was now 1993, and I had begun receiving disability income with back pay that would make it possible to buy my own car. In an effort to try to help myself heal and also keep my son Hunter from having to walk to his High School in the rain, I tried driving him there since it was only two blocks away. Suddenly, I would have a full-blown panic attack just thinking of driving back home alone before he even got out of the car. With my feelings of sheer terror and impending doom, Hunter would have to come back home with me and then walk back to school. When he got to school, he would be punished and sent to in-school suspension for being tardy. I didn't like the way he was treated because of my disability. I called the High School office and tried to explain that it wasn't his fault, but I was informed that it didn't matter since it was the school's policy for dealing with tardiness. I wanted so much to be able to function normally, but the thought of being left alone terrified me and made me physically and emotionally ill.

Because I was drawing disability, I thought I would have to move, so I began making plans about where we would live. I finally had the equivalency of a high school diploma, so if I moved out of the "projects," I would move near Dalton State College, which was about three miles away. I wanted to continue my education because I believed knowledge is power. I had spent so many years of my life feeling powerless. I rented an apartment next to the college called, Wood Valley apartments and it was beautiful with a swimming pool. However, once I moved there, my nights were torment. I panicked so badly from being away from my old apartment—my safe place was forever gone. This place was so much nicer than the cold cement floors at the projects, but that didn't matter; I just wanted to go back home.

Dr. Sandvi advised me to not watch the news or anything on television with violence because it would trigger my terrifying panic attacks. I started watching a lot of Disney movies to try to keep my mind off of the overwhelming river of fears that tried to pull me under. My favorite movie was a 1948 movie called, "*So Dear to My Heart.*" As it came on, John Beal's, deep, soft voice would sing the title song. It would show an adorable cottage with flowers around it as beautiful snow fell late at night. It was as soothing and calming to my nerves as any drug I was ever prescribed.

79

Loving But Never Being Loved

JACOB CALLED ME and asked if I would pay his $268 phone bill. Jacob made plenty of money but was quick to spend it, and since he had often been late with his payment, the phone company was going to disconnect his phone service. He said he would pay me Tuesday when he came in from working in Atlanta.

I often loaned Jacob money, and he would pay me back, but this time was different. He didn't come to pay me on Tuesday as promised, and when he wouldn't return my phone calls, I realized he wasn't going to pay me back at all. I needed to pay my own bills, so I called the phone company and was surprised to find out the clerk was someone I knew. When she told me the check I had written was still on her desk, I knew God was watching out for me. I asked her to hold it until I got there. I also asked her to please wait as long as she could before disconnecting Jacob's phone service since that was his business phone. From Wednesday until the following Sunday I never heard a peep from Jacob. On Monday morning his service was disconnected, and he finally called me, cursing and threatening me with every breath. He lied to Karen and told her I was planning to take his money for a bill I didn't pay and had no intention of paying for him.

It was not uncommon to be mistreated and ganged up on by my

siblings. I had loaned Jacob my vacuum cleaner and television set a while back, and when I went to get them from him, his girlfriend had my vacuum cleaner at her home. I needed him to carry the twenty-seven-inch TV to my car, but he wouldn't. Instead, as I carried the extremely heavy television from his bedroom through his living room, he began cursing me with his fist in my face as though he was going to hit me. I stumbled on his outside walkway and fractured the heel of my foot. It was some of the worse pain I had ever felt in my life. Regardless of the pain I was having Jacob immediately asked me not to charge his land owner with the bill and so I didn't. My foot was in a cast for a long time and it was a very slow healing process.

80

Adversaries of My Heart

I STARTED TAKING classes at Dalton State College and I was very happy about that but I was really having a struggle with my anxiety and panic attacks. Even though my apartment was right next door to the college it was so hard to be in the crowd of students. Then I met Sara Jo. who was also a student and surprisingly enough, she was the ex-wife of Albert. I can't help but believe God placed her in my life at a time when I really needed a friend. She went home with me one day for a visit when mother was at my apartment. I had made a home-made cassette of me singing and played it for Mother. When I put it in my tape player, she quickly told me to take it out; she said my singing was making her head hurt. I was so hurt because I wanted Mother to like my singing and her reaction embarrassed me in front of my friend. Yet, when I walked out of the room in tears, she told my friend Sara Jo, "I think the reason Yvette cried is because she finally realized for the first time that she can't sing." In her heart she only had one daughter, Karen, and they both did their very best to tear me down.

I sang "Help Me Make It Through the Night," back in Indiana and Karen would walk around singing it as she pinched her nose with two fingers to make the song sound terrible, mocking my singing.

I had always loved to sing even as a little girl. I recall walking home from school every day when I was in third grade happily singing as loud as I could while walking up East Morris Street. I began encouraging and comforting myself when my heart was sad, and I believe my Heavenly Father placed that ability in me because He knew no one else would instill any confidence in me to face whatever lay in store for my life here on earth.

Mother and Karen spent the day together, and during their visit, Mother told Karen I was writing my autobiography. Karen angrily sent word to me by Mother that I had better not mention her in the book because she would sue me in court. She must have been very aware of her cruelty toward me; otherwise, why would she think there would be anything negative to say about her?

I had bought a new car with the back paycheck from disability, so Karen told me she needed to borrow it to drive to Adairsville, Georgia. I couldn't seem to say no for fear of making her mad at me, so I let her take my new car and drive away in it. Before she left, she asked me to pick up the new snow village trinket at Proffitt's Department Store for her. If you collected all the pieces, you would end up with a little Christmas village, and each trinket was only five dollars. While she was in Adairsville (getting a speeding ticket in my new car), her daughter Pamela asked me to loan her five dollars to buy some eggs and milk for her kids, and so I did. When Karen returned, I asked her for the five dollars for the trinket I had picked up for her. Later she called and told me how disgusting I was because I was trying to collect from her twice, since Pamela told her she had already paid me the five dollars. It was horrible the way Karen talked to me, and it very hurtful. It was also just a few days after Jacob had attacked me.

When she hung up, I called Pamela and asked her why she told her mother I had already collected the five dollars from her. She said, "Because you did; I gave you five dollars!" I replied, "That was for the money you borrowed from me to buy eggs and milk for your children." She said, "Oh, Yvette, you're right; I forgot. I'm so sorry."

Pamela would later tell me what was said at her mother's that day when she hung up with me:

When she got off the phone, she told her mom she made a mistake. Karen sat at her kitchen table with Pamela as Stacy stood in the kitchen doorway. Karen said, "Well, what would you do? Call and tell Yvette she and Amanda can come to Thanksgiving dinner?" Stacy quickly said, "No! If you let her come for dinner, Uncle Jacob won't come, and I want him here. If Uncle Jacob doesn't come, then I won't either!"

I had asked Karen weeks earlier if I paid her five dollars a plate, could Amanda and I eat Thanksgiving dinner at her house since we had no place to go. Thanksgiving week I would be moving into the Holly Brook apartments up the street from Dalton College and wouldn't be set up for cooking yet. Nevertheless, this was a way of her uninviting us, so we never ate at Karen's on Thanksgiving.

Josh was a quiet, soft-spoken man and had always been Mother's favorite child. However, he carried so much pent-up anger for what he went through in the church, it wouldn't take much to set him off. He worked very hard at keeping his feelings in check. Still, when it came to me and mother was mad at me, he would come at me like he could physically hurt me, and I have no doubt he could have. It was only after Mother died that he and I were able to have a wonderful relationship as brother and sister. Josh was closest to my heart because I understood just how he felt. Mother had three children that she deeply loved. She had so much respect for Jacob because no one told him what to do, not even her, and he also always gave her money. Josh was her baby boy and very close to Mother's heart, so she waited on him hand and foot.

I wanted to have a good relationship with my sister, Karen, but there were very few times she was ever kind to me. She and Mother were very close, and I was always treated like the outsider, I was the topic of their conversations, and nothing had to be true as long as it belittled me. When I had first married Albert, Karen asked me to buy her a new dress to wear to a wedding. It was expensive but she promised to pay me when she got her check. She knew I purchased it with the credit card Albert had given me, yet, when it was time to pay me, she said in an ugly tone, I'm not paying you anything because that was Albert's credit card you purchased it with. Being so disrespected was a common occurrence with her and mother. Even to the extent, when I was laid off from work and applied for food stamps mother told me she took them from my mail box and gave them to my Karen. How hurtful it was for me was of no importance to her. Between the two of them I always felt defeated and unloved. My memories of my mother and my relationship with my siblings were very unhappy ones.

81

My Soul Cries Out, "Oh Lord, How Long?"

MOTHER LIVED IN an apartment I had helped her get, and of all places, they rented her the apartment right across the hall from me. I would be sleeping peacefully in my bed late at night when the telephone would blast in my ear and I would awake in a panic to the sound of my mother's voice screaming at me from the receiver. She was accusing me of stealing her eighty-eight-cent can of Breck hair spray. I was a grown, forty-five-year-old woman still being jarred awake from a sound sleep in a panic by my mother, just as she had done when I was five years old.

She also called in the middle of the night to say I had stolen her rent money order and that she would have me arrested. After begging her to believe me, she would hang up the phone with her angry threats lingering in my room like a heavy cloud hovering over my bed. Being emotionally drained with anxiety, there was no way I could fall back to sleep. I was so tired, yet all I could do was lie there and stare at the ceiling. Karen laughed one day as she told me Mother found her hair spray, and that's when I began to realize Mother would never admit to me that she was finding all the things she had accused me of stealing. Instead, I was left believing that she believed I was stealing from her. I had never been a thief, but Mother began stealing shoes for her sister at school as a poor kid in the mountains of Harlan, Kentucky.

One day I walked over to Mother's apartment and tried to talk to her. I told her I didn't understand why she acted like she hated me because I loved her with all my heart. I remember being on the floor in front of her chair, sobbing into my hands and begging her to tell me why she didn't love me. She just looked at me with no emotion as though I wasn't even there. I will never forget that day as long as I live.

I wanted so much for Mother to love me and be proud of me for the poetry I had written. When I showed her my poems, she looked at me with such anger and an accusing finger. She told me I could go to jail for stealing someone else's poems. I told myself that was kind of a compliment; she must have thought they were pretty good for her to think I had stolen them. Nevertheless, her message to me was I wasn't good enough to write poetry or anything else for that matter.

I have no memories of Mother attempting to build up my confidence about my future, of being capable to be successful in the business world or doing anything worthwhile with my life. She had labeled me a thief, a liar, and a whore, and had said I was not good enough to be a poet, a singer, or a writer, and not good enough "to be loved." Her treatment of me rubbed off on my siblings, and my sister already hated me for just being alive. Mother belittled me to anyone who would listen and didn't hesitate to tell them I didn't have a good mind. There were never words of encouragement or that she was proud of me in any way whatsoever.

I loved the cards at Cracker Barrel and would go there to choose one for Mother on her birthday or Mother's Day. The cards would speak of love, closeness, precious memories, and kindness, but as I stood there reading the beautiful words, I would quickly wipe my cheeks so the other customers wouldn't see my tears. I would then close the card and put it back in its place because I knew it did not apply, even though I desperately wanted it to. When I attempted to buy a serious birthday card for my sister that spoke of fun times, love, and closeness, I sometimes chuckled out loud as I would say to myself in a soft voice, "Yeah, right." Then I would find a funny card to just make her laugh. Oh, how I wished I had a family that loved me, but I knew Mother and Karen didn't love me or even like me as a person. Nevertheless, I longed for the love and closeness these cards conveyed.

82

The Seed of Satan Invades My Home

I NEEDED NEW tires so I took my car to Taylor Tire on Morris St. As I stood there waiting, a man from the Church Assembly was waiting also. I recognized him to be Raymond Edwin, the grandson of a woman who was friends with my mother from the Indiana feeder church. He began telling me how he would love to see my sister and her family. Unbeknownst to me, he had apparently also been friends with my sister's husband, Lance. After a lot of chatter, he asked if I could possibly show him where my sister lived. My driving was very limited, but my willingness to help was always extensive. Karen only lived about three miles from my home, so Raymond followed me to where I lived and then got into my car. I wasn't afraid at all because he was from the church. I drove him to my sister's, and afterward he went his way and I went mine.

Early the next morning I opened my front door to discover a large gift bag with lots of flowers. The card was thanking me for driving him to my sister's home. I didn't like him leaving me flowers, regardless of his reason. The following day he showed up at my door and told me he had a little free time and offered to fix my closet door. In our conversation when I drove him to my sister's, I had mentioned I was trying to fix my closet door. During his extensive chatter, he told me that the ministers at church had physically punched him, and he had even crawled underneath the pews to try to get away from them.

He told me one horrible story after another, and I had no reason to doubt what he said considering my history with the church. He said because of the rebuking at church he wasn't going back to the Church Assembly, so his wife told him he had to leave their home. He had nowhere to stay and asked if he could sleep on my sofa until the next day. I told him he should call a friend instead, but he said all his friends where members of the Church Assembly. I told him it wouldn't look appropriate, especially since he was married. He said he and his wife were legally divorced and had never remarried, only continued to live together. He had a ready answer for everything I would say.

With his continued pressure, I told him he could stay the night. I didn't want him staying; I didn't want to be around people at all, much less a man. He ended up staying two nights, and my anxiety had already kicked in, wondering how I could get him out of my home. I decided to call his wife and tell her without Raymond knowing it. I called Sister Moreen Stratton's home, and without giving my reason, I asked for his wife Melba's phone number. I was told they did not have the number. I was so nervous and panicky having him there. I got up in the middle of the night to go to the restroom, and the next morning he said he saw me in the hallway in my nightshirt and told me how good I looked. I felt that old sick feeling, rise up inside of me, and I just wanted him to leave.

Each day I encouraged him to go back home, and each day he kept bringing me cards and telling me how he had been in love with me ever since he first met me in Indiana at his grandmother's home. He told me he wanted to marry me, but the only thing that kept running through my mind was how to get him out of my home. He had already talked against the church people in such horrible ways, so if I made him angry, what would he say about me to them? More importantly, what disparaging things would he say about me to Chaney?

I was so afraid of saying no or anything that would make any person mad or upset with me. I don't know "why" I couldn't just say, "Get the hell out of my house!" I felt it and I thought it but to open my mouth and say the words out loud, to say "anything" that would make someone angry with me terrified me. Furthermore, staying silent only tore down my own self-esteem even further. I was such a "people-pleaser" and so afraid, always afraid. I always talked myself into agreeing with the other person since I didn't have the courage to be confrontational. My irrational thinking was I could marry him temporarily and get a divorce shortly thereafter. That way I wouldn't look bad in the minds of the church people for allowing him to stay in my home. While carrying all my sick, fearful, and emotional damage right along with me, he took me to the justice of the peace. I wasn't in love; I wasn't even in like. I wasn't even attracted to him whatsoever, not even a little. As always, fear was the officiator of this train wreck, and Raymond was the bully in the conductor's seat.

Before he came along, I had prayed and asked God to take all the desire for a man from me. I even stopped taking the hormone shots the doctor's give women that's had hysterectomies because one of the things it does is increase a woman's sex drive and that's the last thing I wanted. I didn't trust men at all and I certainly didn't want to feel any need or passion for the most deceitful thing that had ever walked across my path. So, when Raymond pushed his way into my home and my life, I had nothing for him, I was empty inside. Instead, like so many times before, I found myself in a situation I didn't know how to get out of.

After two rapes and being married before, I had learned how to disconnect my body and go to a place of peace in my mind when it came to sex. I had a deep mistrust and hatred for men anyway, so I felt nothing, only contempt for his breed. I know there are small men, but I think Raymond was deformed because I had never seen a man small to this extreme, especially with the rest of his body being so big. I kept wondering how a man like that could ever get a woman pregnant. No wonder he drove such a big truck!

One day he picked up my manuscript off my desk, opened up a page, and read where I had been raped. He looked at me and laughed as he said, "Did you like it?" This man carried the title of church deacon, and this was how his mind operated? This man was so depraved and sadistic; surely Satan must have given birth to Raymond himself. I truly believe the only way a man could even grasp how a woman feels when she's raped is if he is a heterosexual male and he's raped by another man. Then and only then do I believe a man can understand how a woman feels when she's been raped!!

Right away he brought his filthy movies into my home and insisted I watch them with him, and I was well trained to do what I was told. I would tell the church members I loved him when they would ask, but that was all connected to my fear of what the church folks would think. His wife seemed to be a nice woman and was one of many ladies that were randomly chosen to be Homecoming Queens for The Church Assembly. Nevertheless, he told me about going with his wife to places where people performed sex on stage, and that was a world I knew nothing about. It did, however, give me insight into the lengths Melba had went to in order to please him. I learned long ago that many people wear mask of one sort or the other especially at church.

I discovered he had molested a girl of thirteen in the church. He was perverted and proud. There were many stories of rape and sexual perversion that happened within the Church Assembly. One friend told me her young daughter was raped by one of the deacons, but the ministers told her to remain silent because it would look bad for the church. My daughter came to visit me, and Raymond made a sexual pass at her when I walked out of the room. Because of my mental illness, I couldn't scream and curse at him like a normal woman. Nevertheless, the underlying pressure I was feeling inside came dangerously close to blowing his head off his sadistic shoulders. As with so many times before, God had held me close and stayed my hand.

Raymond's ex-wife came to my home to talk, and I knew she wanted him to come back to her. I told her it was all my fault, and he was innocent of any wrongdoing. I didn't want her to hurt each day she had to look at his sorry face for the rest of her life. Nevertheless, it was not uncommon for me to immediately take the blame in any given situation in my life. We were married and divorced within three months. The blame I carried on my shoulders was the fact that I was too afraid to stand up for myself or my daughter. I know it hurt her (and me) when I remained silent, but she doesn't know how close I came to getting retribution. Only God was powerful enough to calm the rage within my soul.

83

When Churches Abuse

I HAD NEVER seen nor heard of the passion play, but the radio announcer said there was going to be one at Tyler Baptist Church in Chatsworth, Georgia. This was the church Karen and her children attended. Unfortunately, I couldn't drive myself that far from home because of my agoraphobia. It was ten miles away and at the last minute I called Doug, whom I used to work with. He was a good Christian man and said he would be glad to drive me there. During the entire ride to Chatsworth, I kept thinking, "I have jeans on, and they might try to throw me out of the church." Still, I told myself I would sit in the back of the church by the door, and I could run if the churchmen started toward me. My past experience with the Church Assembly reminded me that I might very well be physically attacked if I walked into the house of God wearing a pair of blue jeans. Yet, something inside of me was drawing me, pulling me to go see this passion play about Jesus Christ.

The life and crucifixion of Christ was so lovingly portrayed, and the people were so nice that it made me want to return. I did visit the church again the very next week and when I returned home, I wrote this song:

This Family Is for Me

I heard the plan of my salvation, as I stepped within the door;
all the burdens that had grieved my mind were not heavy anymore.
Through this family I can feel the love of God is oh, so real; in this
church of faith, I'll do His will. This family is for me.
(Chorus)
This family is for me.
The spirit here is pure as gold, a pleasant rest for my weary soul.
This family is for me.
A far cry from a life in doubt, that the flame within had faded out,
but your love has made the spark and saved me from the dark.
This family is for me.
I watched a hope give life new meaning as her tears fell on the floor.
When she knelt down at the altar, where so many prayed before,
I heard her cry, "I've been set free, through the blood that stained
Mount Calvary," only to realize that child was me.
This family is for me

Written and composed by Yvette Lidy

My life was so limited because of my agoraphobia, but I knew if I could do it once, I could do it again. Each time I went somewhere that I hadn't been before, the first time was always the hardest, and each time afterward would gradually get easier.

My psychiatrist had told me no matter how hard it was to keep moving forward. Dr. Green said when you drive somewhere, don't turn around and flee because it will get easier if you don't run back home. After being driven to Tyler Baptist Church many times, I finally struck out on my own to make the ten-mile drive for the Sunday morning service. I was praying all the way and believing God would be with me since I was going for His honor and glory. When I would get to the service, there was a little time period when everyone went around shaking hands and hugging each other, and that's when I began to feel like I would smother. I would quickly head to the bathroom as fast as I could and stay there until that part of the service was over.

Crowds made me extremely nervous, so interaction with lots of people was impossible, not because I didn't want to participate but because I was terrified! As time progressed, I didn't feel so panicky at some services, so I would put on a big smile and start shaking people's hands. By the time I returned to my seat, the back of my head would hurt so badly that it felt like it would explode off my shoulders.

I loved to sing so I began singing with the choir, and the pastor's favorite song was "I've Got a Feeling" on which I sang the lead. Choir practice was on Wednesday night, but as I drove to Chatsworth, I didn't take into consideration that it would be dark when it was time to drive home.

As I sat there at church during practice, glancing out the window, I realized the sun was going down, and the tension within me began to mount. All the terrible possibilities of what could happen to a woman driving home alone at night if her car should break down began racing through my mind, and this was before everyone had cell phones. I felt the dreaded panic pour over me like ice-cold dripping fear, and I quickly jumped up from my seat and headed toward the door. Without the embarrassment of explaining anything to anyone, I quickly drove toward my home. I was begging God all the way to please not let it get dark before I could get to my safe place, and I knew I could never go back to choir practice if it meant driving home in the dark.

Karen and Stacy were close friends of Pastor Victor Gray and his wife, Stella. Karen wrote a check to the church regularly in addition to giving dinner parties for Pastor Vic and Stella and lavishing gifts and birthday presents on them. They also went to the same places on vacations. When the church offerings were collected, the pastor would have the congregation hold their check or money up in the air for all to see. The pastor knew who was giving and who was not, so it's understandable why Pastor Vic and Stella were very interested in pleasing my sister.

My niece Stacy had a friend named Chrissie, and one Sunday morning as Pastor Vic was preaching, he said, "There are people here who don't like each other, and I want you to go to them right now, right now, right now!" As I stood there at my seat in the second row facing the altar, Chrissie Bryson walked up in front of everyone and, in a condescending tone, told me she didn't like me. She didn't even know me outside of what Stacey and Karen had said to her. Furthermore, she had never even tried to have a conversation with me. We were complete strangers outside of attending the same church.

It was so embarrassing having everyone stare at me. For a long time afterward, I felt such anger inside over how she humiliated me in front of the church people. Nevertheless, I was raised to believe that no matter how unkind a person is to you, to be unforgiving is not an option. As the months progressed, I finally got up the nerve to go to Chrissie after church and ask her to forgive me for harboring resentment toward her for how she talked to me that Sunday morning. She was hateful as she crossed her arms, shrugged her body, and snapped at me like a bulldog.

As I stepped into the aisle heading to the door to go home, Karen was walking out too. I looked at her and asked, "Did you hear how ugly Chrissie talked to me?" Karen replied in a cold and unloving voice, "Well, you must have gone to her in the wrong spirit!"

Like so many times before, I drove home with tears streaming down my face and asking myself *why* I kept going back to church. There was no answer other than God would send me to hell if I didn't.

Each time I attended church, Pastor Vic used his platform as a weapon to attack me, reminding me of that same God of fear who sat on the throne with the big stick in His hand just waiting for me to do something wrong so He could hit me over the head with it. I had been taught about Him all my life and now He had returned with a vengeance to punish me once more.

Where is the Big Stick?

Last night I dreamed of heaven, a place I've never been.
St. Peter opened up the gate and bade me to come in.
I moved in trepidation; I dared not say a word,
For misery awaited me from all that I had heard.

Then suddenly I saw Him, He softly called my name,
He said my child I love you and I'm so glad you came.
Yet, fear welled up inside me, to turn and run away.
But where is the big stick, is all that I could say.

Where is the "big stick"? I know you've got it here.
Where is the big stick that's caused me to live in fear?
I know you want to hurt me just like the preachers did.
They beat me with the big stick when I was just a kid.

He reached and held my trembling hands, my eyes still wet with
tears.
His peace I felt throughout my soul replaced a life of fear.
All it took was just His touch that healed my scares beneath,
I fell before the Kings of Kings and kissed his nail scared feet

So now my cross I'll carry as I think of Calvary
And that blood-stained big stick he hung on just for me.
I've put my trust in Jesus as down this road I trod
Till one day I will find myself safe in the arms of God.

Written and composed by Yvette Lidy

I sang the lead in Pastor Vic's favorite gospel song, "I've Got a Feeling." The problem was when the choir went to different churches to sing, most often I had to stay behind because my panic attacks and agoraphobia were so debilitating. Pastor Vic had no tolerance for my situation; instead, he just saw me as not being committed. I didn't want to go to church there anymore. Just like at the Church Assembly, I saw Pastor Vic as a man speaking for God, so if he wasn't pleased with me, God wasn't either. Each Sunday I would drive to church to be emotionally kicked in the face by this preacher. He made me feel like his God hated me and was going to send me to hell where I belonged. He even told me he believed I had a demonic spirit and continued to use his platform to rip me to shreds. Each time I went to church hoping today would be different, yet once again, I would cry all the way home.

It was a fight to try to save my sanity by positive self-talk, but I made it three weekends in a row without attending church. In the three weeks I stayed away from church, my nerves began to calm down as I talked to the God of Love who loved me back. I told Him I would go to church and sing in the choir just for Him and not let anything that had been done to me bother me. As I drove toward Chatsworth, I felt a smile come across my lips. It felt as though God was putting His arms around me, letting me know I wasn't alone and that He loved me.

Jesus said, "Come unto me…and I will give you rest."
Matthew 11:28 (KJV)

When I stepped down off the platform from the choir loft and found my place in the second-row pew, Pastor Vic looked at me and shouted, "YOU HAVEN'T BEEN HERE IN THREE WEEKENDS IN A ROW, AND THEN YOU COME D-R-A-G-G-I-N-G UP HERE TO THIS CHOIR! YOU'RE NOT COMMITTED TO THIS CHURCH!! WHY DON'T YOU L-E-A-V-E- H-E-R-E ? YOU'RE JUST TAKING UP SPACE ON A PEW!!"

I had called his office weeks before to arrange a conference with him and try to explain the problems I was having driving to church for choir practice, but he never took my call.

He went on to say, "IF YOU WANT TO TALK TO SOMEBODY, DON'T CALL ME, TALK TO GOD! And if you leave the church, all I have to say about that is"—and with his hands tucked in his pants pockets, he kind of danced/skipped across the rostrum and began to sing the Roy Rogers song: Happy trails to you, until we meet again..."

It was a long process, but after about seven years of abuse I finally walked away with no desire to go to church anywhere anymore.

I was happy being alone because no one could hurt me. I watched Trinity Broadcasting Network (TBN) with Matt and Laurie Crouch, plus my other favorite programs, such as Joyce Meyer, Charles Stanley, Jentezen Franklin, T. D. Jakes, Joel Osteen, and Michael Youssef, and other ministers who helped me so much. I would entertain myself with singing, writing poetry, or watching old black-and-white movies.

84

Love Shined in My Mother's Eyes

IN AUGUST 1999, Mother was gradually becoming very sick and always complaining she was freezing to death. It seemed she just couldn't get warm no matter how many quilts I put over her. I made her an appointment with my doctor's office, so she went to see Dr. Coker. She explained to him that she had been on thyroid medication for many years, but her doctor had moved to Florida and she had been going without it. She knew she needed the thyroid medication, but Dr. Coker assured her she didn't, and he refused to give her the prescription.

I will always remember Dr. Coker with sadness as the doctor who refused my mother the life-saving thyroid medication she had taken for many years. Most of my family, including me, take thyroid medication. I didn't know much about thyroid problems when Mother was sick; otherwise, I would have taken her to a different doctor. Unfortunately, for the next three years, Mother became progressively worse.

Mother and I had never been close until the last two months before she died. She had a new doctor now, and he put her on the antidepressant called Prozac. He also gave her the thyroid medication she so desperately needed, but it was too late to reverse the damage that had been done to her organs.

One night, as she lay in her hospital bed, she finally allowed me to talk about and ask her why she had treated me like she hated me. For years she would say I was lying and it didn't happen, it was all in my mind, or change the subject. This night she finally allowed me to express my feelings and all the hurt from what she had done to me, and she didn't deny any of it. She simply asked me to forgive her, but it meant the world to me that she acknowledged what she had done. She even let me sing a song to her I had written about little Timmy Sanders, who had died from the snake bites in Arizona many years ago. She said it was beautiful.

When she heard the words of the song, she said she didn't realize his death and what happened to him had affected me so deeply. For years I had told myself that once she was dead, she couldn't hurt me anymore. Now she was so different since she was taking antidepressants. She finally looked at me with love in her eyes, the look I had waited for all of my life.

I brought her back home from the hospital for about two weeks, and she slept in the room next to mine. One night, as I was leaving her room, I said, "I love you," and she said, "I love you too," Then she softly whispered,

"I just didn't know how much until now."

I fed and bathed her until the very end, and three days before she died, she was admitted to the hospital once more. I had even taken the bed she slept in off the frame so it would be easier to care for her. It's hard for me to write these words without tears starting to fall because what I shared with her those last days was priceless.

I made a long, blue plaid, flannel gown that Mother just loved, and I would rewash it every time I bathed her so she could wear it every other day. I felt so happy that she liked something I had made with my hands, and she looked so pretty when she looked up at me with that big smile on her face. I had just given her a bath, put on her blue flannel gown and was attempting to sprinkle baby powder in the top of her gown as she sat on the edge of her mattress. We were telling each other we loved each other, and then we both got tickled and began to laugh because it was so strange for us to be saying loving things to each other. We laughed so hard as I knelt in front of her with my arms hugging her waist, and she was hugging the top of my head. I finally knew what it was like to feel my mother's love and see the gentleness in her eyes when she looked at me. I could tell she too had discovered a love for me that she had never felt before.

Karen may have stolen Mother's love for all those years, but God had given me the best during the last days of Mother's life. I wouldn't have traded it for the world. I say "stolen" because Karen had done everything, she could to discredit me in my mother's eyes, but she couldn't do it anymore. God had given me complete healing from everything that Mother had ever done to hurt me. I was able to not only forgive her, but I also was able to forgive myself for every angry word I had ever spoken to her out of my own pain. And now, here I was sitting at the foot of Mother's hospital bed, watching her struggle to breathe, with Aunt Sheila on my left and my brother Josh on my right.

Suddenly, Mother's breathing was no longer labored. As I walked up close to her, she took about four short, quiet breaths and then stepped into eternity, into the waiting arms of Jesus, never to suffer anymore. She arrived in heaven on a Wednesday night, October 29, 2003.

As they covered my mother's face with the sheet and began pushing her bed down the hospital hallway, it was so very quiet. The light of my mother's spirit had returned to the God of creation, leaving only a feeling of absence, as the earth seemingly stood still out of respect for the transition. I walked behind her bed and thanked God that I had stayed with her until the very end.

IN LOVING MEMORY OF OUR SWEET MOTHER
VIRGINIA CAROLYN COOPER
born: Sept. 3, 1932. died: October 29, 2003

We came for you today, to show the love burns bright
Sweet memories of long ago, still clinging to so tight
I wonder if you see us, can you hear our words of love
Do you know how much we miss you, can you see us from above

You sought the Lord, he heard you cry, he delivered you from your fears
There must be a heavenly fountain, that's filled with Carolyn's tears
But joy comes in the morning, as you dance down golden streets
And a smile that knows no sorrow, will replace your tear-stained
cheeks

You walked your path with Honor, in this life you suffered so
God knew what he was doing, when He said it's time to go
But soon will come the morning, when you hear the Trumpet sound
And death will lose its power, when our God will shake this ground

The birds will sing each morning, the sun will warm the sod
I'll plant you, yellow roses, while I wait to hear from God
This place is for your honor, sleep well beneath the tree
For when your eyes will open, I'll be beside of thee

Written and composed by: Yvette Lidy

85

Hatred Wears a Smile

I WENT TO Peeples Funeral Home to fix Mother's hair with the waves on the top front as she liked it. She looked beautiful with her still dark hair and a streak of peppered gray down the side. My mother was not only beautiful but she was an elegant lady too. I had picked out a green casket and ordered a lovely Fall Floral arrangement to blanket the top, created by Marty Akins of Bobbie's Florist. Pastor Vic said it was the most beautiful casket he had ever seen.

We laid Mother to rest on a Saturday, and now it was Sunday. I had stayed with Mother until the very end and was now ready for the "Ladies of Faith" Christian retreat in Pigeon Forge, Tennessee. Since I still had agoraphobia, I know it was psychological, but I felt safest with my sister. So, I had asked Karen if I could ride up there with her, and she said I could. However, the day before we were to leave, I called her to see what time I should be ready to go. She hadn't even called to let me know that she had already left without me. She said she had decided to leave a day early and take some decorations up to the resort, and there wouldn't be any room for me anyway. By not calling me, I'm sure she knew she would knock me out of going with someone else. I had also asked her if we could room together on other retreats, and she would say yes. At the last minute she would give me some excuse as to why I had to find someone else to room with. Sometimes I would end up staying behind at home alone and cry.

Time after time Karen was so unkind to me. The first time I went to the Christian retreat I was terrified to be away from home, but my psychiatrist encouraged me to go. Dr. Green said no matter how bad the panic attacks get, just keep going if you want to get better. "You must face your fears."

It was dark shortly after we arrived at the mountain resort, and I felt the fear began to surge through my body. Karen had disappeared, so I stood out on the balcony trembling as I called out her name. I was unaware that most of the church ladies brought special snacks and food to eat the first night. They had gathered together on a lower-level balcony.

Later, some of the church ladies told me Karen heard me. When I called out to her, my voice trembled with fear, and she laughed as she told the church ladies I sounded like a scared rabbit. I roomed with another church lady since Karen didn't want me with her, but with God's help, I got to go to the retreat that time.

When I sang at church, there were times she would get up from her seat and walk out of the sanctuary. She would go to the nursery because she hated me so much she didn't want to sit through my singing. If there were dinners at church, she would always avoid me and never invite me to sit at her table. It was always another church lady who invited me to go and never Karen. I was never a part of the inner circle so most often I never knew the ladies were having "Tea Parties" or other special dinners unless my friend Betty told me. At home I would sit and write my feelings in poems of what was happening in my life. This poem was one of those times:

My Empty Plate

Christmas is coming with hearts all aglow
But not only the weather is feeling so cold,
I chose to take part with the ladies at Faith,
So, I drove to the church with the pie that I baked

The food all looked tasty as I sat down my dish
Yet, escaping in silence is all that I wished
My sister just sits there and I feel I can't breathe
I love her so deeply but she has none for me

If servings of love were on these plates that I see
My plate would be empty cause she has none for me
Her coldness is breaking my heart and my soul
She's patiently waiting till I finally go.

Written and Experienced by: Yvette Lidy 1997

I ran into her daughter, Pamela, at the Red Food grocery store one day and asked her why she wouldn't speak to me at church. She said it was because her mother/Karen made her feel like she was betraying her if she was friendly toward me. Since we were born on the same day, for several years I would take her a dozen red roses to her job but would never be given a gift in return. Once when I took her a beautiful Sunflower arrangement to the hospital, she told my mother, I'd get Yvette some flowers too but she might think I just bought her flowers because she did me. So, she got me nothing which made no sense to me.

I painted Karen's bedroom and bathroom and cleaned it. She sent me home, and then invited her friends over. I went to the movies with the church folks from Tyler Baptist. I sat on the opposite end of the row with my heart aching. My sister would sit on the other end with her church friends, eating candy and laughing as though I wasn't even there. It was amazing how her influence caused other church people to treat me coldly, without even trying to get to know me. She invited people to go to the Apple Festival in Elijay after Sunday church service and my heart ached as she and her friends walked passed me without inviting me to go along.

I tried to earn, buy, and work for Karen's love. Still her hatred for me was so intense it seemed like even the sound of my voice angered her.

Dedicated to My Sister

So many years were stolen from love I gave for free
To a heart that was wretched and hidden from me.
My sister, my precious, my love went so deep.
My spirit was hated, stomped under your feet.
Your children, they loved me, but you changed that too.
They'd turn their face from me before you were through.

Dear Bradley, sweet Bradley, his smile turned to stares.
A love once burned brightly, no longer is there.
He said that he loved me and made his own choice,
But something has changed him and silenced his voice.
Two daughters, two angels, who both praise the Lord,
But if you look deeper, you'll find so much more.

Stacy and Carlie oh, it's such a shame
To know that your poison now runs through their veins.
You've taught them to hate me, to loathe and despise,
But one day you'll answer for all of your lies.
At church you amaze me, pretend all of the while.
You think they don't know what is hidden under that smile.

Wouldn't it be tragic if you'd been at Calvary,
And you looked up at Jesus, and He looked just like me?
Would you still feel hatred or would love take its place?
Be careful, my sister, He might be wearing my face.

Written and composed by Yvette Lidy, 1997

A few years before Mother died, we were all sitting at Fuddruckers restaurant. My brother Jacob said he wouldn't be going to Hilton Head that year to the house on the beach he'd had access to for many years. However, he wanted Mother to get to go. Karen immediately said she would take her. I wanted to go so badly and felt like I was well enough emotionally to make the trip since Mother and Karen would be there.

Karen told me there wouldn't be room for me. I said I could sleep on the sofa, and she angrily said some of her friends were going and they would need the sofa. I said I would be willing to sleep on the floor to go to the beach with Mother. She looked at me with such hatred and shouted, "No, you're not going!" When Karen, her daughters, and their friends, along with Mother returned, I saw pictures of my mother in the pool with a big hat on and everyone laughing and having fun. I cried many tears over not getting to go with my mother that no one heard, no one but God. That was mother's last vacation before she died. Every year Karen went to see the NutCracker and I would tell her I would love to go too but she would always leave me behind. Finally, I ask if I could go the next year when she went to see it in Atlanta. She said I could but when it came time to go she took Stacy, Chrissie and the pastor's wife, Stella and left without me. That was the last time I would ever ask Karen if I could go along. I could have underdstood Karen's hatred for me if I had slept with her husband, beat her children or stolen from her. Nevertheless, there was nothing at all to warrant her hatred towards me. Yes, I was smaller and built differently but that wasn't my fault any more than it was her's. She had a different father than I did so her gene's were different. I loved her so much and I was always so good to her.

I could have never imagined having a sister as cruel to me as Karen and to have loved her as much as I did. Sadly, this is only a very small glimpse into a lifetime of tears I shed from the unkindness of my sister. For years, I tried so hard to figure out why but I couldn't until one day I found the answer in my Bible. **Solomon 8:6 Set me as a seal**

upon your heart, As, a seal upon your arm; For love is as strong as death, Jealousy as cruel as the grave; Its flames are flames of fire, A most vehement flame.

When Mother died, Karen completely shut me out of her life because she didn't feel a need to pretend anymore. I sent her a lovely Susan Bristol red cape, beautifully wrapped, for Christmas that I had let Mother wear and mother had told me Karen loved it. She kept the cape but never sent any acknowledgment to me, no response at all.

I wrote Karen a letter asking her to forgive me if I had ever said or done anything to hurt her, even though I knew in my heart I had always been good to her. I kept trying to have a relationship with her, thinking I could somehow fix whatever kept her from treating me like I was family too.

I took the letter to Karen's office at Hamilton Medical and stood in front of her while she used the copy machine, As the tears streamed down my cheeks, I asked her why she couldn't love me and that if I had ever done anything to offend her, to please forgive me.

As soon as I left her cold and silent frown, she called her three daughters and said I verbally attacked her at her job. She lied without shame. Time passed, and Karen's daughter Carlie eventually admitted to me that she and her sisters discussed and determined that Pamela should be the one to confront me for attacking their mother, since she was the oldest. Months after my visit to Karen's office, she admitted to me that she simply threw the letter in the trash with no curiosity to even open it. That spoke such volumes of the depth of her hatred toward me.

On mine and Karen's birthday, her children gave her an elaborate "50s theme" birthday party. I got my sewing machine out and made four poodle skirts for my girls with matching blouses. I also bought pointy pink glasses, pink bows for their hair, and bobby socks for my daughter, two granddaughters, and daughter-in-law. For the guys, I made four Elvis T-shirts with sparkling guitars on them for the party given for a sister who hated me. I stood at my doorway and waved goodbye to my kids and grandkids as they all started for the party to celebrate my sister's birthday. If she had loved me as I did her, we would have celebrated together since we were born on the same day.

Everyone was in the family picture, even my grandchildren and two brothers, everyone but me. As the years moved on, I was always reminded of that heartbreaking event by continually seeing that same huge family photo on Facebook and even at Ken Elders's funeral, where it was placed out for everyone to see.

To the world Karen was so sweet and easy to love, yet there was such hatred in her heart toward me that she was really good at concealing in front of others. For most of my life I loved her so much that I believed there was something unlovable about me that she could see and I could not. It surely could not be Karen, not Karen with the gentle voice and sweet, quiet demeanor everyone loved.

It took many years, but eventually I realized the problem dwelled somewhere inside of her, and just like Mother, there was nothing I could ever say or do to make her love me in return; only God could fix this. When it came to loyalty in my family, it was nonexistent, and Karen's rejection of me was so commonplace that no one challenged her.

On Easter in 2010, my children and grandchildren attended her family Easter party. As I looked at pictures on Facebook of my two-year-old granddaughter and three-year-old grandson picking up Easter eggs in the yard, my heart shattered into pieces. I cried out loud in the silence of my apartment because I wasn't welcome to share in the fun with my own grandchildren. I remember crying myself to sleep that night. The memory of my grandbaby Madison picking up and staring at that Easter egg as the picture was taken is forever burned in my memory.

I didn't want to stand in the way of my children having a relationship with their cousins, so I remained silent and in the shadows over the years. However, I felt it was a slap in the face from my sister because

Madison was *my* family, *my* granddaughter. Before Facebook, I never had a window into all the events I was excluded from, so the pictures that were posted there were like a knife to my heart. I could have never had a sister who treated me more unlovingly than Karen.

86

Finding God's Beauty in an Unkind World

I WAS NOW medically referred to as a functioning agoraphobic. When I went somewhere in the car, I would always take the same streets and never a different one; otherwise, I would panic. I could come and go short distances alone and do what was necessary to take care of myself in regard to grocery shopping, etc. On the outside I appeared normal, and most people didn't know I hadn't driven alone but ten miles from home in the last nineteen years.

Most of my time was spent upstairs in my apartment. Through the nightmare of my existence, I found beauty in so many things that many people either ignore or simply take for granted. There's nothing that will bring you to a closer relationship with God than living a life of having no one but Him to depend on. To have such fear that dictates every move you make in life is hard to even articulate.

I was afraid of people and would agree with whatever they said just to keep from having a confrontation. I was quick to take the blame to either keep the peace or make the other person feel better. Growing up with Mother and confessing to things I wasn't guilty of—and then having to confess at the Church Assembly for things I wasn't guilty of—taught me at a young age to be a people pleaser and reinforced my own inferior existence.

It's truly a humbling existence when you're powerless to fix yourself, but it's in that valley you realize there's *no one but God* who can bring you through. That's when I believe you develop a heart of gratefulness and understanding for even the least of things, whether it's the grass you walk on or the drunkard sleeping under the bridge. You don't judge; you just quickly ask yourself, "What can I do to help?" Although it doesn't rhyme, I want to share something I wrote to express where I was in my gratitude toward God:

God's Gift's to Me

Yesterday I walked up the beautiful green hillside that I so often gaze
at from my upstairs apartment window.
I felt the need to be close to the trees, the bark, and the vines
crawling up through the forest.
How can I help you to see the dark-green leaves blowing quickly
in the wind as though they were waving to me, welcoming my
presence?
How can I help you smell the scent of freshly mowed grass and
honeysuckle hanging on their vines?
Blackberry bushes were everywhere with a promise of a pie.
Little red wild strawberries nestled quietly at my feet.
I stood silent for a moment looking all around me,
trying to absorb all of the beauty that was so close, I could reach out
and touch it.
I began to walk on this beautiful hillside and
with each thing spotted by these eyes God has blessed me with, I said,
"Thank you, God, for this grass.
Thank you, God, for these trees.
Thank you for these honeysuckles and this wonderful woodpecker
that has chosen to make his home so close to mine."

Suddenly, dark clouds gathered in the sky,
only enhancing the beauty around me. The now shaded trees began
to dance for me.
The floral scent of the forest grew stronger with the blowing of the
wind.
I noticed at least five trees that were now bent to the ground
as though they were bowing to me, and I felt so unworthy.
I took a pair of scissors and began clipping daisies to keep for my
own.
As I did this, a voice within me became loud and said,
"I believe if God was choosing one thing about me that He loved the
most, it would be
my love and appreciation for the beauty He created in the flowers,
trees, vines, etc.
As I thought these thoughts, I began to cry, and my heart was full.

Written, composed, and experienced by Crusonda Yvette Lidy, May 1997

87

The Scene of the Crime

IT WAS 2008, and after all these years, I stood on the steps of the Church Assembly. As I reached to turn the knob of the front door, the voice in my head asked, "*Why* are you here?"

It was the ministers meeting with standing room only, as the minister asked Al Gantry to stand to his feet. Everyone began clapping until it turned into a standing ovation, and someone informed me that he had been in the hospital. As everyone was smiling, I felt tears quietly run down the sides of my face as I thought to myself, "Wow, how good would it feel to be loved like that," and my heart ached within me to know the answer.

My life was so lonely that I continued to go to the Church Assembly. I knew in my heart if I didn't come to terms with the pain from my past and forgive the abusers, I would never completely heal emotionally and make it to heaven. I had heard a Christian song at Tyler Baptist Church called "I Went to the Enemy's Camp and I Took Back What He Stole from Me," so here I was again at the scene of the crime.

Everyone was so nice to me, and yes, as I had heard for several years, the church had changed for the better in many ways that were easily noticeable. Most all of the women had cut their hair and wore makeup and pants, so outwardly they looked like anyone you would see in most any church. Through the invitation of others, I begin to sing in the choir and loved it, especially with my desire to feel I belonged.

One night after choir practice, I was sitting in my car with two other girls singing a song we all liked, when the choir director, Dade Barber, walked past my car. Melody Gage shouted to him to come and hear me sing. At the next choir practice, Dade wanted me to perform the song I had sung in the car for the church homecoming service, which was August 8th. The next day I went to the Christian music store and requested the music only to discover it couldn't be bought.

I informed Dade at the next practice that even though I couldn't buy the music, I would find someone to make a recording for me. He said he knew someone who could do it, and I said great because there were other songs, I wanted the music to also. In a stern voice he said, "For a price!" and I said, "I know. I was intending to pay for it."

On the following Wednesday night, Dade brought his son Jake, who lived in Carterville, Georgia, to the church service. As Dade introduced him to me, I assumed Jake was also a member of the church. Jake said he could give me a much better price if I bought his package deal for $1,500 for five songs, and I agreed. He said he would first bring me the sample tracks for approval and then the final product.

I had such overwhelming trust in the church and Dade Barber, who was also assistant pastor, because I believed above all else that they represented integrity. I didn't think for a moment I would be scammed. Jake brought me the sample tracks, which were not only scratched but they also weren't the quality he had promised. I paid Jake the entire $1,500 after receiving the sample tracks, but not the final product, because he kept talking about how he was struggling and desperately needed the money, and so did his father.

The months continued to go by with Jake not returning my calls or answering when I called him, and I didn't want to take him to court since it involved the church. The entire point of the track was so I could sing the solo at the August church homecoming, yet Dade never even mentioned me singing again once they took my money. It was all for nothing. I stopped going to choir because I was so hurt by the way I had been treated.

The following spring of 2009, the ministers meeting was to include a very special singing event. The Church Assembly choir members from several states were participating. My brother Jacob, who wasn't a member at the time, told me he wanted to come to the Church Assembly with me. My aunt Sheila said she also wanted to come because she had friends coming from Kentucky whom she hadn't seen since she was a young girl. Sheila had suffered such abuse at the Church Assembly in her youth that she carried a lot of wounds and hatred in her heart due to how she had been treated.

Jacob and Sheila both knew I loved to sing, and if they came and I wasn't in the choir, they would have known something was very wrong. I didn't want my family to know how dirty I had been done by the church people I trusted. Because of its bad history, the church was still trying to live down the negative accusations, so I went to choir practice on Tuesday night.

In front of the entire choir, Dade Barber said, "I don't want to make anyone mad, but some people only show up for choir when we have a special event going on, so they can be seen in the spotlight." It was insultingly obvious he was referring to me because he went on to say, "Lisa called and *asked* me if she could come back to choir!" At this point I raised my hand and said in a dispirited tone, "I wasn't aware that I had to call. I just assumed I was welcome to be here." He immediately started to backtrack, and everyone could hear as he said, "And you're absolutely right, Sister Yvette."

After waiting a year, I finally went to see an attorney to file suit against Jake Barber. I paid $2,500 for the attorney plus fees. I paid the high price not so much because of the $1,500 that he scammed from me, but because I was so tired of people walking all over me and getting away with it. My former attorney had died, so I hired a very young Simon Sellers in Dalton, Georgia, to represent me. After taking my money, he put me off for almost two years because he had bigger and more important cases than mine. When we finally went to court, my case was thrown out because the judge said too much time had elapsed.

It's hard to swallow when you finally attempt to protect your rights only to lose in the end, but that's been my life experience. I ended up without even the sample tracks because I had returned them to Jake by way of his father months earlier. With the money Jake took from me, court costs, and my attorney's fees, I ended up paying almost $4,500 just to sing in the church choir. Always when I was angry or upset I would write that person a letter to try to resolve the conflict. This was because of my inability to be confrontational. So, I did write a letter to Pastor Troy Carnes, since Dade Barber was the assistant pastor, but the pastor never responded. I had been foolish enough to take the assistant pastor's son to court, and even though they were successful in stealing my money, I would now pay the religious price for defending myself.

So often in modern-day ministries, the preachers will use members as props in their sermons in an attempt to help the listener get a visual of the message they are trying to convey. During one service, as Pastor Troy began his message, he called on Rev. Dade Barber to walk up to the rostrum, the very man I had trusted and whose son Jake had taken my money. He said that Dade Barber was going to be representative of Jesus in his sermon.

Sitting there in the front row, I never dreamed this sermon was going to be directed at me. Pastor Troy said several critical things that made it obvious he was talking to me. Then, in a stern yet demanding voice with his hand placed affectionately on Rev. Dade Barber's shoulder, he said, "Jesus (inferring Rev. Barber was Jesus) is only about twelve steps away, and *you* need to come to Jesus!" I was beyond insulted as I sat there determined not to make a scene by getting up and walking out the door. That would really have given him a bullet to shoot me down with. As emotionally damaged as I had become from past years of abuse by the church, I knew I was strong enough now that I would only take so much.

After leaving the church again, four years later at a restaurant, Pastor Troy asked me to forgive him. He said he thought if he ignored the letter, I wrote him and the problem, it would just go away. One of the main repercussions of the church's history is, in my personal belief, because of all the damage that was done to members in the past. The current pastors are unwilling to resolve any issues within the church for fear of making someone mad and causing them to leave the church.

88

The Prodigal Returns Once More

IT MAKES NO sense why a person would want to go to a church where anxiety would bleed through their skin like sweat. Yet, here I was, walking in the side entrance of the sanctuary again, hoping with each step I took that I would be viewed as acceptable and good enough to be loved by these heaven-bound saints.

As I looked around the room, vivid memories returned of the exact spots where I had been grabbed by my head when I was fourteen years old and shaken violently as they told me I was going to hell, and where I had stood terrified when I was seventeen years old and confessed to having a spirit against Julie Stratton. I confessed to a sin I had not committed just to appease my accusers.

Wanda Stratton had already screamed at me in front of the entire church to "clean out my heart." Furthermore, John Stratton Jr. and the church were waiting for me to confess my shame, whatever that was. Mother had told me that she was forced to confess to a sin she wasn't guilty of at the Harlan, Kentucky, church. They made her confess to having a lustful spirit toward a minister at church after my father died, and this man was someone she had no interest in or thoughts about at all. Now history had repeated itself. Oh, the many, many times I buried my tear-stained face in that altar praying to a God I was terrified of, almost as much as the two faces I would see when I attempted to raise my head. I will never understand how the Stratton's justified having their own picture in such a sacred place as the altar in God's sanctuary.

The fear, the horrible fear, penetrated through every part of my trembling body and spirit. The loud shouting of so many people made my skin crawl with fear. It wasn't just that God was going to hurt you; it also was the fear of being grabbed physically by the minister representing God's opinion of me.

When I was seventeen, I had a friend who went to Chattanooga to a party and was killed in a car wreck. They made it sound like God killed her because she wasn't living their version of a righteous life. I had seen so much abuse in the church; much of it I don't even talk about. I was so beaten down by Sister Moreen Stratton's handpicked ministers, whom she used as her own personal weapons. Time and time again they used the sanctuary to try to destroy me. More than once I was told by members and ministers that I wasn't good enough for Chaney Stratton, even though I was a virgin.

Not good enough for them meant I wasn't good enough for God. Yet here I was again, still confused in my mind just *why* I kept coming back to this dreadful place. It was as though I was stuck and didn't know how to move forward and leave the past behind.

In a room full of people, I felt nervous and out of place because life had convinced me I was inferior to everyone else. I had worn the best mask at this party we call life as I smiled once more for the congregation.

They just didn't have a clue about all the broken pieces inside me that were continually cutting at my heart. The only way I could cope with the fact that I wasn't good enough was to dress as nice as anyone in the church, and that way no one would know I felt like I was dirt inside. I was nice to everyone, but I didn't want anyone to get to know me because they would see right through my facade.

I felt as if my youth had been stolen from me like a thief in the darkness as I lay in the silence of my room. The sounds of my groaning through my tears whispered to me that I would die alone. The haunting memories of my past and all the things I wish I had done differently arrived each night to torment my already defeated spirit. I lived alone and was calm when I wasn't around people. But the loneliness felt unbearable, as I sobbed into my pillow until my eyes were swollen.

I had learned years earlier to entertain myself whether it was singing to God, the birds, or me; writing my poetry and songs; or sewing. So, when daylight came, I stayed busy. I would wallpaper or paint my home almost as much as I rearranged my furniture. God was my everything because He loved me deeply and knew me completely. I felt so connected to God and His creations that I saw beauty in things that many people might never pay attention to.

One day I saw a tree with such beautiful flowers that I was inspired to write a poem about it because even though it was a tree, it looked like a bouquet of flowers. Here is the poem:

Love's Bouquet

If I were young and pretty with love for some nice man,
my wedding would be special with these flowers in my hand.
But though I'm growing old now and love left me behind,
I know there's someone waiting a little further down the line.
He can hardly wait to see me, and my love grows more each day
because He will always love me and never go away.
He's done so much already though I've never seen His face,
and the letters that He left me says He's preparing me a place.
When I look into my future as the bride I'll finally be,
I will hold these pretty flowers that my Love has made for me.
Dedicated to my Lord and Savior Jesus Christ, 2011.

Written and composed by Yvette Lidy

89

In Love with Jesus

IT WAS THE spring of 2014, and I was walking along the path at Harlan Godfrey Civitan Park. Oh, how I loved my morning walks there among the trees because this was my favorite place to talk with God. He always seemed so near to me as I began thanking Him for this lovely place to enjoy. I would look up at the beautiful trees swaying in the breeze, and of course, my eyes always made their way up toward heaven because I knew He was there.

There was a stream that flowed alongside my path, and what a wonderful peace I felt in my spirit, just to be there with Him. When life's hopes and dreams have been shattered by the reality of your life, when you've never known what it feels like to marry a man whom you love and who loves you in return, when you never have the love of family that you so desperately long for, and when you've battled a spirit of fear all of your life, *that's* when you sense an overwhelming feeling of love and gratitude toward the only one who does love you, the only one you can pour your heart out to, and the only one you know understands exactly how you feel and why. I was truly walking in the sunlight of God's amazing grace. My heart would love no other; no one could take His place.

God had my trust, my time, my affections, and my commitment to read His word and do what I could to help others here on earth.

If I gave you just one of my reasons, it would be because God had been by my side and pulled me up from the raging storms in my mind that tried to drown me in a sea of tormenting memories, a river of fears. I didn't have to keep the secrets of my life from God because He already knew them, and He loved me anyway. Yes, He knew it all and not once did He ever whisper, "You're not good enough."

God knew the road that was before me even before I was conceived, and He knew what His purpose was for my life even though I still don't. He knew I had to be broken, so He allowed every bad thing that happened to me bring me to the love I feel for Him today. If my life had been easy, I would never have the heart for His children that I know is inside of me. When I think of where I started, what I have survived, and where I am today, how could I not praise Him and love Him with every fiber of my being. He was all I had, but He was all I needed.

90

Love Unexpected

ONE DAY, AS I was walking in the park, a man by the name of Allen Ferguson was walking close by. He said good morning and I reciprocated. I knew who he was, not only from the church but also because his uncle was married to my cousin in Texas. I had seen him there many times over the years, but I usually kept my distance because I wanted to be alone so I could enjoy my time with God. He began talking to me, and it felt nice. I had no personal interest in him or anyone, but I knew he was single, and the thought came to me that he and my aunt Sheila might make an attractive couple.

My uncle Vincent had passed away, and I knew Aunt Sheila was very lonely. After walking with Allen for a few weeks with just basic chitchat, I asked, "How would you feel if I set you up on a date with someone?" He said, "Who, you?" I was startled at his response, which caught me totally off guard. I said, "No! I was talking about my aunt Sheila!" He got quiet as he softly said, "I didn't think so. I've wanted to ask you out for three years but didn't think someone as pretty as you would have anything to do with me."

At this point I was embarrassed, feeling red-faced yet thinking, "Aw, how sweet."

I had never considered dating anyone, especially at age fifty-nine. When we parted that morning, I couldn't seem to forget how good it felt being in his company. He was gentle and soft-spoken, and from the talk that went around church for years, he had gone through a lot in the Vietnam War resulting in post-traumatic stress disorder (PTSD). Then he returned home to a very controlling and unfaithful wife, whom he had now been divorced from for many years. He had gotten remarried to Jolene Parson, and they had a son named Trace Ferguson, but now they were divorced and had been for eight years.

We began walking and talking together every day, and each time we parted, I looked forward to next time I would see Allen again. He seemed harmless, which made me feel very much at ease in his presence. Allen seemed so broken from all he had been through in life, and honestly, I could totally relate to those feelings. I know that's why I liked him so much. He told me the tale of his sad life, and everything he said about both of his ex-wives was negative. I've always looked for the good in people even when it's hard to find, so I'm normally wary of people that can't find something good to say about another person. That should have immediately thrown up red flags for me, but instead I felt terribly sorry for him and what he had suffered. I believed he just needed someone to be good to him, and besides, he truly acted like he adored me.

I loved to cook, so I invited him over for dinner and he accepted. After dinner, we were standing in the dining room when he reached out to me, and I quickly backed away. Finally, after fourteen years of not being held or kissed, I let Allen kiss me, and it ignited something inside of me I thought had died long ago. We were like two teenagers falling in love for the first time. It was crazy wonderful! As the weeks passed and we walked together daily, Allen told me he loved me and that he had never loved any woman as much as he did me. It had been forty-two years since I had felt like this about a man (Chaney Stratton), and I truly believed he was a gift from God.

Allen still lived in the projects where he had cared for his mother and father until they died. His apartment was tiny, and he said he wasn't allowed to lay carpet on the cold cement floors or use nails to hang pictures on the walls because it was a government apartment. The bathroom had black mold on the walls; he said he used bleach to keep it clean because the mold kept returning.

His need was my area of expertise, and I honestly got excited about making his life better. I thrived on helping anyone I could since I had been there myself. I knew what it felt like to live at the poverty level, and it made me so happy to feel like I had made one of God's children happy. Where I lived, there were a few income-based apartments, so I suggested I'd get him an application since it was much nicer there, and he agreed.

Allen told me he wanted to marry me, and I couldn't have been happier. I had never married someone I was in love with. We could have lived in a shack and I still would have wanted him in my life. He said for many years, when he drove to different states to deliver carpet, he would be so sad and lonely that he didn't care if he made it back home. He said he was so happy now to know I was there waiting for him to return. Allen said he would lie in bed at night, look up at the ceiling with tears streaming down his face, and beg God to send him someone he could love. He believed God had finally answered his prayers.

I was so gullible to every kind word he said to me because I was starved for love from someone I could love in return. His sadness had been my own as I recalled all the years of lying in bed at night crying and talking to God, wishing I had someone to love and hold me so I wouldn't be so lonely. Now, just when I thought I would die alone, God sent me Allen. I was so happy with him, yet even then, I knew in my spirit that I was taking time away from God for this new man in my life. I wasn't reading my Bible every night like I always had, and even my thought life was stolen from my God, my first love. Nevertheless, Satan comes in many forms, and how could he not despise the deep love and relationship I had for the one who created heaven and earth.

Allen was going to his son's wedding, but I was understanding when he didn't invite me to go with him. He said his second ex-wife, Jolene, had a violent temper and was prone to make a scene. I took Allen to Chattanooga and bought him over $1,000 in new clothes since his were so old and dated. I put it all on my Belk credit card. He never once mentioned that he had a Belk credit card that he could have used to buy his own clothes. On the day of the wedding, I pressed his mint-green shirt to wear with the new suit I had bought him. He added a new belt, new shoes, and Ralph Lauren socks, which I purchased on my credit card. I felt kind of sad when he left without me, but I believed he loved me so I would wait at home while he went to the wedding.

The following weekend his granddaughter was graduating somewhere in Tennessee, and he called and told me his first ex-wife, Rachel, wanted to ride up there with him because of an issue with her car. He reassured me she meant nothing to him, and I believed him without question.

For the first few months we were seeing each other, I had asked him to wait about telling everyone about us. I wanted time to get comfortable with our relationship, and I knew how people were at the church when it came to gossiping and destroying relationships. If you ever made a mistake in your life, even if it was before you were saved, you could rest assured that everyone at church would pass around that information.

Anything negative always seemed to move faster from state to state since the Church Assembly had locations in several states. Even if there was nothing to discredit you with, they would still judge you and talk bad about you. So, many Christians were eager to spread the gossip and believe lies. They did so without question because the dirtier the gossip, the more pleasing to the ear. For many years there was so much sexual immorality within the church. Unfortunately, those beaten down by rebuke and mentality abused worked very hard to make you look bad in order to feel better about themselves. Self-righteousness was like a disease with so many judging and gossiping about each other.

Allen was persistent about wanting to tell everyone we were in love and going to be married. He said his grandson was going to be honored at Crossing Path Church on Sunday, June 1, 2014, and he invited me to go with him. I agreed. We were both dressed in black suits and a white shirt/blouse that I had bought.

As we walked hand in hand into the sanctuary, his son, Stanley Ferguson, was down the hall. As Allen called out to him, Stanley was disinclined to walk up to where we were standing. Allen said, "Yvette, this is my son Stanley. Stanley, this is Yvette."

As I reached out my hand to shake his, I said, "Hi, I believe you know my daughter, Amanda, who works at the hospital, and you also went to school with her at Southeast High School."

He responded with such fierce, ugly sarcasm as he said, "I don't know your daughter!" He could have spit in my face and not shown any less contempt for me than he did. That same day he went home and deleted my daughter from his Facebook page and stopped speaking to her at the hospital where they both worked.

Stanley was part of a gospel group called Harmony Voices, with his two brothers, Scotty Ferguson and Jarrod Ferguson. Jarrod was also the state overseer of the Florida church and pastored at the Church Assembly in St. Petersburg, Florida. His brother, Scotty, was different from any of them. He was very nice and polite, so different that you would have thought he wasn't related to the other two young men.

Since I loved their father, I wanted so much for Allen's adult children to like me. However, if this encounter with Stanley was representative of what I was to expect from his other sons, it certainly didn't look promising. After we left the church at Crossing Path, Allen and I headed to Ryman Hall where a catered dinner was planned for his grandson, Hudson Ferguson, to celebrate him going into the navy. Allen had gotten permission from his first ex-wife, Rachel, for me to attend. Allen had four sons and a daughter, yet only his son Scotty spoke to me at the dinner. I loved to take pictures so I used my photography as a means to interact with Allen's family. That was the day I finally posted a picture of Allen and me on Facebook, saying we were in a "relationship."

Before the sun had set, Allen's second ex-wife, Jolene, called him and was calling me ugly names. In a fit of rage, she told him I was a lesbian, with no basis for her accusation. Anything she could pull out of the air to make me look bad was her intent, even if she had to distort the truth and outright lie. I now realize Jolene had noticed that in the six years I had been at the church I had not dated anyone. In our church, relationships between men and women were like playing musical chairs, always jumping to the next one. What she didn't know was it is almost an impossible feat for me to trust any man. On Sunday mornings when I walked in the church door, I deliberately never made eye contact with any man. I kept my eyes focused on the front roll seat where I would sit.

I had never been called a lesbian in my life and what a mean-spirited thing to say about someone just to try to hurt them. Nevertheless, it was hurtful because Jolene was supposed to be a Christian, and I expected better from her than that. It seemed I was under constant attack now that we had made our relationship public, which was not that surprising.

Rejected

It was getting close to Father's Day when Allen told me he didn't like to go to restaurants because there was always a long wait on holidays. I loved to cook, so I suggested that we get together with his family and all bring a dish. His children absolutely refused; instead, they invited Allen out for dinner but insisted that he leave me behind. They also took him out for a Father's Day breakfast but said I wasn't welcome to come along.

Jarrod was friends on my Facebook page, and he would post pictures of him and his wife. I would "like" the pictures and even comment that they were really good photos. Jarrod would go down the line clicking "like" on all the positive comments on the photos, but when he would come to my complimentary comment, he would skip me. It was so obvious he didn't like me at all, even though he didn't know me. Stanley had deleted me as soon as he knew his father was seeing me, so I knew it was just a matter of time before Jarrod deleted me also.

I had never held a conversation with Allen's daughter, yet her grandmother informed me that the daughter was announcing to the family that she didn't like me either. Stanley informed his father that he didn't want me around his children. None of this was helping my already low self-esteem, which I tried so hard to keep hidden. The Ferguson's were completely unaware of the underlying danger of raining down havoc on my already extremely damaged mental health, and with no presence of conscience, they were more than willing to bring on the storm.

It was June 20, 2014, my daughter's birthday. It was also the day Allen told me his children (by Rachel) didn't want him seeing me anymore. I knew they were very controlling of his life from what he had already told me.

Sixty and Sad

My children threw me a 60th birthday party on June 28, 2014, at Ryman Hall. Allen never showed up for the party, and my heart ached inside. Allen and I broke up because his children wouldn't accept our relationship, so I didn't see him for a couple of weeks. He quit coming to church and even stayed away from the Church Assembly ministers meeting in July, which was totally out of character for him, especially since he was a deacon in the church.

I became very worried after church was over at the Northwest Georgia Trade and Convention Center, where our minister's meetings were now held. So, I put my own feelings aside and went to check on him. He was very depressed, and he told me he loved me with all his heart. He was going to confront his children and tell them he wasn't going to stop seeing me. He said in the past, he always attempted to stand up for what he wanted but would always cave to their wishes. I told him that maybe for the time being, we could just keep our relationship a secret so he wouldn't have to fight with his adult children.

In August 2014, Allen received confirmation that he had been selected to receive a subsidized apartment he had applied for with my help. The apartment was seven rooms, counting the bathroom and laundry room. The walls were white but clean. I loved Allen so much and wanted only for him to be happy when I agreed to decorate his apartment.

Working day and night, I painted all seven rooms in three days even though I had severe neuropathy in my hands and arms. I had extreme nerve damage and severe carpal tunnel syndrome also in both arms and hands. Because of this, I had to wear splints at night.

I brought my toolbox over with my drill and hung curtains in every room. What curtains I didn't give him, I picked out at the store. We went to Kirkland's in Chattanooga and bought pictures for the rooms, as well as matching shower curtains and rugs for the bathroom.

Allen asked me to spend the "first night" in his new apartment with him, and I agreed. He said he just wanted to hold me in his arms all night. Late Wednesday evening, Allen's youngest son, Trace, by his second wife Jolene, helped Allen bring in the sofa. I had just gotten up from the floor after painting the baseboards, and he told me I was welcome to come over with his dad and eat supper. Jolene's son, Trace, was much nicer than Rachels boys. His dad told him we wouldn't be coming since it was so late; however, Allen told me he was going to take Trace home and would be back shortly.

After they left, I went to my apartment, which was just across the driveway, took a shower, and put on my long cotton pajamas and robe with the intention of falling asleep in Allen's arm. I was exhausted from painting all day. As the minutes turned into hours, I finally fell asleep on his sofa.

About three hours later, Allen returned, and I confronted him about being gone so long knowing I was waiting for him. He said he decided to stay and eat with them and play with his grandson. I couldn't help but feel when he left me behind that he knew exactly what he planned to do. It was shocking to me to think about how hard I had worked to paint his apartment and decorate it beautifully, plus he knew I hadn't eaten anything. Yet he appeared unconcerned about how selfish his actions were. He was controlled by his children but wanted me to finish the labor of love I was doing for him before he dropped me permanently.

I had given him a $700 reversible comforter with throw pillows I had bought at Dillard's Department Store in Atlanta, as well as matching sheets and accent curtains for his bedroom. I had packed his kitchen glasses, bowls, etc., neatly in newspapers at his old apartment. I had worked all week getting him moved, loading my Toyota Avalon to the brim with his belongings. I brought them to his new apartment, unloaded them, and put them in place, even rewashing his kitchen glasses, etc.—and this was the kind of consideration he afforded me.

He didn't even bring me a plate of leftovers.

Disenchanted

Show me an honest man,
and I'll show you a story in some old book,
with its pages all torn and tattered
and its binder all covered in soot.
I'll blow the dirt from its cover
when I find it hid on the shelf,
and I'll know somewhere deep within me,
just words is all there is left.

It starts out with its fairy tales
of knights and their ladies fair,
of hardships and of struggles,
yet a man would prove that he cared.
He'd work from beginning of morning
until the sun rose high in the sky.
His words were something you could believe in,
not ever the reason you cried.

Your tears fell only from happiness,
so freely to you he would give,
not of bruises or of heartaches
like a woman of today has to live.
And the words "Happily Ever After"
to me were truly a joke,
and I believe Nicole felt the same way,
when the man she loved cut her throat.

Written and composed by Yvette Lidy 06-12-1994

Again, and again, I was reminded of how unimportant I was, yet I was blind to believing he didn't love me as I continued to make excuses for his thoughtless and cruel behavior. He stopped sitting with me at church immediately after his adult children told him they wouldn't accept me. Harmony Voices was a local well-known gospel group and even sang on television a few times, so Jarrod and Stanley exhibited a superior attitude toward me anyway. Allen continued to make excuses to me, and I was always quick to believe him. I was too trusting of Allen to ever be mad at him.

He truly had his hooks in my heart, yet his actions were no longer reflective of the passive, kind-hearted man I believed God had sent me. Nevertheless, Allen would give me short moments of sweetness and affection that would keep me from giving up. He had convinced me he loved me in the beginning, and that's something I had waited for all my life.

So, I wasn't willing to give it up without trying my best to be patient and understanding. I had invested all my energy into making his life better and convincing myself that his unkind actions were because of his children. Just as with Karen, I never blamed him for his cruel and ugly behavior. I continued to have faith that with time we would eventually have our "happily ever after."

It was now September, and I had once again planned to go to Kissimmee, Florida. For several months, Allen led me to believe that he was going to Florida with me, and I was very excited. We would be away from his adult children. He would have his separate quarters at the condo, and I had everything well planned. Even though I had wanted to make love to Allen, I never did because I was living for the Lord. I knew if that happened without marriage, I would feel very ashamed afterward. I was so excited because I was going to take him to the Holy Land Experience, which was my favorite place, and the condo was only two miles from Disney World. The Holy Land Experience had great gospel music, as well as a wonderful and moving depiction of the life and death of Jesus Christ. I had never been this excited planning a vacation in my life.

After five months of preparation and dreaming, Allen waited until a few days before we were to leave to tell me he was not going, dropping hints that his children had intervened in his plans. I was beyond disappointed leaving for Florida without him. I couldn't make the trip alone because of my agoraphobia so I invited a couple of wonderful ladies/friends from our church. Even with the ache in my heart, it proved to be an awesome vacation. Cindy and Delana kept me laughing and that was just what I needed.

I went shopping at Dillard's in Orlando and bought some Under Armor shirts for Allen since I knew he loved them...yes, just call me stupid! It's hard to believe that when you think you're in love with someone, they can treat you so unkind, yet you continue to make excuses for their thoughtless behavior.

I have always heard that love is blind, but no one bothered to tell me it also erases the commonsense part of your brain that determines good and evil in another human being. I have learned that love is an addiction just like any other drug. Even when you know it's destroying you, you can't seem to give it up.

Jarrod, Judge, and Jury

In October 2014, Allen was planning to go to Chicago for his grandson's naval graduation ceremony. Pictures were posted on Hudson's Facebook page, and Hudson's grandmother, Wanda Stratton, had been my close friend before she died. Allen and I were still keeping our relationship away from his adult children whom he had fathered with Rachel.

When I saw the picture of Hudson on Facebook with Jarrod on one side and Tess (Wanda Stratton's daughter) on the other side, I commented, "Congratulations, Hudson. Your grandmother would be so proud of you, and I can see your mother is beaming with pride." I never acknowledged Jarrod in the photo only because Allen had wanted me to keep my distance, and besides, this was a photo on Hudson's site.

Jarrod immediately deleted me as a friend and blocked me from his site, and his wife deleted me also. When Allen returned home, he told me that when Jarrod saw my comment, he grabbed his phone in anger and walked over to his dad in the restaurant. He angrily pointed at the comment on his phone and said, "Just look at this. She never said one word about me!"

Inside me, it was almost laughable to think his ego was that inflated. However, I can't say it wasn't hurtful because it was since I was still wishing they would like me.

In late November, I walked into the church office to chat with my friend Alice. Suddenly I noticed Rev. Jarrod Ferguson in the hall. I called out to him and he stopped. I said, "I would like to talk to you." I have no doubt that he wouldn't have agreed if it hadn't been at the church office, so I kind of had him in a corner. I asked Jarrod, "Why don't y'all like me? You deleted me on Facebook and then blocked me as though you hate me."

Then I began telling him how much I loved his dad, and what I had done for him financially so he would know my intentions were honorable. His first excuse was regarding that first day I came to the dinner at Ryman Hall in honor of his son Hudson. Jarrod said, "First of all, if Dad was going to introduce us to someone, he shouldn't have done it at the dinner. "Personally, I just didn't think you had a right to be there!" Jarrod continued, "My son was going off to the navy and my heart was broken, and you never said one word to me!"

I responded, "I tried to be friendly with you; that's why I took all those pictures for you and your family."

He said, "Well, when you were leaving, you came by the kitchen and thanked my mother and said you really enjoyed yourself. We were at the other side of the kitchen, and you didn't say one darn word to us!"

At this point I'm thinking, is this all you've got? I then asked him why he blocked me as a friend on Facebook, and he said, "Well, I have the right to not be friends with anyone I choose." Jarrod could see the tears in my eyes, yet he was as cold and unfeeling as he could possibly be. He ended up saying in a nasty tone, "I've heard talk about you!"

Immediately my internal radar was going into overdrive as I asked myself, "What has he heard?" I hadn't had sex in years, so, it couldn't be that. Does he know about my agoraphobia? Does he know I've been raped and ended up in a psychiatric hospital? What does he know? I suddenly felt like I would smother. With everything that had happened in my life and the shame I felt and the feelings of not being good enough, suddenly it was like a damn had burst through all the walls I had worked so hard to build. I had to get out of there. I should have been asking this minister/state overseer why he would be listening to gossip to begin with, but like so many times before I just stuffed it.

With tears streaming down my face, I quickly walked out of the church office and drove down the road sobbing. He had dashed what hope I had held onto against his self-righteous and religious wall! It felt like he knew every horrible thing that had ever happened to me, and the shame was gut-wrenching!

The worst part of it all was that he had exposed what I believed about myself—I wasn't good enough! I wasn't good enough for the Stratton's and now I wasn't good enough for the Ferguson's! I felt like I had fallen into a time warp, as all the horrible memories of the past attacked me at once. I suddenly realized that all I had been going through during my relationship with Allen was a repeat of when I loved Chaney Stratton. "Not good enough" meant "not valuable," just someone to step on at your leisure.

Broken Dreams

Life came but passed me by,
I see no reason I should not die,
the seasons change just as I grow,
I once was young but now I'm old.
I see no reason for why I'm here,
to suffer pain and live, in fear,
just what's the reason for my birth,
for my empty life and what it's worth?
If I had searched in the right place,
would love have passed me and left no trace?
What is it then that others find
makes life complete but is not mine?

I once saw light and felt life's song,
then blinked my eyes and all was gone.
I've lost my hope and live, in doubt;
my light grows dim and soon burns out.
if I don't find this thing I long,
I'll leave this world and soon be gone.

Written and composed by Yvette Lidy

91

Fair-Weather Friends

FIRST, SISTER JENNIFER Douglas from the church was having an affair with Roy Bradley, who was also a member of the church. She asked me if I would notarize her divorce papers, and I told her I would. When we met, her husband, John, who was also a church member, was with her. He began to curse me, calling me a bitch, and came toward me in such anger because he didn't want me helping her. I felt threatened and wondered if he was going to hit me, which caused me to have a panic attack.

Secondly, I had posted a nice random post on Facebook and tagged several people I knew because I wanted them to see it too. John and Jennifer, the couple who were divorcing, had names that both started with the same letter, so when I clicked on their names, they were side by side in the tag.

Roy was extremely jealous when it came to Jennifer, and he became angry when he saw their names side by side. Even though John and Jennifer were still legally married, Roy text me some very ugly and filthy messages because I had tagged John and Jennifer in the same post.

Thirdly, shortly afterward, another incident occurred when Sister Bertha viciously attacked me after a church service one night because she said I had mixed up the T-shirts that were being sold at church. Marlana, the lady who was giving out the T-shirts, had asked me to help her because the line had become so long. The lady who attacked me threatened my life. As I was leaving the next morning for my vacation in Florida, she texted me and told me she would be waiting for me when I returned. She suggested she was going to physically hurt me and this was only some of the attacks I received from church folks...My nerves couldn't take it anymore.

Finally, so far, (1) I had been cursed for notarizing divorce papers for a lady who couldn't afford an attorney; (2) been attacked for accidentally mixing up the sizes of some T-shirts at church; (3) received filthy messages from Roy Bradley for tagging the names of Jennifer and her husband, John, in the same sentence; and (4) been called a lesbian by Jolene Ferguson because she didn't want me dating her ex-husband whom she had divorced eight years ago. In addition, (5) Rev. Jarrod Ferguson had heard talk about me, so he didn't want me seeing his father; and (6) Allen refused to sit with me at church because he was afraid of what everyone would think.

It was all centered around church people, and through the advice of a friend, I had talked to Pastor Scott at the Church Assembly about Jolene calling me a lesbian. He said I should talk to Jolene first, and if she refused to listen, we would have a meeting. I followed the complete protocol that Pastor Scott had set forth. However, Jolene refused each request to meet with me. After church on a Wednesday night, Pastor Scott looked at me and said, "You can't be having a spirit against her for what she did!"

I told him I didn't have a spirit against her, but I thought if we had a meeting, the problem could be resolved. He was unwilling to follow through with the very biblical protocol he had set forth in the first place. With all the drama that was slapping me down at church, once again I went to talk to Pastor Scott, but with no resolution. Instead, he said he could bring me up in front of the entire church for having a spirit against Jolene! I finally had to accept that there was not any accountability for anything at the Church Assembly church. I always left his office feeling defeated, devalued, and criticized. I eventually learned that Jolene Ferguson, the woman who called me a lesbian was Pastor Scott's relative.

I had gone to him on several occasions in hopes of resolving what I was going through, but not one time was he supportive of me. He always made excuses for their bad behavior and criticized me instead. Not once did he bring the parties together to try to bring peace to the situations. With Rev. Jarrod Ferguson being an overseer for the State of Florida, and also the pastor in St. Petersburg, Florida, you would assume he, of all people, would have been held accountable for listening to gossip about anyone. It was too much for me to cope with emotionally, so, I gave up trying to find resolution.

Fair-Weather Friends

The bright sun was shining from the warmth in my soul
when you called me your friend that would never let go.
My phone kept ringing for invitations to dine.
Let's meet at The Longhorn if you've got the time.

My days were so sweet as we chatted and ate,
not ever expecting what would soon be my fate.
If someone had told me in a year I would know
the backs that would face me like what happened to Job.

I'd never believed them, just what was my sin,
that forgiveness was banished from those I called friend.
The storms kept on raging, the love has grown cold,
from fair-weather friends I had to let go.

I'm learning so much in this world growing dark,
the ones who's authentic and those with no heart.
They tell you they love you, but silence is loud
as I stand here alone faced down by the crowd.

Remind me, dear Jesus, why I must go to church
when Christians have caused me such heartache and hurt.
You know where I'm living; you spoke to my heart.
I listen for guidance alone in the dark.

Though church friends forsook me and trampled with blame,
it's you who still holds me and loves me the same.
Yet, all I am seeing is coldness in man,
who stands in the shadows with rocks in his hand.

Is rejection the message they wish to convey,
instead of just kneeling and bowing to pray?
Just how are they different from the sinners they seek,
forgetting the message and how to be meek?
I miss their sweet voices I'll hear not again.
Life taught me the meaning of fair-weather friends.

Written and composed by Yvette Lidy

For we wrestle not against flesh and blood, but against principalities, against powers, against the rulers of the darkness of this world, against spiritual wickedness in high places.

Ephesians 6:12 (KJV)

Trying to Help

During the services at the Church Assembly, I often noticed that people's backsides would be exposed when they were on their knees praying. Also, at one service in particular, the ministers were trying to find a cloth to pray over for someone who was very sick and couldn't attend. I wanted to help, so I decided to make some prayer cloths and altar cloths to donate to the sanctuary. I chose three colors for the altar cloths: royal blue for the Holy Spirit, deep red for the blood of Jesus, and purple to represent the King of Kings. The beige prayer cloths were fancy, trimmed in lace. I thought it would be a nice keepsake for the family if the person didn't survive, and it would also be a nice keepsake for the person if they improved.

When I brought them to Pastor Scott, he said he didn't like the lace on the prayer cloths, and also, they preferred having the church logo stamped on them like they had seen on the internet. He felt the altar cloths were too big, and he only wanted red. He said the ones I made weren't the right color of red because it didn't match the new upholstered pew cushions in the sanctuary. He then suggested we go into the church area so he could show me what color of red he required.

The cording I purchased was expensive, plus fabric, gas to and from Atlanta, bringing the total cost of my contribution to around $300. I had sewn about forty prayer cloths and twenty altar cloths and he rejected them all. I had worked so hard, and now he expected me to redo it all. In a polite voice I suggested they order some online and that way they would get exactly what they wanted. As I left, I felt so dejected and disappointed. I wanted him to be pleased with my efforts, but instead I was criticized for a few flaws in my sewing. I did, however, donate it all to two different churches, and they were very grateful for the gifts.

92

Jesus, the Love of My Life

THE RELATIONSHIP BETWEEN Allen and me continued to deteriorate since he continued to treat me as if I was inferior to him and his adult children. My six-year-old grandson's best friend from school was shot and killed by his own father, and Allen wouldn't even go into the funeral with me. Instead, he parked his Jeep up the street, only close enough so we could see the people going into the funeral home. It's an awful feeling to be sitting there watching the funeral from a distance with the man you love and he tells you he loves you too. It was especially hard knowing he was afraid and ashamed to be seen with me for fear of making his adult children mad. He excluded me from all the events where his sons were performing the entire year and a half of our relationship.

Our last date was when he invited me to go to his brother's anniversary party at Ryman Hall. He knew people were talking about how cruel he was treating me, and oh, how he always worried about what the church people thought of him.

I was so happy, believing things were going to change, but I didn't realize at the time that he was doing it to make himself look favorable in the eyes of the church folks. As we sat at the party in Ryman Hall, his son Stanley and family walked in and wouldn't even come to the table where I was sitting with Allen. Instead, they sat at the other end of the dining room. Later, that same evening, his daughter walked in the door and asked her uncle to go to our table and get her father. She wanted Allen to come over to the other side of the room so she could speak with him. It was terribly unkind the way they treated me.

At Christmas I made very expensive gift baskets with lots of different kinds of homemade candies. I had spent days making them, and I sent them by their father to a party I wasn't invited to attend. My relationship with Allen was a constant shredding away at my self-esteem, which was tearing me down again inside.

Once again Allen had said he wanted to go to Florida with me to Disney World and the Holy Land Experience, but at the last minute and for the second year in a row, he cancelled his plans to go. I had so looked forward to taking Allen to Disney World since he said he had never been there.

When I was on Facebook the following week, I saw pictures of him at Disney World with his son and family. I was crushed inside. I remember saying, "I hope he gets killed in a car wreck coming home." Later, I deeply regretted saying such a horrible thing. I had never in my life been the kind of person who wanted anything bad to happen to anyone who had hurt me. I felt Allen had finally destroyed the trusting part of me that believed there was such a thing as "a good man."

When Allen returned from his vacation, I had written this poem and asked him if I could read it to him. I had hoped it would give him some insight about how much he was hurting me. Yet, when I read it, he became extremely vicious in the way he talked to me, and that's when our relationship finally ended.

My Broken Heart

Once long ago in years gone by,
I learned that love would make you cry,
So, I grabbed my shell so young and thin

to put my broken pieces in.
As time went by, I closed all parts,
no one could reach my broken heart.
The shell grew hard, so firm and strong.
I found it best to walk alone.

My joy, my peace worked out as planned
as long as God held tight my hand.
My days were sweet and so sublime
for I was His and He was mine.
We walked through forest and shadows dim,
And He held me close beside Him.
But then one day on the path I trod
and had my morning talk with God,
there came a man up next to me
who called my name and spoke to me.

He wasn't like all the men before;
his heart was kind and he loved the Lord.
He said all things I once had felt
and caused my broken heart to melt.
Oh, was this God, this gift so sweet
that brought me love that I could keep?
He spoke all things; how could he know
the deep desire inside my soul.
Just like two kids we laughed with joy;
this older man became a boy.
He called to me, "Let's tell the world
for I am yours and you're my girl.

So, hand in hand with smiles so great,
we'd share our joy; we could not wait.
But like sweet lies to pave the way

his whispers came and go my way.
Hard to believe it wasn't real
when Satan comes your soul to steal,
and like a dream crushed at my feet
just what it means to sift as wheat.

So, piece by piece I once called love,
this heart I gave to God above.
The pain still clings, the tears still fall,
while I wait to hear my lover call.
He taught me well with poison kiss
that in this world love don't exist.

Written and composed by Yvette Lidy

My heart was broken because of the faith I had placed in Allen. I had believed he was broken inside too, and we would be perfect for each other. Inside it felt like someone had died. I always reluctantly refused to make love to him, but oh, I wanted him so much, and now we would never be together. I had been like a schoolgirl with her first crush, having feelings and emotions I thought had died long ago. When he held me in his arms, I was in heaven and didn't want to leave. I knew, because of my age, this had been my last chance for happiness, and it was breaking my heart.

After it was finally over, I would watch love stories and remember how it felt to be in love with him, and I would cry knowing that kind of love between a man and a woman would never be mine. I was sixty-one years in age but twenty-one in my heart, longing to be loved by a man.

In my favorite movie, *Something's Gotta Give*, Diane Keaton sees Jack Nicholson with another woman. Remembering that their lovemaking was so passionate, it made them both cry, and she says to him with tears in her eyes, "What am I supposed to do with all this?"

as she waves her hands up and down at her body. I cried right along with her because I knew exactly what she meant. He had awakened the passion within her and then left her to her loneliness.

Every day the tears would come and not leave me alone. I didn't want to see anyone, and I certainly didn't want to go to church and be around people. The most heartbreaking events in my life had started in church. I couldn't seem to stop grieving over Allen because when I lost him, I lost the hope of "me too," the hope of proving to myself that I was good enough to be loved by what was considered a good man. He was a well-respected deacon in the church who would finally validate my worthiness to be loved. It would prove to me that I had value as a human being while dispelling the memory of Mother and Sister Moreen's judgment of me.

I remembered how I used to read my Bible and talk to God all the time. My relationship with Allen had taken my thoughts in another direction and stopped me from reading God's word. I had unconsciously closed my Bible when I opened my heart to a man whom I truly believed loved me. If Allen could expose himself to be the cruel, unkind, and selfish person that he was, there was no hope of a good man in this life, at least not for me. I couldn't help but believe the man I thought God had sent me was actually Satan's attempt to destroy me, and as the Bible says, "sift me as wheat."

All the signs were evident; I just wasn't able to see them clearly for the stardust in my eyes. I awoke on a Monday morning, and as with each previous day, my first thoughts were "He's gone, he's really gone! The love of my life is *gone*!" Then, suddenly, as though someone poured cold water over my head, I heard a voice say, "He's *not* the *love* of *your* life!" It was as though someone flipped on a light switch inside my head.

With a sudden sense of urgency and an overwhelming ache in my heart, I knew what I had to do. I knew I had to be in the presence of the one who had patiently waited for me to see the light, *His light!* I had to go to the park to see His beauty in all He created for me to enjoy, that special place where I loved to talk with God. That's where I could renew my strength in the presence of the only one who had ever truly loved me. I remember how I used to look up at the trees with the gentle breeze kissing my face and whisper, "Thank you, God, for these trees, the clouds, and the sound of this brook singing a song only you can interpret."

No one had ever really loved me in my life, and what little kindness I was given growing up only allowed me a glimpse into what many were experiencing in abundance. But with God, I was completely accepted and loved, and He knew *everything* about me and loved me all the more! The more life had ripped away at my identity, the more my soul and spirit clung to God. He judged my heart and not my failures, so with tears streaming down my face, I wrote this poem:

Jesus, the Love of My Life

Early in the morning while the sun was hidden from me,
I heard his sweet voice calling, "Oh, come and walk with me.
I've sent a breeze to greet you while the trees will sing a song
to take away these heartaches you've carried way too long."
So, I grabbed my shoes, jumped in my car, and down the road I trod
to find our secret meeting place where I loved to talk to God.

The squirrels and the rabbits were laughing out my name
and said the Father's waiting and He's so glad you came.
The trees all looked so lovely as they bowed down at my feet,
I felt the presence of the Lord, and I began to weep.
But the teardrops weren't from sadness; it's this heavenly love I
know.
He sent the wind of love to me that came rushing through my soul.
I told Him of my struggles with the faith and love I gave
to the man I thought God sent me on one lovely summer's day.

He was gentle and so loving like a furry little sheep;
he surely came from heaven that God sent me to keep.
But wolves come in sheep's clothing to tear away and steal
the precious one God's chosen who desires to do His will.
Withdrawn from me the blinders, I finally understood
that even though I'm broken, God can use this for my good.
I've learned of selfish children and a father full of pride;
I never would have pleased them no matter how I tried.

Yet love won't die so easily if it's honest and sincere.
It's a cold heart without repentance that never sheds a tear.
I'll hang the precious scriptures from my bathroom and my bed
to remind me of His promises and the healing words He said.

Today they say a miracle has happened in the park.
Some claim it was an angel they had seen at dusky dark.
Her feathers were all scattered, her wing was ripped away.
I thought I heard her crying; I know I heard her pray.
So battered and so beaten, she limped through shadows dim
as I saw another angel and she flew away with Him.

Written and composed by Yvette Lidy

93

Afraid of Church

AS THE NEW Year 2017 rolled in, I made a few attempts to go to church somewhere. I would get up on Sunday morning with the dread of going to church anywhere, but the scripture that had been drilled into me since childhood would play over and over in my head like a threatening recording: "Fail not to assemble yourselves," meaning you *had* to go to church if you wanted to please God. I would drive to the intersection of Waugh Street and Thornton Avenue and ask myself, "What should I do? Turn right and go to the Church Assembly or go straight ahead to Tyler Baptist Church?" I had been abused and mistreated in both these churches but I would be so afraid that God would be mad at me, so, I forged ahead. As I drove toward the Church Assembly on South 41 Highway, I began to feel like I was smothering, like I couldn't breathe. I pulled into the parking lot and drove toward the back of the church, and in a sudden panic I cried out loud, "I can't do this! I can't go in there!" I pulled back onto the street and headed toward the church in Chatsworth.

Why does a woman who has been abused by a man always return to her abuser, declaring she loves him? That's how I saw myself; I kept returning to the scene of the crime. On countless Sundays, I would get dressed and drive to that same intersection crying and praying—and at times crying out loud to God, "Why am I like this? What's wrong with me? Why can't I go to church like normal people?" I never remembered my father, who was a minister, but I had encountered cruel ministers who professed to speak on behalf of God. The God who wanted to beat me over the head with a stick ever since I was a child and remind me that I wasn't good enough to be loved by anyone, not even Him.

I knew I loved the Lord and wanted to please Him, but the thought of going to church was more than I could bear. It was as though a cage was dropped down over me when I sat down on the pew and I couldn't breathe.

I felt as though as soon as I walked in the doors, I was being sized up and judged, and sadly, like many others, I had been.

Just from being inside this church, where I not only had been mistreated but I had also watched from a young age countless men and women being physically attacked and emotionally ripped to shreds came flooding back into my memory as though it were yesterday. When I walked in the doors, it would trigger my PTSD. The choir's singing sounded like someone had died, and the depressing looks on the choir members' faces only reassured me that there was no joy in serving God here.

It had been that way growing up, and although the members could now cut their hair and wear makeup, many were still emotionally programmed from the past. They were struggling to embrace any form of change within the church. Furthermore, since church members had been stripped of their hard-earned money for so many years, many had such reluctance and resentment to put money in the offering plate, including myself. Most of the songs were the same ones I had heard in the sixties at church, with the same forlorn expression on each face. I didn't understand why I couldn't just leave here and never return, but the pull that kept dragging me back was like a rope connected to my heart that I had never been able to cut. I felt so uncomfortable and out of place that I would scurry toward the door as soon as the service was dismissed and many times even sooner.

Dark Oblivion

Satan has a foothold on the church.
He troubles minds and causes hurt,
he blinds their eyes and seals their fate,
he's working fast, it's getting late.
When Christians fight, don't think it strange.
They've set their ways and refuse to change.
They don't like this; they don't like that,
the pastor's wrong, the music's flat.
They've built their house on sinking sand;
they call it God but live for man.
They stick their fingers in their ears;
the word of God they cannot hear.
They scream and shout to get their way,
forgotten God, forgot to pray.
The servant holds his tray of sin,
fed lies to sheep that rot within.
The cloud of doubts they stand beneath,
their sacred vows they did not keep.
How sad, how sad, they did not know
about the plan to steal their soul.
They step inside God's holy place
with sour looks upon their face.
Expecting songs to entertain,
but if not moved they look to blame.
Where is their joy, where is their praise?
These poor lost souls live in the haze.
In these last days His spirit will pour
for the humble few who serve the Lord.
"Repent, repent," my soul cries out.
"Don't stay in sin and be left out."
Spirits run, infiltrate,

while Satan works to seal your fate.
Put self aside, all strife and doubt,
Let God of Heaven back in His house!
And one last thing I hope you'll do—
Make your praise about God and not about you!

Written by Crusonda Yvette Lidy, 2015

I had to find a way to break free from the influence this church had over me, and with God's help I knew I would do whatever it took to release that hold it had over my life. My need for emotional peace and healing was so threatened at this point, but I believed God would make a way for my escape. Nevertheless, I had to be willing to finally walk away. I went to therapy twice a week in addition to going once every two months to my psychiatrist.

94

Picking Up the Pieces

TODAY, THE CHURCH Assembly has changed considerably in its way of thinking. However, the majority of its members are related since they have spent so many years marrying within the church. They work very hard at presenting themselves as a different version of their past, and I think that's very commendable.

The Stratton descendants are not responsible for their parents' choices, and it is regrettable that they must live down the shame of what happened when they were only babies. The parents and relatives that they deeply love who made some horrible decisions that hurt a lot of good people. The current generation would prefer the abuse was either forgotten or kept secret, and their weapon of defense is that "we are not forgiving" like the Bible requires. Unfortunately, they can't seem to understand, why the victims can't just get over it! If they could walk in the shoes of the members who were emotionally traumatized like myself maybe then they would understand the lasting negative effects abuse can have on a person. Nevertheless, my scares were not only created by my church experience because what I was coping with at home and my personal life was just as damaging. Like many others, my mother was a product of the church abuse and brokenness sewn into the hearts of so many who just wanted to please God. So, I can fully understand why she was not emotionally whole.

Her parents giving everything to the Stratton's leaving a child so poor she had no shoes, yet, when she stole the shoes, she gave them to her sister. My mother wasn't perfect but she would give her last dime to keep someone else from doing without. Unlike the Stratton's, she wasn't a taker, she was a giver with all she had.

I know with certainty I have forgiven those who mistreated me, and the best way I can explain my thoughts is this: If someone broke my legs and I forgave that person for doing it, my legs would still be broken, and I would have to live with the pain and injury until it would one day heal. However, some injuries last a lifetime.

My brother Josh has such a loving heart and would do anything he could to help anyone. Growing up without a father was very difficult for him but it only created in him a love for children. Yes, he still silently carries wounds from growing up in the Church Assembly and living on the church farm but he's a survivor. He's a great teacher with an intellect far above anyone I know. He speaks several languages and teaches Spanish. He and I have a wonderful relationship; he's my best friend, and I am truly grateful.

My brother Jacob has such a generous heart like our mother did. Since 2006, when he received Christ into his life, there has been a drastic change in his attitude. He has transformed into a man who's soul purpose in life is to please God. He is well loved for the many delicious cakes he bakes and gives away.

Karen has a huge circle of friends with whom she enjoys life, and I'm happy for her. For several years now she has dedicated her life and time to feeding the homeless. Regardless of her Severe Rheumatoid authoritic knees she keeps right on moving forward and I think that's very admirable. Sadly, the hope of a close, loving relationship between two sisters, which I had pursued for so many years, has simply vanished with time. Maybe, she loves me now in some way, but I honestly don't know her heart. Maybe it's just that she's grown accustomed to those friends with whom she invested so many years building a relationship. I pray for her every night and only want the best for her. As for me, my mother's baby sister, Sheila and my aunt May, is the closest and dearest friends I've ever had. It's the kind of close friendship I would have loved to have shared with Karen.

For those of you who have been emotionally damaged by a similar experience with the church, I want you to know you are not alone. I've shared many of the heartaches and deeply personal experiences I've suffered along my journey in order to help you if you're willing to consider the power of prayer.

For many years, when I visited West Hill Cemetery, I would walk over to the headstone with Moreen Stratton's name on it. This woman ripped the man I loved from my arms and my life. She was also responsible for so many of the violent and humiliating rebukes I endured at the Church Assembly. I promised myself that as soon as she exhaled her last breath and took up residency in the West Hill Cemetery, I would return to spit and dance on her grave. That was the depth of my hatred for her because that's how deeply she hurt me. I can count on three fingers how many people I have ever truly hated in my life. Unfortunately, they all went to church where I did, and Sister Moreen Stratton was at the top of my list. However, a wise friend once told me the hardest thing you can ever do is pray for someone for whom you feel hatred.

I knew in my heart, regardless of how Sister Moreen treated me, I would never make it to heaven if I didn't find a way to forgive her. I told my friend if I prayed blessings over Moreen's life, God would know I didn't mean a word of it, but my friend said to pray for her anyway and the healing would come. Through gritted teeth I prayed, and I prayed, and I prayed until my heart began to soften, and I knew I finally meant what I was praying. I didn't want to go to hell, and now I didn't want Sister Moreen Stratton to go to hell either.

I learned that in the last years of her life, she had terrible panic attacks. A source said she was afraid to go to sleep, afraid she would go to hell for all the lives she destroyed. They said she had ministers sit by her bedside while she lay there terrified to fall asleep. Now, I only felt love and compassion for her, and I knew how it felt to have a dreaded panic attack. Maybe God allowed me to find out about her panic attacks to show me the extent of Sister Moreen's grief and remorse over how she treated me and others. I choose to believe she was genuinely repentant for the heartaches she caused over the years before she died. I said many prayers for Sister Moreen before she passed away, and I felt compassion for her when she finally closed her eyes in peace. I have no doubt God has forgiven her just like we all need His forgiveness.

For many years Rev. John Winston Stratton Jr. was our Overlord and oppressor while living in sheer luxury. Unfortunately, when he fell from grace, he fell hard. He lost everything he had and died an extremely obese, alcoholic. As true with all of us, there's more to his story than his mistakes. There was a good side to him too and God loved him just as much as He does you or I. He loved his children with all his heart and he was broken when his wife died. He suffered dearly for his mistakes and we are not to be his judge. His behavior within the church was a learned behavior. If we are to make it to God's heaven we all must learn forgiveness and I assure you, that has been a struggler for me. Remember, with God all things are possible. After his death, his young children were not always greeted with a warm reception because of the resentment many members felt toward their father. Nevertheless, life's hard knocks and struggles taught the kids to be strong as they grew into young adults any parent would be proud of.

As far as the way he mistreated me, I have totally forgiven him and I believe I'll see him in heaven someday.

Today I can finally say, I thank God I did not marry Chaney Stratton. I have come to realize he was too emotionally attached and controled by his mother. Most importantly, I know medical treatment would have been withheld from me, and because of that, I would have died in childbirth. God was protecting me all along.

And we know that all things work together for good to them that love God, to them that are called according to his purpose.
Romans 8:28 (KJV)

What a beautiful scripture. God truly is faithful!

There is so much I haven't shared that happened within our religion, but those events are not my story to tell.

95

Taking Care of Me

As I turn the page to 2018, I realize that unbeknownst to most people, I have only driven alone a distance of thirty-two miles from my home since 1988. My home, my safe place, keeps me anchored and away from the noise of the world, and I find my security in talking to God and reading His Word. The highlight of my world each month is going with a friend to Atlanta to shop and eat. As soon as we pull onto the interstate leaving Dalton, I feel like a bird let out of my cage because for a day I am leaving my memories at the Whitfield County line.

Even though I can't make the trip alone, the security of a good friend is all I need. I never take different roads because I would have a panic attack if I accidentally got on an unfamiliar road. So, I always, always, travel the same roads I am familiar with. Driving is my favorite sport because it calms my nerves, and it's one of the few things in life I have control over.

Going shopping is my "drug" of choice. It's my way of shutting out the ache in my heart to feel loved. I still struggle with fear of the crowds and going to church without the pain that tries to smother my existence. Nevertheless, I cling to my faith in Christ Jesus because I know "through Him all things are possible."

96

Rockbridge, A New Beginning

FOR SEVERAL YEARS, when I walked at the Harlan Godfrey Civitan park, that special place where I loved to talk to God, there was a man named Dan Lawson who also walked there with several of his friends. One day as I passed them on the track, he called out to me and asked if I attended church anywhere. I gave him a flat no while mumbling that I didn't believe in organized religion. He invited me to Rockbridge church and seemed to make it his mission to invite me each time he had the opportunity. Finally, on one very lonely Sunday morning, I slipped in the door at Rockbridge church.

I didn't want to be in a crowd of people, but I desperately needed something from God. I loved the fact that I didn't really know anyone, and also there were no bright lights shining in my face. I was relieved to discover my PTSD was not triggered there; instead, I felt pleasantly calm inside. There was no heaviness or smothering weight that seemed to blanket the room as it did at the Church Assembly. I slipped out before the service concluded, but I knew I wanted to return.

I attended several services, and with each message preached, I began to feel a peace inside that was wonderful. The best way I know to describe it was I felt like a baby being born and someone was finally cutting the cord so I could breathe. I knew for the first time that

I would never feel the need to return to the Church Assembly.

The best thing that happened to me at Rockbridge church was experiencing the God of Love who had been with me all my life—the one who gave me strength to walk into church, the one who was in my apartment when I was crying from the abuse that had been so much a part of my life experience. He was with me both times when I was raped on my birthdays. He comforted me and helped me keep my sanity during the most devastating events in my life. He was at Rockbridge church speaking to me through the mouth of a young minister named Rev. Matt Evans.

As I sat there in the dimly lit sanctuary, I felt a smile come across my face. The words to my poem "River of Tears" flashed through my mind as I heard the choir in the distance singing powerful words that felt so healing to my soul. The song is called, "What the Lord Has Done in Me." In that moment the words I was hearing said. "Into the river I will wade, there my sins are washed away, from the heavens mercy streams, of the Savior's love for me....**I will rise from waters deep, into the saving arms of God, I will sing salvation songs, Jesus Christ has set me free.**" In my mind's eye, I could see Jesus pulling me from the river of my despair and the breath of life rushing into my lungs.

Wow, it was such a revelation for me to go from seeing the waters taking my life to giving me new life and washing away all my pain. It felt as though the Holy Spirit was speaking directly to me in that song. I felt so loved in that moment as though Jesus was wrapping His arms around me and loving me completely. It was truly an amazing experience.

What greater hope could I ever need than to know Jesus Christ is holding me and carrying me, and I would never drown through the storms in my life, my river of tears. He has a plan for me, and every event that He has allowed to occur in my life will serve a greater purpose for His honor and glory. If, I had not developed agoraphobia and was emotionally able to travel to pursue a career in country music for example, it may have pulled me away from God. If I had not been raped, beaten, mistreated, and rejected, I believe I would not have the love and compassion for other people that I know is in my heart. I don't hate anyone, even those who hurt me most.

The things I've suffered have only humbled me and brought me to my knees to completely depend on God. I have walked through the fire in my life, but His word says, **"He knoweth the way that I take: when he hath tried me, I shall come forth as gold" (Job 23:10).** Furthermore, I always remind myself of another scripture that says, **"For my thoughts are not your thoughts, neither are your ways, my ways, saith the Lord" (Isaiah 55:8).** So, when we face trials in this life and we don't understand why God doesn't handle it differently, remember this scripture because God's plan is far greater than anything our minds can comprehend—just like heaven is more glorious than we can possibility imagine—but, praise God, we have an invitation.

I count each day a blessing that He allows me to wake up each morning. I'm excited for the day whether here on earth or in heaven when it will be revealed in me why this was to be my path in my journey home.

The End